"This book will serve as a valuable source for the digital transformation of the financial industry."
— **Dr. Zamir Iqbal**, *VP Finance and Chief Financial Officer (CFO),*
Islamic Development Bank (IsDB)

"An essential resource for financial accounting managers and students of financial management."
— **Professor Mehmet Huseyin Bilgin**, *Istanbul Medeniyet University, Turkey*

"A comprehensive coverage of emerging intelligent technologies in finance."
— **Professor Ohaness Paskelian**, *University of Houston-Downtown, USA*

T0384026

The Essentials of
Machine Learning in
Finance and Accounting

This book introduces machine learning in finance and illustrates how we can use computational tools in numerical finance in real-world context. These computational techniques are particularly useful in financial risk management, corporate bankruptcy prediction, stock price prediction, and portfolio management. The book also offers practical and managerial implications of financial and managerial decision support systems and how these systems capture vast amount of financial data.

Business risk and uncertainty are two of the toughest challenges in the financial industry. This book will be a useful guide to the use of machine learning in forecasting, modeling, trading, risk management, economics, credit risk, and portfolio management.

Mohammad Zoynul Abedin is an associate professor of Finance at the Hajee Mohammad Danesh Science and Technology University, Bangladesh. Dr. Abedin continuously publishes academic papers in refereed journals. Moreover, Dr. Abedin served as an ad hoc reviewer for many academic journals. His research interest includes data analytics and business intelligence.

M. Kabir Hassan is a professor of Finance at the University of New Orleans, USA. Prof. Hassan has over 350 papers (225 SCOPUS, 108 SSCI, 58 ESCI, 227 ABDC, 161 ABS) published as book chapters and in top refereed academic journals. According to an article published in *Journal of Finance*, the number of publications would put Prof. Hassan in the top 1% of peers who continue to publish one refereed article per year over a long period of time.

Petr Hajek is currently an associate professor with the Institute of System Engineering and Informatics, University of Pardubice, Czech Republic. He is the author or co-author of four books and more than 60 articles in leading journals. His current research interests include business decision making, soft computing, text mining, and knowledge-based systems.

Mohammed Mohi Uddin is an assistant professor of Accounting at the University of Illinois Springfield, USA. His primary research interests concern accountability, performance management, corporate social responsibility, and accounting data analytics. Dr. Uddin published scholarly articles in reputable academic and practitioners' journals.

Routledge Advanced Texts in Economics and Finance

For more information about this series, please visit: www.routledge.com/Routledge-Advanced-Texts-in-Economics-and-Finance/book-series/SE0757

The Essentials of Machine Learning in Finance and Accounting

Edited by
Mohammad Zoynul Abedin,
M. Kabir Hassan,
Petr Hajek, and
Mohammed Mohi Uddin

LONDON AND NEW YORK

First published 2021
by Routledge
2 Park Square, Milton Park, Abingdon, Oxon OX14 4RN

and by Routledge
605 Third Avenue, New York, NY 10158

Routledge is an imprint of the Taylor & Francis Group, an informa business

British Library Cataloguing-in-Publication Data
A catalogue record for this book is available from the British Library

Library of Congress Cataloging-in-Publication Data
A catalog record has been requested for this book

ISBN: 978-0-367-48083-7 (hbk)
ISBN: 978-0-367-48081-3 (pbk)
ISBN: 978-1-003-03790-3 (ebk)

Typeset in Adobe Garamond Pro
by codeMantra

Contents

3 Improving longevity risk management through machine learning

SUSANNA LEVANTESI, ANDREA NIGRI, AND GABRIELLA PISCOPO

4 Kernel switching ridge regression in business intelligence systems

MD. ASHAD ALAM, OSAMU KOMORI, AND MD. FERDUSH RAHMAN

Figures

Tables

Contributors

Mohammad Zoynul Abedin is an Associate Professor of Finance in the Department of Finance and Banking at Hajee Mohammad Danesh Science and Technology University, Bangladesh. Dr. Abedin earned the Doctor of Philosophy in Investment Theory from the Dalian University of Technology, China. Prior to this, Dr. Abedin completed BBA and MBA in Finance from Chittagong University, Bangladesh. Dr. Abedin's contributions appeared in major indexing journals such as *IEEE Access, Journal of Business Economics and Management, Risk Management, Journal of Credit Risk,* and *International Journal of Finance & Economics.* His research interest includes data analytics and business intelligence. Moreover, Dr. Abedin served as an ad hoc reviewer in the Web of Science indexed journals.

Md. Ashad Alam is a Professor at the Department of Statistics, Hajee Mohammad Danesh Science and Technology University, where he serves as a bridge across teaching and research. His research interests include theoretical and computational aspects of statistical machine learning, representation learning, combinatorial algorithms, robust statistics, and their applications to biomedical data science. Alam's work is published in peer-reviewed journals including *Neurocomputing, Computational Statistics and Data Analysis, Journal of Neuroscience Methods,* and *POLS one.* By the work on statistical machine learning, he received the PhD degree in Statistical Science from the Institute of Statistical Mathematics at the Graduate University of Advanced Studies, Tokyo, Japan, in September 2014.

Mohammad Sarwar Alam has been engaged in teaching as an Assistant Professor in the Department of Management at the University of Chittagong, Bangladesh. He completed his BBA in Management and MBA in International Management from the Department of Management, University of Chittagong. Mr. Alam's research interests include ERP adoptions, artificial intelligence, supply chain management, and information analytics.

Lubomir Benko received the MS degree in Applied Informatics from Faculty of Natural Sciences, Constantine the Philosopher University in Nitra, Slovakia, in 2014. In 2018, he received the PhD degree in Applied Informatics from University of Pardubice, Czechia. From 2014 to 2018, he was a researcher in the Department of Computer Science, Constantine the Philosopher University. He is currently an Assistant Professor in the Department of Computer Science, Constantine the Philosopher University. His research interests are in the field of web usage mining and natural language processing.

Petra Blazekova is currently an external PhD student at the Faculty of Management, Comenius University in Bratislava. She works at a commercial bank in Slovakia as a risk management specialist. Her research interests are in the field of risk management, reporting, and regulation.

Roberto Casarin is currently a Professor of Econometrics at Ca' Foscari University of Venice researching on Bayesian inference, computational methods, and time series analysis. He is the director of the Venice Center for Risk Analytics and a member of ECLT, GRETA, Econometrics Society, and International Society for Bayesian Analysis. He was an Assistant Professor at University of Brescia and a research assistant at University of Padova. He received a PhD degree in Mathematics (2007) from University Paris Dauphine, a PhD degree in Economics (2003) from the University of Venice, an MSc degree in Applied Mathematics from ENSAE-University Paris Dauphine, and an MSc degree in Economics from the University of Venice.

Emon Kalyan Chowdhury is an Associate Professor of Accounting at Chittagong Independent University, Bangladesh and the head of the Department of Accounting. His research focuses on stock market risk, capital asset pricing model, financial reporting, and corporate governance. Professor Chowdhury earned a PhD degree in stock market risk in 2016 from the University of Chittagong, Bangladesh, where he had received an MBA degree in 2007 and a BBA degree in 2006. He received a second MBA degree in Finance and Human Resource Management from the University of Bangalore, India in 2009. He has more than 25 scholarly publications in different renowned national and international peer-reviewed journals.

Salma Drissi received a PhD degree in Management Science from the Laboratory of Research in Performance Management of Public, Private Organizations and Social Economy, University Ibn Zohr, Morocco. Drissi works as an Assistant Professor at the EMAA Business School, and as a lecturer at the National School of Commerce and Management in Agadir. Dr. Salma holds in her research portfolio several articles published in indexed international journals.

Alessandro Facchinetti received his bachelor degree in Foreign Languages and Literature from Catholic University of Milan in 2014. He then shifted his academic interests to economics and received a second bachelor degree in Business and Administration from Ca' Foscari University of Venice in 2017 and an MSc degree in Finance in 2020 with a thesis on machine learning methods. After a short internship in the data production team of HypoVereinsbank-UniCredit, he obtained a fixed-term position as a research assistant at the Venice Centre for Risk Analytics on machine learning methods.

Petr Hajek is an Associate Professor with the Institute of System Engineering and Informatics, Faculty of Economics and Administration, University of Pardubice. Dr. Petr received the PhD degree in system engineering and informatics from the University of Pardubice, Pardubice, Czech Republic, in 2006. He is the author of three books and more than 90 articles. His research interests include soft computing, machine learning, and economic modeling. He was a recipient of the Rector Award for Scientific Excellence both in 2018 and 2019, and six best paper awards by the international scientific conferences.

Richard L. Harmon is the Managing Director of Cloudera's Financial Services Industry Vertical. He joined Cloudera in May 2016 and has over 25 years of experience in capital markets with specializations in risk management, advance analytics, fixed income research, and simulation analysis. Prior to Cloudera, Dr. Harmon was the Director of SAP's EMEA Capital Markets group for six years and also held senior positions at Citibank, JP Morgan, BlackRock, and Bank of America/Countrywide Capital Markets. Dr. Harmon holds a PhD degree in Economics with specialization in Econometrics from Georgetown University.

M. Kabir Hassan is Professor of Finance in the Department of Economics and Finance at the University of New Orleans. He currently holds three endowed Chairs – Hibernia Professor of Economics and Finance, Hancock Whitney Chair Professor in Business, and Bank One Professor in Business – in the University of New Orleans. Professor Hassan is the winner of the 2016 Islamic Development Bank (IDB) Prize in Islamic Banking and Finance. He received his BA degree in Economics and Mathematics from Gustavus Adolphus College, Minnesota, USA, and an MA degree in Economics and a PhD degree in Finance from the University of Nebraska-Lincoln, USA.

Md. Shah Azizul Hoque is currently pursuing his MBA, major in Human Resource Management (HRM), from the University of Chittagong, Bangladesh. Earlier, he received his BBA degree from the same institution. Apart from this, he has completed a postgraduate diploma in HRM from the BGMEA Institute of Fashion & Technology, Bangladesh. Mr. Hoque feels keen interests in technological and environmental aspects of HRM practices.

Md. Kaosar Hossain is a graduate in Human Resource Management (HRM) from the Department of Human Resource Management, University of Chittagong, Bangladesh, and he is pursuing an MBA in the same field. His research interests lie in the adoption of technology in HRM, AI, and green HRM.

Tarikul Islam is a graduate in Human Resource Management from the University of Chittagong, Bangladesh. He finds research interests in the technology-enabled workplace, gender, leadership style, and conflict resolution at work.

Osamu Komori received his PhD degree from the Graduate University for Advanced Studies in 2010. He is an Associate Professor at Seikei University. His research field includes bioinformatics, machine learning, and linguistics.

Susanna Levantesi is Associate Professor in Mathematical Methods of Economy and Actuarial and Financial Science in the Department of Statistics, Sapienza University of Rome, Italy. She obtained her PhD degree in Actuarial Science from the Sapienza University of Rome. She is Fully Qualified Actuary, member of the Professional association of Italian actuaries, member of the Italian Institute of Actuaries, and member of the Working Group on the Mortality of pensioners and annuitants in Italy. Her areas of expertise include longevity risk modeling and management, actuarial models for health insurance, and machine learning and deep learning in insurance and finance risk.

Michal Munk received the MS degree in Mathematics and Informatics and the PhD degree in Mathematics in 2003 and 2007, respectively, from Constantine the Philosopher University, Nitra, Slovakia. In 2018, he was appointed as a Professor in System Engineering and Informatics at the Faculty of Informatics and Management, University of Hradec Kralove, Czechia. He is currently a Professor in the Department of Computer Science in Constantine the Philosopher University, Nitra, Slovakia. His research interests include data analysis, web mining, and natural language processing.

Renata Myskova received her PhD degree in Economics and Management from the Faculty of Business and Management, Brno University of Technology, Czech Republic, in 2003. Since 2007, she has been working as an Associate Professor at the Institute of Business Economics and Management, Faculty of Economics and Administration, University of Pardubice. She has been working with strategic management, management analysis, financial reporting, and financial management. She has published a number of papers concerning economics and finance. She serves as the associate editor of journal *Economics and Management*.

Andrea Nigri is a PhD student in Statistics at the Sapienza University of Rome. Since 2015, he has been working as a biostatistician and co-author of publications in medical journals. In 2016, Andrea was a research fellow at the Local Health Department of Padua (epidemiological surveillance of mesothelioma). In 2017, during his first year of Doctoral School, he attended the EDSD program (European Doctoral School of Demography) at the CPop in Odense. His research interests include mortality forecasting using statistical learning and deep learning methods and the evolution of life expectancy and lifespan inequality.

Vladimir Olej was born in Poprad, Slovakia. In 2001, he worked as a Professor in the branch of technical cybernetics at the Technical University of Ostrava. Since 2002, he has been working as a Professor with Institute of System Engineering and Informatics, Faculty of Economics and Administration, University of Pardubice, Czech Republic. His research interests include artificial and computational intelligence. He has published a number of papers concerning fuzzy logic, neural networks, and genetic algorithms.

Anna Pilkova is currently Professor of Management at Faculty of Management at Comenius University, Bratislava, Slovakia. Earlier, she worked at top managerial positions in a commercial bank in Slovakia. Her research interests are focused on the banking regulation, risk management, and strategic management at commercial banking in developing countries. In addition, she has conducted research on entrepreneurial activities and entrepreneurship inclusivity as a national team leader for Global Entrepreneurship Monitor. She is a recipient of a few awards including the Green Group Award of Computational Finance and Business Intelligence (Best paper) of the International Conference on Computational Science 2013, the Workshop on Computational Finance and Business Intelligence (Barcelona, 2013).

Gabriella Piscopo is Associate Professor in Financial Mathematics and Actuarial Science at University of Naples Federico II. She obtained her European PhD from University of Naples Federico II and Cass Business School of London. She has been Visiting Professor at Renmin University of China, and Visiting Researcher at Cass Business School of London and at Chatolique Université de Louvain. Her areas of expertise are longevity risk modeling, life insurance valuation, machine learning, and neural network in actuarial science. She is Fully Qualified Actuary member of the Professional association of Italian actuaries and a member of the Italian Institute of Actuaries.

Andrew Psaltis previously served as the Cloudera APAC CTO, joining the company through the Hortonworks merger where he was the APAC CTO starting in 2016. He has spent most of his 20+ year career leading from the intersection of business and technology to drive strategic planning, tactical development, and implementation of leading-edge technology solutions across enterprises globally. He's recognized for being an industry thought leader in big data, data analytics, and streaming systems.

Maha Radwan is an Adjunct Professor of Financial Management, Advanced Accounting, and Public Management, and a Postdoctoral Research Fellow at the University of Turin. She holds a PhD degree in Business and Management from the University of Turin, Italy. Dr. Radwan is the Manager of the *European Journal of Islamic Finance*. She has several publications and a monograph in the field of Islamic finance.

Md. Ferdush Rahman is an Associate Professor and Head in the Department of Marketing, Begum Rokeya University Rangpur (BRUR), Bangladesh. As part of his last 16 years career, Mr. Rahman held many leadership roles like Dean of the Faculty of Business Studies, Head of the Department of Marketing, etc., at Begum Rokeya University Rangpur. His research interests include consumer behavior, advertising, and retailing. Rahman's work is published in various peer-reviewed journals including *POLS one, International Journal of Economics & Management Sciences, Journal of Marketing and Consumer Research, Global Media Journal*, etc. He achieved his Bachelor of Business Studies and Master of Business Studies in Marketing from the Department of Marketing, Rajshahi University, Bangladesh.

Silvana Secinaro is an Associate Professor in Business Administration, Islamic Finance, and Accounting at University of Turin. Since 2001, she has been an expert in Public Sector Accounting. She is a member of several groups of study and author of papers focused on public sector accounting. She is included as an external expert to support the implementation of structural reforms in Member States in European Commission.

Md. Shajalal received the BSc (Eng) and MEng degrees in Computer Science and Engineering from the University of Chittagong (CU), Bangladesh, and the Toyohashi University of Technology (TUT), Japan, respectively. He is currently a lecturer in the Department of Computer Science and Engineering at Hajee Mohammad Danesh Science and Technology University, Bangladesh. He is also leading a research group working on IR and NLP (IRLP Research Group). He also served as a faculty member at Bangladesh Agricultural University and Bangladesh Army University of Science and Technology. His research interests are in the field of web search, information retrieval, sentiment analysis, and natural language processing.

Domenico Sorice earned his bachelor degree in Business Administration with specialization in financial intermediaries from Ca' Foscari University of Venice in 2017. Afterward he did an internship in the Global Operations Center of General Electric supporting the development of the information system of healthcare, power, and renewable business processes. He received his MSc degree in Economics and Finance in 2020 with a thesis on random forests for time series forecasting. He is currently a Capital Markets Research intern in the Economic Group Research of Allianz SE.

Stefano Tonellato is currently an Associate Professor of Statistics at Ca' Foscari University of Venice, researching on Bayesian inference, classification, and statistical inference from spatio-temporal stochastic processes. He received an MSc degree in Economics from the Ca' Foscari University of Venice and a PhD degree in Statistics from Padua University. He was previously an Assistant Professor at Ca' Foscari University of Venice and a research associate at the University of Lancaster and the Athen University of Economics and Business. He is a member of the Italian Statistical Society.

Md. Aftab Uddin has been teaching as an Associate Professor in the Department of Human Resource Management, University of Chittagong, Bangladesh. Apart from scoring BBA and MBA from the University of Chittagong, Dr. Uddin was also awarded an MBA and a PhD from the Wuhan University of Technology, China. He researches corporate greenization, creative engagement, innovative behavior, intelligence, leadership, positive psychology, technology-driven workplace, etc.

Mohammed Mohi Uddin, PhD, is an Assistant Professor of Accounting at the University of Illinois Springfield, USA. He received a Bachelor of Commerce and a Master of Commerce from the University of Chittagong, an MBA degree from the University of Leeds, and a PhD degree in Accounting from Aston University. His primary research interests concern accountability, performance management, corporate social responsibility, and accounting data analytics. He secured external research funding, and published scholarly articles in reputable academic and practitioners' journals. Dr. Uddin served as an ad hoc reviewer of internationally reputable accounting journals such as *Accounting, Auditing and Accountability Journal*, and *Journal of Accounting in Emerging Economies*. He is a fellow of Higher Education Academy, United Kingdom. In the past, Dr. Uddin held academic positions at Queen's University Belfast, Aston University, and University of Chittagong.

Veronica Veggente received her bachelor degree in Economics and Finance from Roma Tre University in 2018 writing a thesis on an econometric analysis of the investment choices of households. She then moved to Ca' Foscari University of Venice and completed her MSc in Finance in 2020 discussing master thesis on random projection methods in statistics. During her studies she did a short internship in the Financial and Credit Risk unit of Generali Italia and she obtained a fixed-term position as a research assistant at the Venice Centre for Risk Analytic. Her current project focuses on dimensionality reduction techniques for entropy estimation.

Chapter 1

Machine learning in finance and accounting

Mohammad Zoynul Abedin, M. Kabir Hassan, Petr Hajek, and Mohammed Mohi Uddin

1.1 Introduction

Machine learning (ML) is a type of applied artificial intelligence (AI) that enables computer systems learn from data or observations, and automatically improves predictability by utilizing ongoing learning. It is generally featured in computer science discipline but can be applied in disciplines such as social sciences, finance, accounting and banking, marketing research, operations research, and applied sciences. It utilizes computationally intensive techniques, such as cluster analysis, dimensionality reduction, and support vector analysis. ML has experienced a rise in recognition among academics, researchers, and practitioners over the last couple of decades because of its ability to help predict more accurately. Many applications of ML across diverse fields have emerged. Particularly, its applications in major disciplines such as finance, accounting, information systems, statistics, economics, and operations research are noteworthy. In the context of rapid innovations in computer science and availability of big data, ML can change the way practitioners make predictions, and researchers collect and analyze data.

Computational finance is an interdisciplinary area that integrates computing tools with numerical finance. By utilizing computer algorithms, it can contribute to the advancement of financial data modeling systems. These computational techniques can successfully be utilized in important finance areas, such as financial risk management, corporate bankruptcy prediction, stock price prediction, and portfolio management. For example, ML can be utilized to prevent and detect credit card frauds. Taking into consideration the availability of huge volume of unstructured data, such as customer reviews and social media posts and news data, ML can

1

provide "new insights into business performance, risks and opportunities" (Cockcroft & Russell, 2018, p. 324). ML tools can be utilized to process these unstructured data in order for making better business decisions. Managers can use ML tools in preventing and detecting accounting frauds (see Cockcroft & Russell, 2018). It can also be used in accounting areas such as auditing, income tax, and managerial accounting.

ML can be successfully utilized in accounting and finance research. For example, content analysis is a widely used research method in accounting research. ML algorithms can provide "reliability, stability, reproductivity and accuracy" (see Bogaerd & Aerts, 2011, p. 13414) in data processing. Accounting researchers in corporate social responsibility (CSR) frequently use textual analysis, a sub-category of content analysis, for identifying themes. ML algorithms can successfully be used to classify texts or generate themes (see Bogaerd & Aerts, 2011). Accounting scholars (Deegan & Rankin, 1998; Gray, Kouhy & Lavers, 1995; Neu, Warsame & Pedwell, 1998) used algorithms in classifying texts from corporate social and environmental reports. Bogaerd and Aerts (2011) used LPU (learning from positive and unlabeled data) ML method in classifying texts with 90% accuracy. Behavioral finance researchers can use unstructured newspaper and social media data to understand market sentiment, and utilize the data in developing models predicting prices of financial products.

The next two sections highlight the motivation and provide the brief overviews of chapters appearing in this book.

1.2 Motivation

ML is an emerging computing tool that can be successfully utilized in large and complex data settings. For example, recently researchers from Warwick University, UK, discovered 50 new planets from existing NASA data by using ML algorithms (Yeung, 2020). These types of opportunities were not available in the past due to the absence of large datasets and the processing limitations of computers. Due to the advancement in computing technology, "big data" are now easily available on various business areas. ML can be used to exploit the immense potential of utilizing "big data" for making improved business decisions. Research on utilizing big data (and ML) has potentials for better "industry practices" and "cross-disciplinary research" (see Cockcroft & Russell, 2018, p. 323). However, although it has tremendous potentials, Goes (2014) argues that finance industry does not have sufficient expertise to exploits the benefits of big data. This book is interdisciplinary in nature. It aims to contribute to the emerging machine learning area and its applications in businesses.

This book will present 12 chapters covering topics including machine learning concepts, algorithms and their applications. More specifically, this book introduces methods such as kernel switching ridge regression, sentimental analysis, decision trees, and random forests. It also introduces empirical studies applying ML in multiple finance and accounting areas, such as forecasting of mortality for insurance product pricing, using kernel switching ridge regression for improving prediction models, managing risk and financial crimes, and predicting stock return volatilities. Given the lack of availability of sufficient books in this area, this book will be useful to researchers, including academics and research students, who are interested in advanced machine learning tools and their applications. The contents of this proposed book are also expected to benefit practitioners who are involved in forecasting modeling, stock-trading risk management, bankruptcy prediction, accounting and banking fraud detection, insurance product pricing, credit risk management, and portfolio management. We believe findings from this book will add new insights into the stream of computational finance and accounting research.

1.3 Brief overview of chapters

In addition to this introduction chapter, there are 11 chapters included in the book. We briefly introduce these chapters in the following sections.

Chapter 2 reviews Breiman's CART algorithm, classification features, and non-parametric methods, i.e., decision trees and random forests (Casarin, Facchinetti, Sorice & Tonellato, 2021). The authors also apply the decision trees and random forests in financial time series in predicting default probability in selected enterprises.

Chapter 3 applies ML to enhance longevity risk management by life insurance companies and pension fund managers. Particularly, this chapter shows how ML can help improve mortality forecasting. The authors used mortality data and the 'forecasted mortality rates' in pricing life insurance products (Levantesi, Nigri & Piscopo, 2021).

In **Chapter 4**, the authors introduced kernel switching ridge regression, an ML method. They argue that the method can make predictions from multiple "regimes of dataset" and "can overcome the unstable solution and the curse of dimensionality" (Alam, Komori & Rahman, 2021, p. 14). By using evidence from an experimental study, the authors show that this method can provide better results than some other popular ML methods.

In **Chapter 5**, the authors utilized sentiment analysis in predicting stock return volatilities. By analyzing textual and fundamental indicators' data from annual reports of a large number of US companies, the authors show that ML methods can help generate more accurate predictions of stock price movements (Hajek, Myskova & Olej, 2021).

Chapter 6 introduces some important concepts and ML algorithms, and applications of machine learning techniques in the fields of economics and finance. By reviewing existing literature, the chapter also provides valuable insights to researchers, practitioners, and readers who seek to understand key algorithms used in ML in the field of finance and economics fields. It also examined the effectiveness of ML methods in time series analysis through a simulation study (Casarin & Veggente, 2021).

Chapter 7 focuses on the use of ML and AI in financial services industry. The authors provide examples where ML and AI can transform how the financial services industry can improve products and services, and minimize risk. They used three business cases on "combating financial crimes," "mitigating risk exposures," and how "regulators understand potential cloud concentration risk exposures" to justify the potentials of ML and AI in financial services industry (Harmon & Psaltis, 2021, p. 1).

Chapter 8 focuses on the importance of using AI in an audit process. It introduces an AI-based audit framework and explains some benefits and challenges of using AI in an audit process. This chapter introduces the uses of AI by leading audit firms in an audit process with reference to developed countries. This study emphasizes on ensuring transparency in audit process for taking decisions and to giving judgments on various audit affairs.

Chapter 9 introduces web usage analysis that integrates Pillar 3 information assessment in turbulent times. By using data from website visits logs, the chapter assessed the "interests of bank depositors on the requirements of Pillar 3 disclosures and Pillar 3 related information" during the credit crunch-related financial crisis in 2009 (Pilkova, Munk, Blazekova & Benko, 2021, p. 1).

Chapter 10 introduces various ML concepts and algorithms, and applications of ML in accounting, finance, and economics. Particularly, it highlights the importance of using ML in "algorithmic trading and portfolio management, risk management and credit scoring, insurance pricing and detection of accounting and financial fraud" (Radwan, Drissi & Secinaro, 2021, p. 2).

Chapter 11 discusses challenges of applying classification techniques in highly class imbalanced dataset. Select techniques including oversampling, undersampling, SMOTE, and borderline-SMOTE to solve class imbalance problems are presented. This chapter also presents different metrics for evaluating performance of classification techniques applied on imbalanced dataset.

Chapter 12 is about the applications of AI in staff recruitment. This chapter applies the lens of combined system of acceptance and usage of technology. By doing so, it highlights the importance of various antecedents of acceptance of AI among HR experts for hiring talents in Bangladesh. It also identifies the determinants of AI adoptions. By employing a deducting reasoning approach, the authors make some interesting empirical contributions. It also provides some insightful comments and notes on opportunities for further research in this area.

References

Alam, M. A., Komori, O., & Rahman, M. F. (2021). Kernel switching ridge regression in business intelligence system. In M. Z. Abedin, Hassan, M. K., Hajek, P., and Uddin, M. M. (Eds.), *The Essentials of Machine Learning in Finance and Accounting* (pp. 17–45). Oxford: Taylor and Francis.

Bogaerd, M. V., & Aerts, W. (2011). Applying machine learning in accounting research. *Expert Systems with Applications, 38*, 13414–13424.

Casarin, R., Facchinetti, A., Sorice, D., & Tonellato, S. (2021). Decision trees and random forests. In M. Z. Abedin, Hassan, M. K., Hajek, P., and Uddin, M. M. (Eds.), *The Essentials of Machine Learning in Finance and Accounting* (pp. 17–45). Oxford: Taylor and Francis.

Casarin, R., & Veggente, V. (2021). Random projection methods in economics and finance. In M. Z. Abedin, Hassan, M. K., Hajek, P., and Uddin, M. M. (Eds.), *The Essentials of Machine Learning in Finance and Accounting* (pp. 17–45). Oxford: Taylor and Francis.

Cockcroft, S., & Russell, M. (2018). Big data opportunities for accounting and finance practice and research. *Australian Accounting Review, 86*(28), 1–12.

Deegan, C., & Rankin, M. (1996). Do Australian companies report environmental news objectively? An analysis of environmental disclosures by firms prosecuted successfully by the Environmental Protection Authority. *Accounting, Auditing and Accountability Journal, 9*(2), 50–67.

Goes, P. B.(2014). *Big Data and IS Research*. Minneapolis: Carlson School of Management.

Gray, R., Kouhy, R., & Lavers, S. (1995). Corporate social and environmental reporting: A review of the literature and a longitudinal study of UK disclosure. *Accounting, Auditing and Accountability Journal, 8*(2), 47–77.

Hajek, P., Myskova, R., & Olej, V. (2021). Predicting stock return volatility using sentiment analysis of corporate annual reports. In M. Z. Abedin, Hassan, M. K., Hajek, P., and Uddin, M. M. (Eds.), *The Essentials of Machine Learning in Finance and Accounting* (pp. 17–45). Oxford: Taylor and Francis.

Harmon, R., & Psaltis, A. (2021). The future of cloud computing in financial services: A machine learning and artificial intelligence perspective. In M. Z. Abedin, Hassan, M. K., Hajek, P., and Uddin, M. M. (Eds.), *The Essentials of Machine Learning in Finance and Accounting* (pp. 17–45). Oxford: Taylor and Francis.

Levantesi, S., Nigri, A., & Piscopo, G. (2021). Improving longevity risk management through machine learning. In M. Z. Abedin, Hassan, M. K., Hajek, P., and Uddin, M. M. (Eds.), *The Essentials of Machine Learning in Finance and Accounting* (pp. 17–45). Oxford: Taylor and Francis.

Neu, D., Warsame, H., & Pedwell, K. (1998). Managing public impressions: Environmental disclosures in annual reports. *Accounting, Organizations and Society*, *23*(3), 265–282.

Pilkova, A., Munk, M., Blazekova, P., & Benko, L. (2021). Web usage analysis: Pillar 3 information assessment in turbulent times. In M. Z. Abedin, Hassan, M. K., Hajek, P., and Uddin, M. M. (Eds.), *The Essentials of Machine Learning in Finance and Accounting* (pp. 17–45). Oxford: Taylor and Francis.

Radwan, M., Drissi, S., & Secinaro, S. (2021). Machine learning in the fields of accounting, economics and finance: The emergence of new strategies. In M. Z. Abedin, Hassan, M. K., Hajek, P., and Uddin, M. M. (Eds.), *The Essentials of Machine Learning in Finance and Accounting* (pp. 17–45). Oxford: Taylor and Francis.

Yeung, J. (2020). Breakthrough AI identifies 50 new planets from old NASA data. *CNN Business*, available at: https://www.cnn.com/2020/08/26/tech/ai-new-planets-confirmed-intl-hnk-scli-scn/index.html, date accessed: August 30, 2020.

Chapter 2

Decision trees and random forests*

Roberto Casarin, Alessandro Facchinetti, Domenico Sorice, and Stefano Tonellato

2.1 Introduction

A decision tree is a non-parametric supervised learning tool for extracting knowledge from available data. It is non-parametric, since it does not require any assumptions regarding the distribution of the dependent variable, the explanatory variables, and the functional form of the relationships between them. It is supervised, since it is trained over a labeled dataset, $\mathcal{L}$, in which each observation is identified by a series of *features*, or explanatory variables, $X_1, \ldots, X_p$, belonging to the sample space $\mathcal{X}$, and by a *target*, or response variables, Y. A generic observation is denoted as $o_i = (x_{1i}, x_{2i}, ..., x_{pi}, y_i)$, where y_i represents the measurement of the response variable on the ith sample item, whereas x_{ji} represents the measurement of the jth feature on the same item, with $j = 1, \ldots, p$ and $i = 1, \ldots, N$. The symbol $\mathbf{x}$ denotes a generic value of the p-dimensional feature vector.

Based on the evidence provided by the data, a decision tree provides a prediction of the target and a relationship between the features and such target.

The engine that powers a decision tree is recursive binary partitioning of the sample space $\mathcal{X}$ as represented in Figure 2.1. The diamond-shaped box identifies the *root node*, which is associated with observations, $\mathcal{L}$. The circles identify the *internal nodes*. At each internal node, a test

---

*This research used the SCSCF multiprocessor cluster system and is part of the project Venice Center for Risk Analytics (VERA) at Ca' Foscari University of Venice.

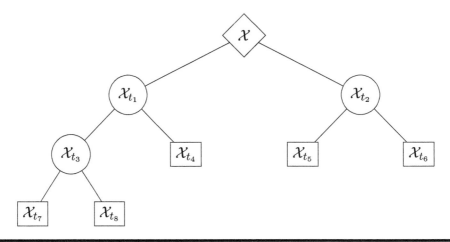

Figure 2.1 Structure of a decision tree, highlighting root node (diamond), internal nodes (circles), branches and leaves (squares).

is performed over some features and an arbitrary observation is associated either with the left or with the right children node, accordingly with the result of such test. The terminal nodes, called *leaves*, determine a partition of $\mathcal{L}$ by means of a sequence of splitting decisions.

Decision trees are discriminated according to the nature of the target they have to predict. A *classification* tree is characterized by the fact that it predicts a categorical response, as opposed to a quantitative and, generally, continuous one in the *regression* case. In the following two sections, the Classification And Regression Tree (CART) algorithm (Breiman, Friedman, Olshen, & J., 1984) will be illustrated. CART is one of the most popular algorithms used in the construction of decision trees. Other valuable algorithms that will not be treated in this chapter are *ID3* (Quinlan, 1986) and *C4.5* (Quinlan, 1993). Section 3 will illustrate some common features of classification and regression trees, with particular emphasis on surrogate splitting, handling of missing values, and feature ranking. Section 4 provides a short discussion of the advantages and disadvantages of decision trees. In Section 5, random forests are presented. Some applications of random forests in classification, regression, and time series analysis are produced in Section 6. The R code used in the applications is reported in the appendix.

2.2 Classification trees

In a classification tree, taking into account the first two nodes t_1 (the left node) and t_2 (the right node), the partition $\{\mathcal{X}_{t_1}, \mathcal{X}_{t_2}\}$ that has been performed must satisfy the following conditions: $\mathcal{X}_{t_1}, \mathcal{X}_{t_2} \subseteq \mathcal{X}$, $\mathcal{X}_{t_1} \cup \mathcal{X}_{t_2} = \mathcal{X}$, and $\mathcal{X}_{t_1} \cap \mathcal{X}_{t_2} = \emptyset$. These conditions must be satisfied by any binary splitting until the very end of the tree, which corresponds to the leaves level, i.e., $\mathcal{X}_{t_l}, \mathcal{X}_{t_{l+1}} \subseteq \mathcal{X}_{t_k}$, $\mathcal{X}_{t_l} \cup \mathcal{X}_{t_{l+1}} = \mathcal{X}_{t_k}$, $\mathcal{X}_{t_l} \cap \mathcal{X}_{t_{l+1}} = \emptyset$, with $k = \tau_{n-1} + 1, \ldots, \tau_{n-1} + 2^n$, $l = \tau_n + 2(k - \tau_{n-1} - 1) + 1$, $\tau_n = 2^{n+1} - 2$, where n is the distance of the leaf from the root. The leaves, in accordance with their role of terminal nodes, perform the ultimate partitioning of the input space, and discriminate among different groups of measurement vectors associating them with distinct response labels. The final tree, trained on the learning sample, can be used to classify any future measurement vector **x** assigning the correct label with the highest accuracy.

The problem of generating a tree consists in the following choices (Breiman et al., 1984):

■ the best partition of the data (*splitting* rules);
■ the size of the tree (*stopping* rules);
■ the label assignment to the leaves (*assignment* rules).

2.2.1 *Impurity and binary splitting*

The rationale behind any split, at any internal node, is to generate two descendant child nodes where the data are increasingly pure. In the classification tree a larger purity level is obtained by partitioning the data into two subsets with homogeneous features within each group and heterogeneous features between the groups. A simple visual representation might clarify the concept. Let us assume we are dealing with a group of 15 people and our target variable, whose behavior we want to unveil, is the color of their eyes: either brown (B) or green (G). The available features are the height of the individuals and the continent they come from. We could identify each person in our sample by the combination of the two-dimensional measurement vector and the response value, $o_i = (x_{continent,i}, x_{height,i}, y_{color,i})$. Let us assume we partition the group of people following alternatively their height or their origin. The resulting partitions are provided by the leaves of the trees in Figure 2.2a and b. In the root node of both trees 60% of the individuals have green eyes, while the rest have brown eyes. Figure 2.2a shows that in the left child (t_L) the percentage is respectively 62.5% and 37.5%, while in the right child (t_R) it is respectively 57% and 43%. In Figure 2.2b the distribution of the response variable in the children nodes is now strongly unbalanced: among the group of people in t_L, 87.5% of the people have green eyes; among the people in t_R, 71.5% have blue eyes. Therefore, we can state that the partition in Figure 2.2a has larger impurity level than the one shown in Figure 2.2b.

According to Breiman et al. (1984) a function that quantifies impurity, regardless of its formal structure, must possess the following properties:

(i)   it must be non-negative;
(ii) it has to achieve its maximum in the case in which the distribution of the response in the node is perfectly uniform, because it is the worst case scenario in terms of acquired knowledge;
(iii) it has to achieve its minimum whenever all the sample items allocated to the node exhibit the same value of the response;
(iv) it has to be symmetric with respect to the frequency distribution of the response; this means that if we permute the labels of the response in two children nodes by keeping the frequencies unaltered, the value of the function does not change.

A split is beneficial whenever it creates two descendant subsets that are indeed more homogeneous with respect to the class distribution, and a way to judge the goodness of a split is to compute the change in impurity that it produces:

$$\Delta\iota(s,t) = \iota(t) - p_L\iota(s,t_L) - p_R\iota(s,t_R), \tag{2.1}$$

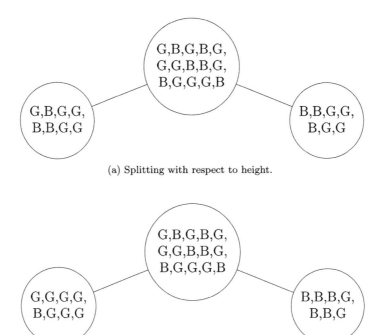

(a) Splitting with respect to height.

(b) Splitting with respect to geographical origin.

Figure 2.2 Examples of alternative splitting rules giving rise to partitions characterized by (a) high and (b) low impurity level. Each symbol represents an individual, G indicates green eyes and B brown eyes.

where s represents a possible split of node t into the left and right children nodes, t_L and t_R; $\iota(t)$, $\iota(t_L)$, and $\iota(t_R)$ denote the impurity level of nodes t, t_L, and t_R respectively. The children impurities are weighted by the proportions of instances that they have collected, p_L and p_R respectively.

The tree T impurity level is defined as

$$\mathrm{I}(T) = \sum_{t \in \tilde{T}} p(t)\iota(t),$$

a weighted average of leaves impurity levels, where $\tilde{T}$ identifies the series of terminal nodes of T. Let us assume we wanted to proceed with one further split at an arbitrary terminal node t. This step would generate a different tree, where the single leaf t would make room for two new leaves t_L and t_R. The overall change in impurity level between the original tree and the newly produced one could be quantified as in Eq. (2.1).

2.2.1.1 Specification of the impurity function

We give now a short overview of the most used impurity functions in the context of classification. For a more detailed discussion see Breiman et al. (1984).

Error-based index is indeed the most intuitive criterion: the best split is the one with the smallest number of misclassifications in the children nodes. From a mathematical perspective we can define the impurity of node t as the *error index* in t, i.e.,

$$\iota_{EI}(t) = 1 - \max_c p(c|t).$$

Equation (2.1) then gives

$$\Delta\iota_{EI}(t) = 1 - \max_c p(c|t) - p_L \left[1 - \max_c p(c|s, t_L) \right] - p_R \left[1 - \max_c p(c|s, t_R) \right].$$

The impurity function based on *Gini index* is widespread and is defined as

$$\iota_{GI}(t) = 1 - \sum_c \left[p(c|t) \right]^2 .$$

It is straightforward to verify that if $p(c|t)$ is close to 1 for some c, the impurity measure will tend to 0, implying that the more the observations tend to belong to a single class, the higher the value of the information conveyed by the split. From Eq. (2.1), it follows that

$$\Delta\iota_{GI}(s, t) = 1 - \sum_c \left[p(c|t) \right]^2 - p_L \left[1 - \sum_c \left[p(c|s, t_L) \right]^2 \right] - p_R \left[1 - \sum_c \left[p(c|s, t_R) \right]^2 \right].$$

Another popular definition of impurity function is based on *Shannon entropy index* (Shannon, 1948):

$$\iota_{HI}(t) = - \sum_c p(c|t) \log_2 p(c|t)$$

The behavior of the function is similar to one based on the Gini index. From Eq. (2.1) we have

$$\Delta\iota_{HI}(s, t) = - \sum_c p(c|t) \log_2 p(c|t) - p_L \left[- \sum_c p(c|s, t_L) \log_2 p(c|s, t_L) \right]$$
$$- p_R \left[- \sum_c p(c|s, t_R) \log_2 p(c|s, t_R) \right].$$

2.2.1.2 Labeling the leaves

A unique category of the response variable is associated with a leaf. Formally, the class c^* is assigned to a terminal node if

$$c^* = \arg \max_{c \in \mathcal{C}} p(c|t), \tag{2.2}$$

where $\mathcal{C}$ represents the support of the categorical response variable. Thus, c^* is the Y-category that most frequently occurs in the terminal node t. This assignment rule is known as majority vote method.

2.2.1.3 Tree size and stopping rules

The choice of the size is a fundamental step in the tree building process (Maimon & Rokach, 2005). A tree that grows too much, generating too many leaves, might fit too closely to the data it has been trained on, without necessarily maintaining the same performance on new independent observations. The reason is that a large tree is likely to give too much weight to possible outliers in the learning sample, becoming overly adapted on past data and losing predictive power on future observations: this problem is called *overfitting*. On the contrary, if a tree is too small (so if the number of leaves is too restricted), there is a chance it is not extracting enough knowledge from the learning sample and performing badly on both past and future observations. This is *underfitting* issue. In order to prevent the tree from becoming too large, we can act earlier by setting a series of stopping criteria (*pre-pruning approach*), or we can let the tree fully expand and delete the parts that seem to add unjustified complexity (*post-pruning* approach). The two approaches are not mutually exclusive: they are fully compatible and might actually speed up the process of finding the optimal size if used together.

Pre-pruning consists in stopping the tree induction process and declaring a node as terminal in the following circumstances:

1. the frequency distribution of either the response or the features is degenerate in such node (these are also called *mandatory conditions*);
2. when any of its possible children contains a number of instances which is lower than a given threshold, or if any further splitting does not determine a decrease of impurity higher than a given level, or when the maximum admissible depth of the tree is reached, i.e., the maximum number of splits has been achieved.

Post-pruning still resorts to a series of stopping criteria, just very loose ones: the aim is to let an excessively large tree grow with few restrictions, and then progressively cut off parts of it monitoring how the performance is affected. The available literature proposes a number of different post-pruning approaches such as reduced error pruning, pessimistic error pruning, minimum error pruning, critical value pruning, error-based pruning, and cost-complexity pruning (Esposito, Malerba, Semeraro, & Kay, 1997). The last one is employed in the Classification and Regression Trees (*CART*) algorithm implemented by the `rpart` package Therneau and Atkinson (2019). The pruning process consists in starting from the overly large tree, let us call it T_{max}, and in trimming the branches, thus generating a sequence of progressively smaller *subtrees*. Up to the smallest one, the root node t_0 itself. The optimal subtree is the one that minimizes the following loss function:

$$L(T) = MR(T) + \alpha(T),$$

where $MR(T)$ represents the misclassification rate, i.e., the proportion of misclassified items in the training set, and $\alpha(T)$, $\alpha(T) \geq 0$ denotes the cost associated with the size of the subtree.

2.2.2 Performance estimation

This section is devoted to the misclassification rate of a tree, $MR(T)$, with the aim of providing its fairest estimate. In particular, three possible approaches will be discussed (Breiman et al., 1984, ch. 2 and 3): the *resubstitution* estimate, the *test-sample* estimate, and the *cross-validation* estimate.

2.2.2.1 Resubstitution estimate

Assuming that the predicted class for leave t is given by $c^* = \arg\max\limits_{c \in C} p(c|t)$, which corresponds to the majority vote method, the estimated probability that an instance falling into the terminal node t does not belong to the predicted class, i.e., the estimated misclassification rate at leave t, is

$$MR^{res}(t) = 1 - p(c^*|t). \tag{2.3}$$

Clearly, $MR^{res}(t)$ represents the proportion of objects wrongly predicted by node t, hence its predictive accuracy. As usual, the behavior of the tree relates to the performance of the single leaves, each weighted by the proportion of total instances they collect. Therefore, Eq. (2.3) generalizes as

$$MR^{res}(T) = \sum_{t \in \tilde{T}} p(t)\, MR^{res}(t) \tag{2.4}$$

meaning that the overall tree misclassification is simply the weighted average of the single leaves misclassification rate. We must highlight a flaw of this method: the performance of a tree is measured in terms of the good fitting only to the dataset over which it has been trained on. In fact, if we had a single set of observations for both training and validation, we would obtain a biased measure of the performance, specifically an overly optimistic one. Intuitively, given the nature of Eq. (2.4), the more we split, the finer the partitions and the lower the misclassification rate estimate. In other words, following this logic, we would be persuaded to keep on splitting until we would be forced to stop by a mandatory condition. This is the reason why alternative approaches should be looked for.

2.2.2.2 Test-sample estimate

The problem of lack of independence between training set and test set suggests to formulate an alternative known as test-sample estimate. The simple step that fixes the issue of coincidence between training and validation sets consists in randomly selecting, from the original learning sample, a number of N_{ts} elements that will constitute what we define as the *test sample* $(\mathcal{L}_{ts})$, and separating it from the remaining N_{nls} that will form the *new learning set* $(\mathcal{L}_{nls})$. Only the observations contained in the new learning set are used to build the usual sequence of trees, while the untouched observations in the test sample are used to assess the predictive performance. More formally, let us define with N_c the number of observations of class c included in $\mathcal{L}_{ts}$, and with N_{dc} the number of observations of class c that, when fed to the tree, are wrongly labeled as d, $d \neq c$. The estimated misclassification rate of the tree T based on the test set $\mathcal{L}_{ts}$ is then given by

$$MR^{ts}(T) = \frac{1}{N_{ts}} \sum_{c=1}^{C} \sum_{d=1;\ d \neq c}^{C} N_{dc}. \tag{2.5}$$

The remarkable feature of this approach is that the random selection ensures that the disjoint sets $\mathcal{L}_{ts}$ and $\mathcal{L}_{nls}$ are truly independent. As a rule of thumb, usually 70% of the observations are reserved for the tree building process, and the rest are employed for validation. Of course, in order to proceed in this way a sufficiently large sample size is required. A quantification of the uncertainty in the estimation of the misclassification rate is given the standard error of MR^{ts}:

$$se\left(MR^{ts}(T)\right) = \sqrt{\frac{MR^{ts}(T)\left(1 - MR^{ts}(T)\right)}{N_{ts}}}.$$

As the size of the test set $\mathcal{L}_{ts}$ increases, the standard deviation decreases, coherently with the fact that the estimation of the misclassification rate becomes increasingly reliable.

This approach can be further generalized by splitting the sample $\mathcal{L}$ in G disjoint training sets and estimating the misclassification rate of a tree using cross-validation.

2.3 Regression trees

2.3.1 Regression

The crucial difference with the classification case lies in the nature of the response variable: a regression tree is meant to predict the behavior of a continuous variable. A regression tree is similar to its classification counterpart and aims at identifying subsets of the feature space $\mathcal{F}$ providing similar prediction of the response variable. Let $\mathcal{P} = \{R_1, \ldots, R_F\}$ represent a partition of the feature space, i.e., $R_f \cap R_{f'} = \emptyset$ and $R_1 \cup \cdots \cup R_F = \mathcal{F}$, where F identifies the number of subsets in the partition, R_f refers to the generic element of $\mathcal{P}$, and $\hat{y}_{R_f}$ is the average value of the response in the subsample $\mathcal{L}_f$:

$$\mathcal{L}_f = \left\{i \in \mathcal{L} : (x_{1i}, \ldots, x_{ip}) \in R_f\right\}.$$

Since $\mathcal{P}_{\mathcal{L}} = \{\mathcal{L}_1, \ldots, \mathcal{L}_F\}$ is a partition of $\mathcal{L}$, the overall model performance can be evaluated by the residual sum of squares (James, Witten, Hastie, & Tibshirani, 2013):

$$S(\mathcal{P}_{\mathcal{L}}) = \sum_{f=1}^{F} \sum_{i \in \mathcal{L}_f} (y_i - \hat{y}_{R_f})^2. \tag{2.6}$$

Our aim is to find the partition $\mathcal{P}_{\mathcal{L}}$ that minimizes Eq. 2.6. Unfortunately, this optimization problem cannot be solved when the number of features is moderately high. Therefore, decision trees based on a binary splitting analogous to the one illustrated in the previous section are built in order to approximately minimize $S(\mathcal{P}_{\mathcal{L}})$ in Eq. (2.6).

We move from the majority vote rationale to a least squares approach: the prediction attached to a terminal node is simply the average of the response variable on the cases it collects. Then, the prediction produced by node t is

$$\bar{y}(t) = \frac{1}{N(t)} \sum_{i \in t} y_i$$

With $N(t)$ we denote the number of instances collected by the node t; the summation concerns only those sample items that are allocated to t.

It is worth to notice that the average minimizes a square loss function. Hence, a suitable impurity function for the generic node t in a regression tree can be defined as

$$\iota(t) = \sum_{i \in t} (y_i - \bar{y}_t)^2.$$

Once we have defined an impurity function, we can grow the tree by looking for those splits that maximize Eq. (2.1).

Suppose we want to predict the value taken by the response y when the feature vector takes the value $\mathbf{x}$. The prediction produced by the regression tree trained on the sample $\mathcal{L}$ will be denoted by

$$\phi_{\mathcal{L}}(\mathbf{x}) = \bar{y}_{\tilde{t}_{\mathbf{x}}},$$

where $\tilde{t}_{\mathbf{x}}$ is the leaf where sample items with feature vector equal to $\mathbf{x}$ are allocated, i.e., $\mathbf{x} \in \mathcal{X}_{\tilde{t}_{\mathbf{x}}}$.

2.3.2 *Performance assessment and optimal size of the tree*

As far as pre-pruning and post-pruning conditions are concerned, the same methodologies applied to the classification task also hold for regression trees. The only exception is made for the mandatory stopping condition introduced in the previous section, which requires a process to be necessarily interrupted in the case of perfect class homogeneity: since we are now dealing with a continuous target variable, the situation in which a node may present identical response values is highly unlikely.

In the classification task, the misclassification rate has a very straightforward interpretation: it serves the purpose of telling us how many times the prediction of the tree corresponds to the reality. The regression counterpart to the misclassification rate is the *mean squared prediction error*,

$$\mathrm{MSE}(T) = \mathbb{E}\left[(Y - \phi_{\mathcal{L}}(\mathbf{x}))^2\right].$$

2.3.2.1 *Resubstitution estimate of* $\mathrm{MSE}(T)$

The resubstitution estimation method exploits the learning sample $\mathcal{L}$ for the double purpose of building a predictor $\phi_{\mathcal{L}}$ and estimating its mean squared prediction error. The resubstitution estimate of $\mathrm{MSE}(T)$ is given by

$$\mathrm{MSE}^{res}(T) = \frac{1}{N}\sum_{i=1}^{N}\left(y_i - \phi_{\mathcal{L}}(\mathbf{x}_i)\right)^2. \tag{2.7}$$

The use of this estimate in the assessment of the performance of T encourages the algorithm to keep on splitting, often raising overfitting issues.

2.3.2.2 *Test-sample estimate of* $\mathrm{MSE}(T)$

As in the classification case, the test-sample approach requires the creation of two disjoint subsamples: the learning sample $\mathcal{L}_{ls}$, used to train the tree, and the test sample $\mathcal{L}_{ts}$, used to assess the predictive performance of the tree. The mean squared prediction error estimate is given by

$$\mathrm{MSE}^{ts}T = \frac{1}{N_{ts}}\sum_{(\mathbf{x}_i,y_i)\in\mathcal{L}_{ts}}\left(y_i - \phi_{\mathcal{L}_{nls}}(\mathbf{x}_i)\right)^2, \tag{2.8}$$

where the same computation of Eq. (2.7) is limited to the N_{ts} observations of the test sample, compared to the predictions provided by the tree that has been trained on the complementary subset $\mathcal{L}_{nls}$. The standard error associated with this estimate can be easily computed:

$$sd\left(\text{MSE}^{ts}(T)\right) = \frac{1}{\sqrt{N_{ts}}} \left[\frac{1}{N_{ts}} \sum_{i=1}^{N_{ts}} \left(y_i - \phi_{\mathcal{L}}(\mathbf{x}_i)\right)^4 - \left(\text{MSE}^{ts}(T)\right)^2 \right]^{1/2}.$$

Again, further refined estimates of the mean squared prediction error can be obtained through cross-validation.

2.4 Issues common to classification and regression trees

2.4.1 Surrogate splits

Surrogate splits are intuitively alternative splits over alternative features ranked by following how well they would be able to substitute and emulate the best original split. More formally, the approach requires to compare the behavior of s^*, the global best split that can be performed at node t, and a sequence of splits s_js performed on the jth feature. Given the jth input variable, and the set of all the splits S_j that can be performed on it, in order to pinpoint the best surrogate s_j among that sequence we must find a way to quantify how closely a split matches the partition produced by s^* itself. The intuition is to keep track of the number of times an observation is sent to the same children node by both the splits: the higher that number, the greater the accuracy of the surrogate in predicting the actions of s^*. More formally, the instances that are directed to the left children by both the best split s^* and the candidate surrogate s_j generate the intersection set $t_L \cap t_L^j$, where t_L and t_L^j identify respectively the sets of observations that are sent to the left by the best split and by the potential surrogate; similar arguments hold for the right children. In order to quantify the dimension of the intersection sets in the classification case, we can estimate the probability for a specific instance to fall into either intersection by

$$p_{LL}(s^*, s_j) = \sum_c \frac{N_c(LL)}{N(t)}$$

for the left direction and by

$$p_{RR}(s^*, s_j) = \sum_c \frac{N_c(RR)}{N(t)}$$

for the right one. By $N_c(t)$ we denote the number of sample items of class c allocated to node t elements that belong to node t, and by $N_c(LL)$ or $N_c(RR)$ the number of those elements that are sent either left or right by both the splits. The summation $\sum_c$ accounts for all classes; hence, at the numerator $\sum_c N_c(LL)$ and $\sum_c N_c(RR)$ identify all the observations whose direction the two splits agree upon, regardless of class membership. At the denominator, $N(t)$ corresponds to the total number of observations allocated to node t. These ratios quantify the probability that, since an observation is temporarily stored in t, it will be directed toward the same child, therefore revealing the correspondence with the ratios of probabilities in the intermediate step. The counterpart estimations in the regression case are

$$p_{LL}(s^*, s_j) = \frac{p\left(t_L \cap t_L^j\right)}{p(t)} = \frac{N(LL)}{N(t)}$$

and

$$p_{RR}(s^*, s_j) = \frac{p\left(t_R \cap t_R^j\right)}{p(t)} = \frac{N(RR)}{N(t)}.$$

Again, $N(LL)$ and $N(RR)$ identify the sets of observations that are sent either left or right by both splits. The overall performance of a surrogate, regardless of the fact that we are dealing with a classification or a regression tree, is given by

$$p\left(s^*, s_j\right) = p_{LL}\left(s^*, s_j\right) + p_{RR}\left(s^*, s_j\right). \tag{2.9}$$

Therefore, given a specific alternative input, the best surrogate that it can provide is the one $s_j^* \in S_j$ that maximizes the function in Eq. (2.9). This approach creates a sequence of the best surrogates that each input can offer. However, regardless of the "best" status, it does not necessarily mean that a specific surrogate split is worth being taken into consideration. In other words, we need a systematic measure to determine whether a split could indeed act as replacement or should, instead, be discarded. Given the globally optimal split s^* of a node t, we denote by p_L and p_R the probabilities by which it directs the instances it contains toward the left or the right child. If a new observation is fed to the node, then our prediction is that it will be collected by t_L if $max(p_L, p_R) = p_L$, or that it will end up in t_R otherwise; the probability of formulating a wrong prediction about the destination of an observation that is missing the primary variable value, based on the primary variable behavior, thus corresponds to $min(p_L, p_R)$. From the surrogate perspective, Eq. (2.9) estimates the probability that a new observation is directed toward the same node by both the primary and surrogate splits. Hence, we deduce that the estimated probability that the two might instead disagree corresponds to $1 - p(s^*, s_j)$. The so-called predictive association between the two splits

$$\lambda(s^*|s_j) = \frac{\min\left(p_L, p_R\right) - \left(1 - p\left(s^*, s_j\right)\right)}{\min\left(p_L, p_R\right)} \tag{2.10}$$

gives a systematic answer to the issue of whether the surrogate split s_j could be worthy of replacing the primary s^*.

2.4.1.1 Handling of missing values

Missing values are a problem that can affect both data in the training sample and in the test set. Applying the logic of surrogates to the issue allows us to simultaneously make the best use of data available in the tree building phase and to make sure that the final tree is able to handle any new observation, regardless of the fact that it might have some input values missing. In particular during the tree construction process, while the unknown best split s^* is being searched for, the investigation over the specific input is restricted to those observations whose value for such input is defined, while the cases whose value is missing are temporarily discarded. The approach allows us to exploit the available information at best, while at the same time not affecting the process with random guesses. However, if a new observation has a missing value for the input variable over which the split is being performed, the approach consists in selecting the best surrogate input whose value is defined (based on the strength of the predictive index introduced in Eq. (2.10)) and directing the case according to that surrogate split. A remarkable consequence of this approach is the robustness of the decision tree method: missing value cases do not affect the tree construction and hence do not influence the path that will be followed by the other observations.

2.4.1.2 Ranking of input variables

The purpose of tree-based methods is to formulate a prediction of the response variable and, possibly, to unveil the nature of the relationship between the variables involved. To do so, we need a way to measure the importance of an input variable. Given the selected optimal subtree T and its specifically employed splitting rule, to quantify the relevance of an input variable X_j we assess, as a proxy, the performance of the surrogate splits it provides. At each internal node the globally optimal split is replaced by the best surrogate split provided by X_j, and the decreases in impurity generated by the replaced splits are added up together giving the total variation of impurity

$$\mathrm{VI}\left(X_j\right) = \sum_{t \in T} \Delta \iota \left(s_j^*, t\right),$$

where $\Delta \iota$ refers to the decrease in impurity (and not the measure of impurity itself), which is a function of the specific parent node t and the best surrogate split s_j^* that X_j can provide in that circumstance. Intuitively, the larger the decreases in impurity that the splits over X_j can guarantee, the higher the importance of the variable in the model. This measure evaluates the systematic capacity of an input variable in providing surrogate splits: the clever implication is that it quantifies the importance of a variable despite the fact that it may or may not have appeared among the selected splits in the optimal subtree, removing the masking effect due to the presence of other more recurring inputs. In order to generate a ranking and make it as visually appealing as possible, another useful step is to normalize the measure as follows:

$$\frac{\mathrm{VI}\left(X_j\right)}{\max_j \mathrm{VI}\left(X_j\right)} \cdot 100,$$

where the denominator is the value of the most important variable and the ratio is multiplied by a hundred, hence ranging from 0 to 100.

2.4.1.3 Input combination

Most often splits are determined by the results of a test on one explanatory variables. In order to make the tree more powerful and flexible, the split can be performed with respect to a combination of several features such as *linear combinations*, *Boolean combinations*, and *features creation*. See (Breiman et al., 1984, ch. 5.2) for a detailed discussion.

2.4.2 Advantages and disadvantages of decision trees

There are a number of reasons why decision trees are so attractive and widespread. A remarkable trait, probably the one that played the major role in decision trees rise to fame, is definitely the ease of interpretation (James et al., 2013, ch. 8.1). They are easy to explain and easy to understand, even for non-expert users. In particular, if the number of leaves is not overwhelming, the visual representation is always appealing, and allows us to appreciate the precise sequence of decisions, their outcomes, and the probabilities in comprehensible and straightforward fashion. Given the fact that the structure closely resembles human decision making, they can also be easily converted in a logical sequence of rules.

Decision trees are a non-parametric inferential technique; hence, there is no need to make any a priori assumptions regarding the distribution of either the input or the output space. They are particularly fit for modeling complex relationships between predictors and target, just by formulating the appropriate sequence of binary questions (Breiman et al., 1984, ch. 2.7). Moreover, they can easily account for missing values and are flexible enough to handle features of heterogeneous nature such categorical and numerical variables.

Finally, decision trees are computationally efficient (Gupta, Rawat, Jain, Arora, & Dhami, 2017), nevertheless, they suffer from some limitations such as overfitting and instability. The performances of the decision trees tend to be generally good on the training sample, but deteriorate on out-of-sample observations. This overfitting problem can be partially mitigated by both pre-pruning and post-pruning. As far as instability is concerned, even a small change in the training data might produce a large change in the optimal tree structure. Random forests, introduced in the next section, use simultaneously different training sets, thus providing a remedy to instability.

2.5 Random forests

In the previous sections, we remarked that large trees tend to overfit the data. Therefore, we expect that predictions produced by such trees are characterized by a low bias (on average they should be close to the target) and high variance: small changes in the learning sample make prediction very unstable and unreliable. Random forests allow us to overcome this inconvenience very effectively. This section illustrates the main features of random forests, focusing attention on regression. With some minor adaptations, the same augments hold for classification problems. A deeper treatment of this topic can be found in Louppe (2014).

2.5.1 Prediction error bias-variance decomposition

Let $\phi_{\mathcal{L}}$ be the predictor associated with a decision tree trained on the set $\mathcal{L}$ that for the moment is assumed to be non-random. A loss function L is associated with the prediction error and we aim at minimizing the prediction risk

$$R(\phi_{\mathcal{L}}) = \mathbb{E}_{X,Y}\left[L\left(Y - \phi_{\mathcal{L}}(X)\right)\right], \qquad (2.11)$$

where the expectation is taken with respect to the joint probability distribution of X and Y, with (X, Y) being independent of $\mathcal{L}$. Analogously, if the prediction is conditioned on $X = \mathbf{x}$,

$$R(\phi_{\mathcal{L}}(\mathbf{x})) = \mathbb{E}_{Y|X=\mathbf{x}}\left[L\left(Y - \phi_{\mathcal{L}}(\mathbf{x})\right)\right], \qquad (2.12)$$

where the expectation is taken with respect to the probability distribution of Y conditioned on $X = \mathbf{x}$. When $\mathcal{L}$ is assumed random as well, the above two equations are written respectively as

$$R(\phi_{\mathcal{L}}) = \mathbb{E}_{\mathcal{L}}\left\{\mathbb{E}_{X,Y}\left[L\left(Y - \phi_{\mathcal{L}}(X)\right)\right]\right\}, \qquad (2.13)$$

(the outer expectation is taken with respect to $\mathcal{L}$) and

$$R(\phi_{\mathcal{L}}(\mathbf{x})) = \mathbb{E}_{\mathcal{L}|X_{\mathcal{L}}=\mathbf{x}}\left\{\mathbb{E}_{Y|X=\mathbf{x}}\left[L\left(Y - \phi_{\mathcal{L}}(\mathbf{x})\right)\right]\right\}, \qquad (2.14)$$

where $X_{\mathcal{L}}$ represents the multivariate random variable generating the feature values in $\mathcal{L}$.

As far as the loss function is concerned, in regression problems L is commonly defined as

$$L(\phi_{\mathcal{L}}(X)) = (Y - \phi_{\mathcal{L}}(X))^2, \qquad (2.15)$$

whereas in a classification context it is usually given by

$$L(\phi_{\mathcal{L}}(X)) = 1 - \mathbf{1}_Y(\phi_{\mathcal{L}}(X)),$$

where $\mathbf{1}_b(a) = 1$ if $a = b$ and $\mathbf{1}_b(a) = 0$ otherwise, $a, b \in \mathbb{R}$.

We shall now focus our attention on the regression context and assume we want to minimize (2.12) when the loss function is defined as in Eq. (2.15). It is well known that, under these assumptions, the optimal predictor is the expectation of Y conditioned on $X = \mathbf{x}$:

$$\phi_B(\mathbf{x}) = \mathbb{E}_{Y|X=\mathbf{x}}(Y).$$

It is straightforward to verify that (2.12) can be rewritten as

$$R(\phi_{\mathcal{L}}(\mathbf{x})) = \text{noise}(\mathbf{x}) + \text{bias}^2(\mathbf{x}). \qquad (2.16)$$

The first term in (2.16) is

$$\text{noise}(\mathbf{x}) = \mathbb{E}_{Y|X=\mathbf{x}}\left[(Y - \phi_B(\mathbf{x}))^2\right] \qquad (2.17)$$

and represents the lowest risk level that can be achieved by the optimal $\phi_B(\mathbf{x})$. The second term in (2.16) is the square of the bias of $\phi_{\mathcal{L}}(\mathbf{x})$, which is given by the difference between the prediction produced by the tree trained on $\mathcal{L}$ and the one provided by the optimal predictor:

$$\text{bias}(\mathbf{x}) = \phi_{\mathcal{L}}(\mathbf{x}) - \phi_B(\mathbf{x}).$$

If the training sample $\mathcal{L}$ is random, we need to consider the risk function introduced in (2.14), which can be rewritten as

$$R(\phi_{\mathcal{L}}(\mathbf{x})) = \text{noise}(\mathbf{x}) + \text{bias}^2(\mathbf{x}) + \text{var}(\mathbf{x}),$$

where noise($\mathbf{x}$) is defined as in (2.17), whereas

$$\text{bias}(\mathbf{x}) = \mathbb{E}_{\mathcal{L}|X=\mathbf{x}}[\phi_{\mathcal{L}}(\mathbf{x})] - \phi_B(\mathbf{x}),$$
$$\text{var}(\mathbf{x}) = \mathbb{E}_{\mathcal{L}|X=\mathbf{x}}\left[\left(\phi_{\mathcal{L}}(\mathbf{x}) - \mathbb{E}_{\mathcal{L}|X=\mathbf{x}}(\phi_{\mathcal{L}}(\mathbf{x}))\right)^2\right].$$

The term bias($\mathbf{x}$) has been redefined in order to take into account the randomness of $\mathcal{L}$, whereas the definition of noise($\mathbf{x}$) is unchanged.

When dealing with complex datasets it is very difficult to identify the optimal predictor $\phi_B(\mathbf{x})$, since this would require a precise knowledge of the data distribution. However, regression trees provide predictors with relatively low bias, at the cost of high prediction error variance, which is related to var($\mathbf{x}$). In the following, we shall introduce some tools that allow us to reduce var($\mathbf{x}$).

2.5.2 *Bias-variance decomposition for randomized trees ensembles*

Suppose that the learning set $\mathcal{L}$ is fixed and there exists a random hyperparameter θ, independent of $\mathcal{L}$, that rules the construction of the regression tree. For instance, at any step the value taken by θ might determine which subset of variables among the available features might be taken into account in order to find the best split. The resulting tree would be the output of a random algorithm and it would be therefore itself random. As we shall see, random trees will play a crucial role in the definition of random forest.

Let us denote the predictor produced by a random tree as $\phi_{\mathcal{L}}(\mathbf{x}, \theta)$ making the dependence of such predictor on θ explicit. The risk associated with $\phi_{\mathcal{L}}(\mathbf{x}, \theta)$ is now defined as

$$\mathrm{R}\left(\phi_{\mathcal{L}}(\mathbf{x}, \theta)\right) = \mathbb{E}_{Y, \mathcal{L}, \theta}\left[\mathrm{L}\left(Y - \phi_{\mathcal{L}}(\mathbf{x}, \theta)\right)\right]$$
$$= \mathrm{noise}(\mathbf{x}) + \mathrm{bias}^2(\mathbf{x}) + \mathrm{var}(\mathbf{x}), \tag{2.18}$$

where noise($\mathbf{x}$) is defined as in (2.17), whereas

$$\mathrm{bias}(\mathbf{x}) = \mathbb{E}_{\mathcal{L}, \theta | X = \mathbf{x}}\left[\phi_{\mathcal{L}}(\mathbf{x}, \theta)\right] - \phi_B(\mathbf{x}),$$
$$\mathrm{var}(\mathbf{x}) = \mathbb{E}_{\mathcal{L}, \theta | X = \mathbf{x}}\left[\left(\phi_{\mathcal{L}}(\mathbf{x}, \theta) - \mathbb{E}_{\mathcal{L}, \theta | X = \mathbf{x}}\left(\phi_{\mathcal{L}}(\mathbf{x}, \theta)\right)\right)^2\right].$$

Both bias($\mathbf{x}$) and var($\mathbf{x}$) take into account the randomness of θ, whereas noise($\mathbf{x}$) is still defined as in (2.17).

The risk in (2.18) is generally higher than the risk in (2.14); however, it can be substantially reduced by averaging over an ensemble of random trees. Let θ_m, $m = 1, \ldots, M$, be M independently and identically distributed hyperparameters that give rise to M random trees. We can then define the *ensemble* predictor

$$\Psi_{\mathcal{L}}(\mathbf{x}, \theta_1, \ldots, \theta_m) = \frac{1}{M}\sum_{m=1}^{M}\phi_{\mathcal{L}}(\mathbf{x}, \theta_m). \tag{2.19}$$

Notice that the individual predictors $\phi_{\mathcal{L}}(\mathbf{x}, \theta_m)$ are identically distributed. Hence, we can write

$$\mu_{\mathcal{L}, \theta}(\mathbf{x}) = \mathbb{E}_{\mathcal{L}, \theta_m}\left[\phi_{\mathcal{L}}\phi_{\mathcal{L}}(\mathbf{x}, \theta_m)\right], \tag{2.20}$$

$$\sigma^2_{\mathcal{L}, \theta}(\mathbf{x}) = \mathbb{V}_{\mathcal{L}, \theta_m}\left[\phi_{\mathcal{L}}\phi_{\mathcal{L}}(\mathbf{x}, \theta_m)\right], \qquad m = 1, \ldots, M. \tag{2.21}$$

And from (2.20), it follows that

$$\mathbb{E}_{\mathcal{L}, \theta_1, \ldots, \theta_m}\left[\Psi_{\mathcal{L}}(\mathbf{x}, \theta_1, \ldots, \theta_m)\right] = \mu_{\mathcal{L}, \theta}(\mathbf{x}).$$

The risk associated with the ensemble predictor can be written as

$$\mathrm{R}\left(\Psi_{\mathcal{L}}(\mathbf{x}, \theta_1, \ldots, \theta_m)\right) = \mathbb{E}_{Y, \mathcal{L}, \theta_1, \ldots, \theta_m}\left[\mathrm{L}\left(Y - \Psi_{\mathcal{L}}(\mathbf{x}, \theta_1, \ldots, \theta_m)\right)\right] \tag{2.22}$$
$$= \mathrm{noise}(\mathbf{x}) + \mathrm{bias}^2(\mathbf{x}) + \mathrm{var}(\mathbf{x}), \tag{2.23}$$

noise($\mathbf{x}$) is again defined as in (2.17), whereas

$$\mathrm{bias}(\mathbf{x}) = \mu_{\mathcal{L}, \theta}(\mathbf{x}) - \phi_B(\mathbf{x}), \tag{2.24}$$

$$\text{var}(\mathbf{x}) = \left(\rho(\mathbf{x}) + \frac{1 - \rho(\mathbf{x})}{M}\right)\sigma_{\mathcal{L},\theta}^2(\mathbf{x}), \tag{2.25}$$

with

$$\rho(\mathbf{x}) = \mathbb{C}\text{orr}_{\mathcal{L},\theta_m,\theta_m'}\left(\phi_{\mathcal{L}}(\mathbf{x},\theta_m),\phi_{\mathcal{L}}(\mathbf{x},\theta_{m'})\right). \tag{2.26}$$

Equations (2.22)–(2.26) explain the usefulness of the ensemble predictor. The squared bias term in (2.23) does not play an important role, since it is usually low for the predictors produced by regression trees. The quantity that plays a crucial role is var($\mathbf{x}$) in (2.23). It is closely linked to $\rho(\mathbf{x})$, the correlation coefficient between the predictors associated with an arbitrary pair of random trees in the ensemble. It can be shown that $0 \leq \rho(\mathbf{x}) \leq 1$ (see Louppe (2014)). Then, equation (2.25) shows that var($\mathbf{x}$) decreases as $\rho(\mathbf{x})$ decreases and the size of the ensemble, M, increases. This result makes ensemble predictors to be preferred to predictors associated with single trees and paves the way to the definition of random forests.

2.5.3 From trees ensembles to random forests

A random forest is a collection of M randomized regression trees indexed by a random hyper-parameter, θ. Such hyperparameter plays two important roles. On one hand, it resamples with replacement from $\mathcal{L}$ the n-dimensional subsample, with $n \in \{1, \ldots, N\}$, on which the generic randomized tree is trained. On the other hand, at each step of the tree growth, it randomly chooses k out of the p features that will be compared in order to produce the optimal splitting in the CART algorithm. Each tree is grown arbitrarily large and no pruning is implemented: the only constraint is that leaves should have a size no less than a given threshold, usually fixed at 5. The ensemble is then generated accordingly with M independent replicates of the hyperparameter θ, say $\theta_1, \ldots, \theta_M$. Let $\mathcal{L}_m \subseteq \mathcal{L}$ be the n-dimensional training set for the mth tree in the forest and $\bar{\mathcal{L}}_m = \mathcal{L} \setminus \mathcal{L}_m$ its complement. The predictor produced by the random forest is

$$\Psi_{\mathcal{L}}^{RF}(\mathbf{x},\theta_1,\ldots,\theta_M) = \frac{1}{M}\sum_{m=1}^{M}\phi_{\mathcal{L}_m}(\mathbf{x},\theta_m).$$

It is worth to notice that, being the θ_i's independent, the individual predictors $\phi_{\mathcal{L}_m}(\mathbf{x},\theta_m)$ are weakly correlated. The reason why this happens is quite simple. Suppose that any tree in the forest was grown using the CART algorithm and that there exists one feature, call it X_1, strongly correlated with the response Y. In such a situation, X_1 would be selected as the variable on which the first split in any tree is produced. This would make the output of the trees in the forest strongly correlated. Since at any step of any tree's growth only a subset of features is randomly chosen as candidate for splitting, such correlation is sensibly reduced. Consequently, the risk associated with $\Psi_{\mathcal{L}}^{RF}(\mathbf{x},\theta_1,\ldots,\theta_M)$,

$$R\left(\Psi_{\mathcal{L}}^{RF}(\mathbf{x},\theta_1,\ldots,\theta_m)\right) = \mathbb{E}_{Y,\mathcal{L},\theta_1,\ldots,\theta_m}\left[L\left(Y - \Psi_{\mathcal{L}}^{RF}(\mathbf{x},\theta_1,\ldots,\theta_m)\right)\right],$$

is generally lower than the risk associated with the predictor produced by an individual regression tree.

Some words need to be spent on the resampling of $\mathcal{L}_m$, $m = 1, \ldots, M$, the n-dimensional training samples of the trees in the forest. Originally, Breiman (2001) fixed n equal to the sample size, N. Under this circumstance, the $\mathcal{L}_m$s are bootstrap samples from the original dataset, and the forest predictor is obtained through a bootstrap aggregating scheme that Breiman called *bagging*. It can be shown that, on average, each tree is trained on two-thirds of the observations in $\mathcal{L}$. The remaining part of observations are referred as *out-of-bag* (OOB) observations. We can predict the response for the ith observation in $\mathcal{L}$ by averaging the predictions of all trees for which that observation was OOB. This can be done for each observation in $\mathcal{L}$, allowing us to estimate the risk associated with the random forest predictor without recurring to any test set independent of $\mathcal{L}$ (Breiman, 1996, 2001). If N is large, we can fix $n << N$, subsample the $\mathcal{L}_m$s independently, and proceed analogously.

Random forests are less interpretable than individual regression trees. However, they allow us to quantify the importance of each feature in predicting the response. The two main tools available are the *mean decrease impurity* (MDI) and the *mean decrease accuracy* (MDA). For each feature, say X_j, we can compute the total decrease in node impurity when splitting on that variable and averaging over all trees in the forest. This average is the MDI of X_j. Features can be ranked in terms of the MDI: the most relevant variables will be the ones with high MDI. Alternatively, we can estimate the mean square prediction error on the OOB prediction. Let us call such estimate $\hat{R}$. If we are interested on the relevance of feature X_j, we can proceed as follows. Permute the values of X_j over the OOB items and estimate the mean square prediction error on the perturbed OOB. Let us call this estimate $\hat{R}^j$. Then the MDA is defined as

$$\text{MDA}(X_j) = \hat{R}^j - \hat{R}.$$

A value of $\text{MDA}(X_j)$ close to zero means that X_j does not affect the prediction, whereas a high value of $\text{MDA}(X_j)$ indicates X_j has a relevant predictive power.

2.5.4 *Partial dependence function*

MDI and MDA are quite useful to catch a glimpse of the perceived importance of the inputs, but they do not tell much about the kind of relationship between the features and the target. Other more useful and refined tools can be employed with that purpose, such as the partial dependence function (Friedman, 2001) which reveals the marginal influence of a feature on the predictive outcome of our forest. Formally, the partial dependence function f_{X_j} of an arbitrary feature X_j can be defined as the expected value, with respect to the remaining features, of the random forest predictor when the jth feature assumes an arbitrary fixed value x_j. It can be estimated by exploiting the observations of the training set. The value of the partial dependence function for an arbitrary fixed value of the jth feature is obtained by forcing all the observations in the training set to assume such value, leaving the other features unaffected, and by computing the average prediction once such modified observations are fed to the forest. Formally,

$$\hat{f}_{X_j}(x_j) = \frac{1}{N_{x_j}} \sum_{i \in \mathcal{L}_{x_j}} \Psi_{\mathcal{L}}^{RF}(\mathbf{x}_i, \theta_1, ..., \theta_M),$$

where $\mathcal{L}_{x_j}$ is the subset of $\mathcal{L}$ containing all the items on which the jth component of $\mathbf{x}$ is equal to x_j, N_{x_j} refers to the number of items in $\mathcal{L}_{x_j}$, and x_j is the punctual value of the jth feature at which the function is computed. The partial dependence plot is the graphical representation of such function, where the feature under investigation is given on the horizontal axis, and the average prediction of the forest on the vertical one.

Similarly, a two-way partial dependence function can be obtained by computing the average prediction of the forest while keeping fixed the values of two features. This function allows for studying the joint effect of two features of interest on the prediction, marginalizing out the remaining explanatory variables.

2.6 Forecasting bond returns using macroeconomic variables

Many studies confirmed the existence of a relationship between macroeconomic variables and bond risk premia, allowing researchers to formulate predictions conditioned on such variables. Relevant references are Ludvigson and Ng (2009), Cochrane and Piazzesi (2005) and Bianchi, Büchner, and Tamoni (2020). We use random forests to make predictions on the ICE BofA US Corporate Index Total Return (retrieved from FRED, Federal Reserve Bank of St. Louis, `https://fred.stlouisfed.org`) which is one of the reference index for the fixed income sector in the USA. The ICE BofA index tracks the performance of US dollar denominated investment grade rated corporate debt publicly issued in the US domestic market.

The input variables are taken from the FRED-MD database which is one of the most used dataset by macroeconomists (McCracken & Ng, 2016). The FRED-MD database contains 130 monthly series divided into eight groups: output and income, labor market, consumption and orders, orders and inventories, money and credit, interest and exchange Rates, prices, and stock market. An exhaustive description of the dataset can be found in McCracken and Ng (2016).

As far as we know, random forests have never been used to study the impact of macroeconomic variables on the US bond market. Therefore, we find interesting to assess whether the implementation of this methodology can improve the flexibility and the accuracy of the existing methods.

The time series cover a sample period ranging from January 1973 to January 2020 and consist of 565 monthly observations. The number of input variables is 128. Since the number of observations is small in comparison with the number of regressors, we removed the covariates for which some data were missing, reducing the number of inputs to 126. The excluded variables are the consumer sentiment, measured by the University of Michigan's Surveys of Consumers (UMCSENT), and the value of manufacturers' new orders for consumer goods industries (ACOGNO). In order to mitigate the effect of non-stationarity, the response variable has been log-transformed and differenced. First differences of all regressors have been used as well. Being the data temporally ordered, the training and test sets were given respectively by the first 75% and the last 25% of sample observations.

Random forests have been implemented using the software environment R and, more specifically, the package `randomForest` (Liaw and Wiener (2002)). The number of trees is 500, the bootstrapped sample size corresponds to the size of the training set, the minimum number of observations in a node in order for a split to be attempted is 5, the number of terminal nodes has no restrictions, and the number of chosen candidate features for splitting at each node is fixed at one-third of the number of explanatory variables. Furthermore, a dynamic analysis through a rolling regression on 40 observations has been performed in order to assess changes in the interactions between the response and the covariates over time.

Figure 2.3 compares the in- and out-of-sample predictions produced by the model to the observed values. The training set residuals in Figure 2.4a exhibit higher dispersion in the periods 1975–1985 and 2001–2003. In the former the American bond market was under pressure in the aftermath of the 1973–1974 oil crisis and the consequent deterioration of the trade balance and deficit conditions. In the latter the dot-com bubble burst gave rise to higher uncertainty and volatility levels in the financial markets. As far as the test set is concerned, in Figure 2.4b we observe a similar behavior of the prediction errors, due to the financial crisis of 2008/2009.

Panels (a) and (b) of Figure 2.4 show the MDA and MDI variable importance scores. Both scores agree in selecting the most relevant variables in the groups of interest and exchange rates, prices, and stock market. The first five variables among them, with some differences in their order, represent interest rates and are described in detail in Table 2.1. The partial dependence plots, shown in Figure 2.5a, provide some interesting insights: the predicted return of the ICE BofA index is negatively correlated with the Moody's Seasoned BAA and AAA Corporate Bond Yield and the Ten-Year Treasury Rate. Some of our findings are in line with the in-sample analysis obtained by Ludvigson and Ng (2009) with a factor model approach. Returns on government and corporate bonds are the main drivers of the bond market returns. In our findings longer maturities from 1 to 10 years are more relevant than shorter maturities. Real variables on employment and production conditions are important following MDI and MDA, respectively. Differently from

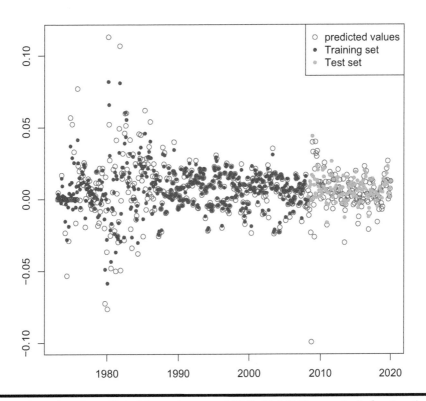

Figure 2.3 Actual and predicted log-returns on ICE BofA US Corporate Index (vertical axis) over time (horizontal axis).

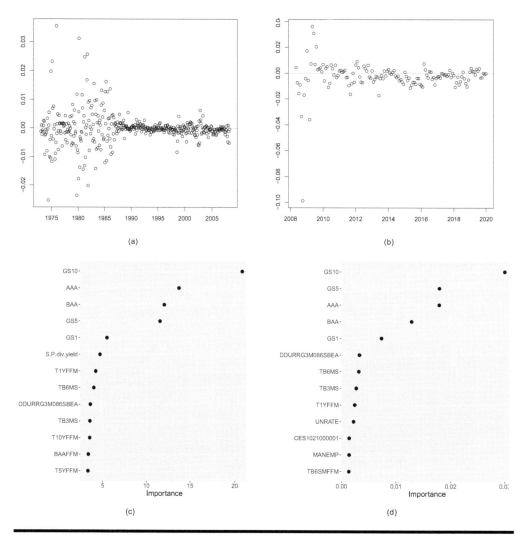

Figure 2.4 **Log-returns on ICE BofA US Corporate Index BofA: residuals on the training sample (panel a, vertical axis), prediction errors on the validation sample (panel b, vertical axis) over time (horizontal axis), mean decrease accuracy (panel c), and mean decrease impurity (panel d) variable importance analysis.**

Ludvigson and Ng (2009), consumption variables (changes in expenditure for durable goods) are relevant following MDI, whereas inflation and price changes are not important. Stock market factors (such as S&P Dividend Yield) are less relevant than real variables and interest rates.

The non-parametric nature of the random forest regression allows us to provide evidence of a nonlinear relationship between the predictors and the response variable (e.g., see the S-shaped curves in Figure 2.5a). The nonlinearity of the partial dependence function is confirmed by the

Table 2.1 Analysis of the log-returns on ICE BofA US Corporate Index: description of the most relevant variables from the FRED-MD database

FRED Code	Description
S&P 500	S&P's Common Stock Price Index: Composite
S&P div. Yield	S&P's Composite Common Stock: Dividend Yield
GS1	1-Year Treasury Rate
GS5	5-Year Treasury Rate
GS10	10-Year Treasury Rate
AAA	Moody's Seasoned Aaa Corporate Bond Yield
BAA	Moody's Seasoned Baa Corporate Bond Yield
CES1021000001	All Employees: Mining
T1YFFM	1-Year Treasury C Minus FEDFUNDS
TB6MS	6-Month Treasury Bill: Secondary Market Rate
T5YFFM	5-Year Treasury C Minus FEDFUNDS
CP3Mx	3-Month AA Financial Commercial Paper Rate
TB6SMFFM	6-Month Treasury C Minus FEDFUNDS
TB3MS	3-Month Treasury Bill: Secondary Market Rate
UNRATE	Civilian Unemployment Rate
DDURRG3M086SBEA	Personal Consumption Expendirture in Durable goods
MANEMP	All employees, manufacturing

two-way partial dependence plot for GS10 and BAA (Figure 2.5b). The plot obtained using the `randomForestExplainer` package (Paluszynska, Biecek, and Jiang (2019)) suggests that a joint increase of the two yields affects negatively the prediction. It is also worth to notice that the GS10 variable has an overwhelming effect with respect to BAA: when keeping BAA fixed, variations in GS10 produce strong changes in predictions, whereas evidence of symmetric effects is much weaker.

In the rolling regression, the variables that most often appeared among the first five positions accordingly with MDA and MDI are AAA, BAA, GS10, GS5, and GS1, which confirm the results of the statics analysis. Furthermore, the sequential analysis (see Figure 2.5c,d) provides further evidence of nonlinearities and new evidence of substantial changes in the shapes of the partial dependence function over the different subperiods considered (Jun. 1973–Sep. 1976, Jan. 1998–Apr. 2001, Sep. 2014–Dec. 2017).

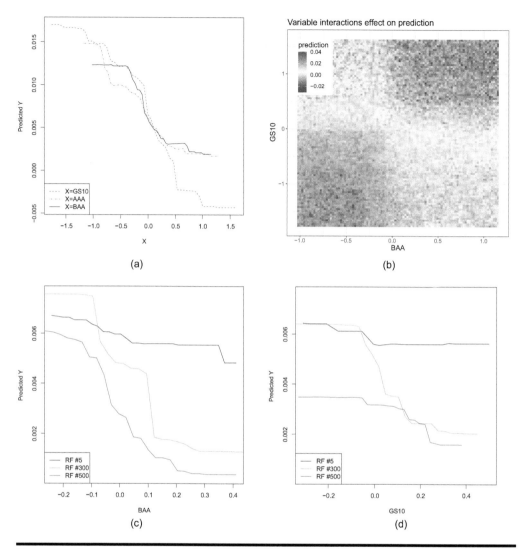

Figure 2.5 **Log-returns on ICE BofA US Corporate Index BofA analysis: two-way partial dependence plot involving Moody's Seasoned BAA Corporate Bond Yield and the Ten-Year Treasury Rate (panel a), static partial dependence plots of BAA, AAA, and GS10 (panel b), sequential partial dependence plots of BAA (panel c), and GS10 (panel d) corresponding to the three different periods: Jun. 1973–Sep. 1976, Jan. 1998–Apr. 2001, Sep. 2014–Dec. 2017.**

2.7 Default prediction based on accountancy data

In this section we present the results of an analysis based on the data retrieved from the Bureau Van Dijk's AIDA database (https://www.bvdinfo.com/it-it/le-nostre-soluzioni/dati/nazionali/aida). We focused our attention on the population of small and medium-sized enterprises (SME) since this type of firms are the backbone of the economic system of many European regions and states (such as Italy and France) and received attention in the credit risk literature (Calabrese, Marra, & Osmetti, 2016; Calabrese & Osmetti, 2013) due to the acute challenges they are facing during periods of economic and financial distress.

We propose an original application of random forest classification to 109,836 firms located in the North-Eastern Italy regions (Veneto, Trentino Alto Adige, and Friuli Venezia Giulia) which published their last financial statements in 2018 or 2019. The analysis is particularly important since these regions are the first ones planning and starting reopening after the lockdown due to the COVID-19 pandemic. An analysis of the weakest companies and of the determinants of their frailty is crucial for studying early warning indicators and making correct policy interventions.

The response variable is the legal status of the companies which is a categorical variable labeled as `Default` or `Active` with some abuse of terminology: under the `Default` category, we include all the enterprises which have been declared bankrupt, the ones that are insolvent or under receivership proceedings. Our purpose is to predict the `Default` state of an enterprise, given the information provided by some salient features of the company, its financial statements, and the main financial and profitability ratios. The number of inputs so defined is 104. Missing values have been estimated through the proximity measure (Breiman, 2003). One important feature of the population is that only 689 enterprises out of 10,9836 are classified as `Default`. This implies that any sample should be strongly unbalanced (i.e., it should contain a very small proportion of `Default` cases) in order to represent the whole population. Such class imbalance problem is common to many classification problems (Lemaître, Nogueira, & Aridas, 2017; Li, Bellotti, & Adams, 2019), and it determines an important undesired effect: while `Active` cases would be correctly classified with high probability, the `Default` ones would often be misclassified. This would happen independently on sample size: on large samples we would correctly identify the `Active` cases with probability close to one, but we would predict as `Active` a high proportion of defaults. We assume this type of classification error is most costly and randomly undersample the majority class to reduce the misclassification rate within the `Default` cases.

We built two random forests with different size and composition of the training set to study the effect of the undersampling rate. In the first one, the training set has size 10,344, with 10,000 `Active` cases, whereas in the second one, the training set has size 688, with 344 `Active` enterprises. Clearly, the latter is far from representing the population, but it is perfectly balanced in terms of legal status categories. Each random forest counts 500 trees, the number of features chosen at each split is the default value of 10 (the square root of input variables), the minimum number of observations in a terminal node in order for a split to be attempted is 1, and there are no restrictions regarding the number of leaves in a single tree; the bootstrap samples have the same size of the training set.

Comparing Table 2.2a,b with Table 2.2c,d, we can notice that when we use the largest training set the overall misclassification rate is 0.015 in both the training and the test set, whereas it increases respectively to 0.096 and 0.054 in the test set when we use the smallest one. However, the misclassification rate within the `Default` class decreases from about 0.345 to 0.137 in the training set and from 0.316 to 0.128 when we move from the former to the latter. Figure 2.6a,b show the ranking of the first 16 variables in terms of MDA and MDI scores. We can notice that overwhelming importance is attributed to the amount of net capital and to the degree of financial dependence on third parties. Furthermore, a joint increase in the two variables produces an

Table 2.2 Out-of-the-box (left) and test set (right) predictions and classification error with a training sample size of 10344 (first line) and of 688 (second line)

(a)				(b)			
	Active	*Default*	*Class. err.*		*Active*	*Default*	*Class. err.*
Active	9961	39	0.004	Active	9956	44	0.004
Default	120	224	0.345	Default	109	236	0.316
(c)				(d)			
	Active	*Default*	*Class. err.*		*Active*	*Default*	*Class. err.*
Active	325	19	0.055	Active	9484	516	0.052
Default	47	297	0.137	Default	44	301	0.128

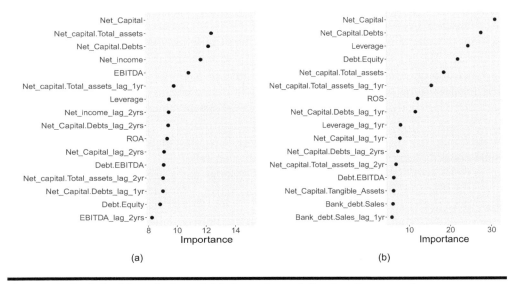

Figure 2.6 Default risk analysis: variable importance following the mean decrease accuracy (panel a) and mean decrease impurity (panel b) score variables' rankings.

increase in the default probability (see the PDP in Figure 2.7a). Figure 2.7b shows the substantial agreement between what predicted by the PDP and what observed in the test set.

2.8 Appendix: R source codes for the applications in this chapter

You need to upload the following libraries at the beginning of each source code:

```
1 library(ISLR)
2 library(vip)
```

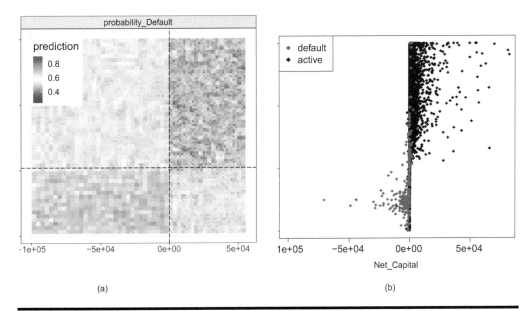

(a)

(b)

Figure 2.7 Default risk analysis: two-way partial dependence of default on net capital and net capital to total assets ratio (panel c); scatterplot of the net capital and net capital to total assets ratio in the test set (panel d, default cases in red, active cases in black).

```
3   library(randomForest)
4   library(iml)
5   library(caret)
6   library(randomForestExplainer)
7   library(Metrics)
8   require(caTools)
9   library(ggplot2)
10  library(MASS)
11  library(pdp)
12  library(plotly)
13  library(plyr)
```

2.8.1 Application to US BofA index

```
14  #-------------------------------------------
15  # DATA IMPORT AND PREPARATION -----------
16  #-------------------------------------------
17  data ← read.csv("Bofa_Fred.csv", header = TRUE, sep = ";")
18  bofa ← ts(data$BAMLCC0A0CMTRIV, start=c(1973, 1), end=c(2020, 1),
         frequency=12)
19  bofa ← log(bofa)
20  data$BAMLCC0A0CMTRIV ← NULL
21  data$DATE ← NULL
```

```r
22  clean_data ← data[ , colSums(is.na(data)) == 0]
23
24  d_bofa ← diff(bofa) # target variable
25
26  d_clean ← data.frame(x=c(1:564))
27  for (i in 1:126) {
28    vec ← diff(clean_data[,i])
29    d_clean ← cbind(d_clean,vec)
30  }
31
32  d_clean$x ← NULL
33  colnames(d_clean) ← colnames(clean_data)
34  #----------------------------------------
35  # DEFAULT RANDOM FOREST -----------------
36  #----------------------------------------
37  d_train ← d_clean[1:round(dim(d_clean)[1]*0.75),]
38  d_test ← d_clean[(round(dim(d_clean)[1]*0.75)+1):dim(d_clean)[1],]
39  d_bofa_train = ts(d_bofa[1:dim(d_train[1])], start = c(1973, 2),
        frequency = 12)
40  d_bofa_test  = ts(d_bofa[(dim(d_train[1])+1):length(d_bofa)], start
        = c(2008, 5), frequency = 12)
41
42  d_rf ← randomForest(formula=d_bofa_train~., data = d_train,
        localImp = TRUE)
43
44  sam_pred = ts(predict(d_rf, newdata=d_train), start = c(1973, 2),
        frequency = 12)
45  plot(d_bofa_train)
46  points(sam_pred, col="blue")
47
48  test_pred = ts(predict(d_rf, newdata=d_test), start = c(2008, 5),
        frequency = 12)
49  plot(d_bofa_test)
50  points(test_pred, col="green")
51
52  plot(d_bofa, ylab="ICE BofA - log returns")
53  points(sam_pred, col="blue")
54  points(test_pred, col="green")
55  legend("topright",legend=c("Training fit","Test fit"),pch=19, col=c
        ("blue","green"))
56
57  # Residuals
58  fit_residuals_train ← c()
59  fit_residuals_test ← c()
60
61  for (i in seq(1, length(d_bofa_train), by = 1)) {
62    fit_residuals_train[i] = (d_bofa_train[i] - sam_pred[i])^2
63  }
64  MSE_train = mean(fit_residuals_train)
65
66  for (i in seq(1, length(d_bofa_test), by = 1)) {
```

```
67    fit_residuals_test[i] = (d_bofa_test[i] - test_pred[i])^2
68  }
69  MSE_test = mean(fit_residuals_test)
70
71  # Residual plots
72  plot(d_bofa_train - sam_pred, main = "Training set residuals", ylab
        = "Residuals", type = "p")
73  abline(0,0, lty = 3)
74
75  plot(d_bofa_test - test_pred, main = c("Test set prediction errors"
        ), ylab = "Prediction errors", type = "p",)
76  abline(0,0, lty = 3)
77  #-----------------------------------------
78  # FEATURES IMPORTANCE --------------------
79  #-----------------------------------------
80  # mean decreased accuracy
81  imp_MDA = vi_model(d_rf, type = 1, scale = TRUE)
82  imp_MDA = imp_MDA[order(-imp_MDA$Importance),]
83  # mean decreased impurity
84  imp_MDI = vi_model(d_rf, type = 2, scale = TRUE)
85  imp_MDI = imp_MDI[order(-imp_MDI$Importance),]
86
87  # plotting all variable importance measures
88  MDA = vip(imp_MDA, num_features = 13, geom = "point", horiz = TRUE,
        aesthetics = list(size = 3, shape = 16), main = "MDA")
89  MDI = vip(imp_MDI, num_features = 13, geom = "point", horiz = TRUE,
        aesthetics = list(size = 3, shape = 16))
90
91  MDA+theme(text=element_text(size=15))+ggtitle("MDA")
92  MDI+theme(text=element_text(size=15))+ggtitle("MDI")
93
94  # PDP plot
95  part_dep_func_BAA ← partial(d_rf, pred.var = "BAA")
96  au_pdp_BAA ← autoplot(part_dep_func_BAA, rug = TRUE, train = d_
        train)
97  plot(au_pdp_BAA)
98
99  part_dep_func_GS10 ← partial(d_rf, pred.var = "GS10")
100 au_pdp_GS10 ← autoplot(part_dep_func_GS10, rug = TRUE, train = d_
        train)
101 plot(au_pdp_GS10)
102
103 part_dep_func_AAA ← partial(d_rf, pred.var = "AAA")
104 au_pdp_AAA ← autoplot(part_dep_func_AAA, rug = TRUE, train = d_
        train)
105 plot(au_pdp_AAA)
106
107 # Two-way dependence plot
```

```
108  plot_predict_interaction(d_rf, d_train, "BAA", "GS10", main = "
        Variable interactions effect on prediction") + theme(
        legend.position="bottom") + geom_hline(yintercept = 2, linetype=
        "longdash") + geom_vline(xintercept = 140, linetype="longdash")
```

2.8.2 SME default risk application

```
14   #---------------------------------------
15   # DATASET -------------------------------
16   #---------------------------------------
17   load("SMETrainC.RData")
18   load("SMETestC.RData")
19
20   nc <- ncol(SMETrain)
21   #---------------------------------------
22   # DEFAULT RANDOM FOREST -----------------
23   #---------------------------------------
24   SMETrain = rfImpute(SMETrain[,2:nc], SMETrain[,1], iter = 5, ntree
        = 50)
25   SMETest = rfImpute(SMETest[,2:nc], SMETest[,1], iter = 5, ntree =
        50)
26
27   # random forest default setting
28   class_randomForest = randomForest(LegalStatus ~ ., data=SMETrain,
        replace = TRUE, nPerm = 4, importance = TRUE, proximity = TRUE,
        oob.prox = TRUE, keep.inbag = TRUE)
29   print(class_randomForest)
30
31   # predictions on the test set
32   SMETest$RF_predictions = predict(class_randomForest, newdata =
        SMETest)
33
34   # predictions on training set
35   SMETrain$RF_predictions = predict(class_randomForest, newdata =
        SMETrain)
36
37   # Confusion matrix and error rates
38   conf_matrix = table(SMETest$LegalStatus, SMETest$RF_predictions)
39   ErrRates <- c(conf_matrix[1,2]/sum(conf_matrix[1,]),conf_matrix
        [2,1]/sum(conf_matrix[2,]))
40   conf_matrix <- cbind(conf_matrix,ErrRates)
41   colnames(conf_matrix)[3] <- "class.error"
42   print(conf_matrix)
43   #---------------------------------------
44   # FEATURES IMPORTANCE -------------------
45   #---------------------------------------
46   # mean decreased accuracy
47   importance_MDA = vi_model(class_randomForest, type = 1, scale =
        TRUE)
48   importance_MDA = importance_MDA[order(-importance_MDA$Importance),]
```

```
49
50  # mean decreased impurity
51  importance_MDI = vi_model(class_randomForest, type = 2, scale =
        TRUE)
52  importance_MDI = importance_MDI[order(-importance_MDI$Importance),]
53
54  # partial dependence importance
55
56  # plotting all variable importance measures
57  MDA = vip(importance_MDA, num_features = 16, geom = "point", horiz
        = TRUE, aesthetics = list(size = 3, shape = 16), main = "MDA")
58  MDI = vip(importance_MDI, num_features = 16, geom = "point", horiz
        = TRUE, aesthetics = list(size = 3, shape = 16))
59
60  MDA+theme(text=element_text(size=15))+ggtitle("MDA")
61
62  MDI+theme(text=element_text(size=15))+ggtitle("MDA")
63  #-------------------------------------
64  ## # FEATURES INTERACTION ---------------
65  #-------------------------------------
66  # 2-way partial dependence plot
67  plot_predict_interaction(class_randomForest, SMETrain, names(
        SMETrain)[9], names      (SMETrain)[60], main = "Joint effect
        on predicted default probability") +     theme(legend.position="
        bottom") + geom_hline(yintercept = 2, linetype="longdash") +
        geom_vline(xintercept = 140, linetype="longdash")
68
69  plot(SMETest[,9],SMETest[,60], col=SMETest[,1],xlim=c(-100000
        ,80000), xlab=aa, ylab=bb, pch=18)
70  legend("topleft", legend=c("default","active"), col=c("red","black"
        ), pch=rep(18,2))
```

References

Bianchi, D., Büchner, M., & Tamoni, A. (2020). Bond risk premia with machine learning. *Review of Financial Studies, forthcoming.*

Breiman, L. (1996, aug). Bagging predictors. *Mach. Learn., 24* (2), 123–140.

Breiman, L. (2001, 10). Random forests. *Mach. Learn., 45* (1), 5–32.

Breiman, L. (2003). *Setting up, using, and understanding random forests V4.0.* Retrieved from https://www.stat.berkeley.edu/~breiman/Using_random_forests_v4.0.pdf

Breiman, L., Friedman, J. H., Olshen, R. A., & J., S. C. (1984). *Classification and Regression Trees.* New York: Chapman & Hall.

Calabrese, R., Marra, G., & Osmetti, S. A. (2016). Bankruptcy prediction of small and medium enterprises using a flexible binary generalized extreme value model. *Journal of the Operational Research Society, 67* (4), 604–615.

Calabrese, R., & Osmetti, S. A. (2013). Modelling small and medium enterprise loan defaults as rare events: the generalized extreme value regression model. *Journal of Applied Statistics, 40* (6), 1172–1188.

Cochrane, J. H., & Piazzesi, M. (2005, March). Bond risk premia. *American Economic Review*, *95* (1), 138–160.

Esposito, F., Malerba, D., Semeraro, G., & Kay, J. (1997). A comparative analysis of methods for pruning decision trees. *IEEE Transactions on Pattern Analysis and Machine Intelli- gence*, *19* (5), 476–491.

Friedman, J. H. (2001, 10). Greedy function approximation: A gradient boosting machine. *Annals Statistics*, *29* (5), 1189–1232.

Gupta, B., Rawat, A., Jain, A., Arora, A., & Dhami, N. (2017). Analysis of various deci- sion tree algorithms for classification in data mining. *International Journal of Computer Applications*, *163*, 15–19.

James, G., Witten, D., Hastie, T., & Tibshirani, R. (2013). *An introduction to statistical learning: with applications in r.* Springer.

Lemaître, G., Nogueira, F., & Aridas, C. K. (2017). Imbalanced-learn: A python toolbox to tackle the curse of imbalanced datasets in machine learning. *Journal of Machine Learning Research*, *18* (17), 1-5.

Li, Y., Bellotti, T., & Adams, N. (2019). Issues using logistic regression with class imbalance, with a case study from credit risk modelling. *Foundations of Data Science*, *1* (4), 389-417. Liaw, A., & Wiener, M. (2002). Classification and regression by randomforest. *R News*, *2* (3), 18-22. Retrieved from https://CRAN.R-project.org/doc/Rnews/

Louppe, G. (2014). *Understanding random forests: From theory to practice.* Retrieved from https://arxiv.org/abs/1407.7502

Ludvigson, S., & Ng, S. (2009). Macro factors in bond risk premia. *Review of Financial Studies*, *22* (12), 5027–5067.

Maimon, O., & Rokach, L. (2005). *Data mining and knowledge discovery handbook.* Springer-Verlag.

McCracken, M. W., & Ng, S. (2016). Fred-md: A monthly database for macroeconomic research. *Journal of Business & Economic Statistics*, *34* (4), 574-589.

Paluszynska, A., Biecek, P., & Jiang, Y. (2019). randomforestexplainer: Explaining and visual- izing random forests in terms of variable importance [Computer software manual]. Retrieved from https://cran.r-project.org/web/packages/randomForestExplainer/ randomForestExplainer.pdf

Quinlan, J. R. (1986, Mar 01). Induction of decision trees. *Machine Learning*, *1* (1), 81–106. Quinlan, J. R. (1993). *C4.5: Programs for Machine Learning.* San Francisco, CA, USA: Morgan Kaufmann Publishers Inc.

Shannon, C. E. (1948). A mathematical theory of communication. *Bell System Technical Journal*, *27* (3), 379–423.

Therneau, T., & Atkinson, B. (2019). rpart: Recursive partitioning and regression trees [Com- puter software manual]. Retrieved from https://CRAN.R-project.org/package=rpart (R package version 4.1–15)

Chapter 3

Improving longevity risk management through machine learning

Susanna Levantesi, Andrea Nigri, and Gabriella Piscopo

3.1 Introduction

Over the last century, the human mortality has declined globally. To live longer is a good thing for people, but it needs to be combined with satisfactory standard of living when they retire. Before 2000 high financial returns sustained consumption and other expenses of the elderly. Later, limited equity market performances and low interest rates together with life expectancy improvements have represented a challenge for the pension industry and insurance sector. It is clear that an increase in the life expectancy is posing many questions for individuals approaching retirement, for insurance companies offering life products, for pension plans, and for governments facing rising pensions and healthcare costs.

The changes in mortality trends strongly impact on pricing and reserve allocation of life annuities and on the sustainability of social security systems. In 2012, the International Monetary Fund estimated that each additional year of life expectancy added about 3%–4% to the present value of the liabilities of a typical defined benefit pension fund. To manage the uncertainty related to future life expectancy, the agents involved are trying to transfer such risk to capital markets. Due to the long-term nature of the risks, accurate longevity projections are delicate and the longevity risk transfer is a difficult process to realize without a theoretical recognized framework among actuaries and industry. In the same time, investors are looking for alternative investment assets with diversification purposes. The capital markets offer a complementary channel for distributing longevity risk and the involved players try to develop financial instruments indexed to the longevity of the population. Longevity bonds and longevity derivatives are designed to transfer the risk of higher life expectancy to investors. As it is clear, a correct quantification of longevity risk is necessary to offer adequate risk premium to investors from one hand, and from the other hand to evaluate insurance liabilities as close as possible to the real obligations and define opportune pricing policies. As the insurers used to say, there are no bad risks, but only bad pricing, meaning that companies are able to offer protections against risks as long as they are good matched in pricing.

Nowadays, many insurers still rely on traditional methods when evaluating risk. As regarding the longevity risk, the majority of actuarial researchers and practitioners make predictions resorting to classical demographic frameworks based on traditional extrapolative models. Among the stochastic models for mortality, the widely used Lee and Carter (1992) model introduces a framework for central mortality rates involving both age- and time-dependent terms. The Renshaw-Haberman model (Renshaw and Haberman, 2003, 2006) was one of the first to incorporate a cohort effect parameter to characterize the observed variations in mortality among individuals from differing cohorts. Other approaches make use of penalized splines to smooth mortality and derive future mortality patterns (Currie et al., 2004).

Recently, Artificial Intelligence (AI) in general and Machine Learning (ML) in particular are appearing on the landscape of actuarial research and practice, albeit belatedly and slowly with respect to other areas such as medicine, industry, finance, and so on. During the last three years, the actuarial literature has presented the first results of the application of ML techniques to mortality forecasts and longevity management. Some early unsupervised methods have been proposed in the context of mortality analysis with application to different fields of medicine, but around lately they have been exploited by demographers (Carracedo et al., 2018) and actuaries (Piscopo and Resta, 2017). As regards the supervised approaches, Deprez et al. (2017) use some ML techniques to improve the estimation of the log mortality rates. The model has been extended by Levantesi and Pizzorusso (2019) which takes the advantage of ML to improve the mortality forecasts in the Lee Carter framework. Deep Learning (DL) techniques have been proposed by Hainaut (2018) who employs a neural network to modeling mortality rates. Richman and Wüthrich (2018) have proposed a multiple-population Lee-Carter model where parameters are estimated using neural networks. Nigri et al. (2019) have integrated the original Lee-Carter formulation introducing a Recurrent Neural Network (RNN) with Long Short-Term Memory (LSTM) architecture to produce mortality forecasts more coherent with the observed mortality dynamics, also in cases of nonlinear mortality trends. In the remainder of the chapter, we focus on the application of ML to longevity data. Our original contribution lies in quantifying the impact of longevity risk modeled with ML on two insurance products; as far as our knowledge is concerned, in the literature there are no empirical analyses to real insurance policies. We show the progress of results in terms of better fitting and projections of mortality with respect to the classical approaches.

This chapter illustrates how ML can be used to improve both fitting and forecasting of traditional stochastic mortality models, taking the advantages of AI to better understand processes that are not fully identifiable by standard models. It is organized as follows. Section 2 introduces the framework of the generalized age period cohort models and the main accuracy measures. Section 3 summarizes the literature on the mortality modeling with ML, also providing a brief overview of the Classification And Regression Trees (CART) approach that has been used until now in mortality modeling. It discusses the improvement obtained by ML in the mortality fitting provided by some canonical stochastic mortality models, to which an ML adjustment factor is applied. It also discusses the benefits of using ML techniques as complementary to standard mortality models rather than as substitutes. This approach is probably likely to meet the needs of many demographers and all the longevity risk managers who are unwilling to use algorithms whose decisions cannot be rationally explained. In Section 4 we present a numerical application based on real mortality data of three European countries: we implement different mortality models in order to show how some ML techniques improve the fitting and modify the forecasts. Some of the forecasted mortality rates are then used to price two life insurance products whose payoffs depend on the future realized lifetime. The time profile of the actuarial reserves is shown to highlight the impact of longevity risk on such products. Final conclusions and some cues for future works are offered in Section 5.

3.2 The mortality models

Many of the stochastic mortality models proposed in literature belong to the family of the Generalized Age Period Cohort (GAPC) mortality models (see Villegas et al. (2015) for further details), in which the effects of age, calendar year, and cohort are captured by the following predictor:

$$\eta_x = \alpha_a + \sum_{i=1}^{n} \beta_a^{(i)} \kappa_t^{(1)} + \beta_a^{(0)} \gamma_{t-a}, \quad \forall x = (g, a, t, c) \in X \tag{3.1}$$

where α_a is the age-specific parameter giving the average age profile of mortality, $\kappa_t^{(i)}$ is the time index and $\beta_a^{(i)}$ modifies its effect across ages so that their products are the age-period terms describing the mortality trends, γ_{t-a} is the cohort parameter, and $\beta_a^{(0)}$ modifies its effect across ages ($c = t - a$ is the year of birth) so that $\beta_a^{(0)} \gamma_{t-a}$ is the cohort effect. The predictor η_x is linked to a function g as follows: $\eta_x = g\left(E\left(\frac{D_x}{E_x}\right)\right)$. The models here mentioned consider the log link function and assume that the numbers of deaths D_x follow a Poisson distribution. All the analyses reported in this chapter consider the Lee-Carter model as proposed by Brouhns et al. (2005). In addition, Deprez et al. (2017) analyze the Renshaw-Haberman model and Levantesi and Pizzorusso (2019) also the latter and the Plat model.

Following to the GAPC framework, the Lee-Carter model is specified by

$$\log(m_x) = \alpha_a + \beta_a^{(1)} \kappa_t^{(1)} \tag{3.2}$$

under the constraints $\sum_{t \in T} \kappa_t^{(1)} = 0$, $\sum_{a \in A} \beta_a^{(1)} = 1$ that allow us to avoid identifiability problems with the parameters. The forecasted probabilities are obtained by modeling the time index $\kappa_t^{(1)}$ with an autoregressive integrated moving average (ARIMA) process. The random walk with drift properly fits the data: $\kappa_t^{(1)} = \kappa_{t-1}^{(1)} + \delta + \epsilon_t$, with $\epsilon_t \sim N\left(0, \sigma_k^2\right)$, where δ is the drift parameter and ϵ_t are the error terms, normally distributed with null mean and variance σ_k^2. Moreover, we briefly introduce the Renshaw-Haberman model, which extends the Lee-Carter model by including a cohort effect:[1] $\log(m_x) = \alpha_a + \beta_a^{(1)} \kappa_t^{(1)} + \gamma_{t-a}$. The model is subject to the constraints: $\sum_{t \in T} \kappa_t^{(1)} = 0$, $\sum_{a \in A} \beta_a^{(1)} = 1$, and $\sum_{c \in C} \gamma_c = 0$, where $c = t - a$; and the Plat model: $\log(m_x) = \alpha_a + \kappa_t^{(1)} + \kappa_t^{(2)} (\bar{a} - a) + \kappa_t^{(3)} (\bar{a} - a)^+ + \gamma_{t-a}$, where $(\bar{a} - a)^+ = \max(\bar{a} - a, 0)$.

This latter model is subject to the constraints: $\sum_{t \in T} \kappa_t^{(1)} = 0$, $\sum_{t \in T} \kappa_t^{(2)} = 0$, $\sum_{t \in T} \kappa_t^{(3)} = 0$, $\sum_{c \in C} \gamma_c = 0$, $\sum_{c \in C} \gamma_c c = 0$, $\sum_{c \in C} \gamma_c c^2 = 0$. The mortality data are taken from the Human Mortality Database (HMD). The accuracy of the models in terms of goodness of fit is measured by the mean absolute percent error (MAPE) and the mean absolute error (MAE), while in terms of goodness of forecasting by the root mean squared error (RMSE) used to compare the forecasted mortality rates in an out-of-sample test. Let N be the data dimension and m_x and $\hat{m}_x$ the observed and estimated values, respectively. MAPE, MAE, and RMSE are expressed by the following formulae:

$$MAPE = \frac{100}{N} \sum_x \left| \frac{m_x - \hat{m}_x}{m_x} \right| \tag{3.3}$$

$$MAE = \frac{\sum_x |m_x - \hat{m}_x|}{N} \tag{3.4}$$

$$RMSE = \sqrt{\frac{\sum_x \left(m_x - \hat{m}_x \right)^2}{N}} \tag{3.5}$$

Mortality forecasting literature provides a rich overview of an increasing number of fine statistical models. Specifically, mortality models may exhibit important drawbacks, concerning demographic and bio-demographic aspects. One of the most suitable examples refers to the fixed age structure over time, which affects Lee Carter's framework, ignoring the population age evolution (Li et al., 2013). In particular, we refer to Levantesi and Nigri (2020) for a detailed description of the limits of the Lee Carter that are not fully able to identify the mortality patterns especially at older ages. ML could help scholars allowing to overcome these limitations by investigating the hidden pattern among data structure.

Deprez et al. (2017) use decision trees to enhance the quality of mortality estimates provided by two stochastic mortality models: Lee-Carter model and Renshaw-Haberman model. They use this approach to back-test a mortality model, allowing to identify strengths and weaknesses of the model with respect to the individual features (age, year of birth, gender, etc.). Moreover, the authors apply the model to improve the mortality fitting of the Lee-Carter and Haberman-Renshaw models with respect to feature components that are not well captured by these models. The case study is based on the mortality data of Switzerland and on the following set of variables $A = \{0, \ldots, 100\}$, $T = \{1876, \ldots, 2014\}$ for both the genders.

Levantesi and Pizzorusso (2019) extend the previous approach to improve the Lee-Carter, Renshaw-Haberman, and Plat mortality projections through DT, RF, and GBM. These algorithms are used to predict the ratio between observed and estimated deaths from a specified model, then obtaining an improvement in the accuracy of the projections of the Lee-Carter, Renshaw-Haberman, and Plat models. The case study is based on the mortality data of Italy and on the following set of variables $A = \{0, \ldots, 100\}$, $T = \{1915, \ldots, 2014\}$, and $C = \{1815, \ldots, 2014\}$ for both the genders. They obtain better results for RF that is more effective than DT and GBM. The application of an ML estimator leads to significant improvement in the quality and level of both fit and forecasting.

Following the same line of research, Levantesi and Nigri (2020) propose to extrapolate the ML estimator on the whole mortality surface using the two-dimensional P-splines, obtaining more accurate mortality projection with respect to the Lee-Carter model. Moreover, the authors develop a sensitivity analysis of the model to predictors, aiming to investigate whether the results are reasonable in a demographic perspective, and a sensitivity analysis on the age range in order to verify the level of the improvement provided by the model on a reduced dataset. The case study is based on the mortality data of Australia, France, Italy, Spain, the UK, and the USA, and on the following set of variables $A = \{20, \ldots, 100\}$, $T = \{1947, \ldots, 2014\}$, and $C = \{1847, \ldots, 1994\}$ and both genders. The authors obtained significative improvements in the mortality projection of the Lee-Carter model by applying the RF estimator. These results hold for all the analyzed countries.

3.3 Modeling mortality with machine learning

The literature on the mortality modeling with ML is still now very scarce. To the best of our knowledge, the only scientific contributions on this topic are from Deprez et al. (2017), Levantesi and Pizzorusso (2019), and Levantesi and Nigri (2020). The common element of these works is to use ML algorithms in order to improve the fitting accuracy in estimating mortality rates of some standard stochastic mortality models. All of these papers apply CART to calibrate a machine learning estimator that is then used to adjust (and to improve) the mortality rates estimated by the original mortality model, showing that mortality modeling can take advantage of ML that better captures patterns that are not easy to be identified with a traditional mortality model. CART is useful to work with categorical variables that identify some mortality features (ages, gender, the year of birth and time).

Deprez et al. (2017) use decision trees aiming to detect the weaknesses of different mortality models, also investigating the cause-of-death mortality. Levantesi and Pizzorusso (2019) use decision trees, random forest, and gradient boosting for the calibration of a machine learning estimator. Finally, Levantesi and Nigri (2020) use decision trees.

CART is tree-based models used for regression and classification, based on the partition of the feature space into a sequence of binary splits segmenting the predictor space (Hastie et al., 2016). The predictive performance of the trees can be improved by aggregating many of them, giving rise to the ensemble methods, which also include random forest and gradient boosting machine.

In the literature, the ML implementation of mortality models refers to four categorical variables identifying an individual: gender (g), age (a), calendar year (t), and year of birth (c). Therefore, the model assigns to each individual the feature $x =$g,a,t,c$\in X$ with $X = G \times A \times T \times C$ being the feature space, where $G = \{males, females\}$, $A = \{0, \ldots, \omega\}$, $T = \{t_1, \ldots, t_n\}$, and $C = \{c_1, \ldots, c_m\}$. The feature space X could be enriched with other information such as the income, the marital status, to be or not to be a smoker. The model requires that the number of deaths D_x satisfies the age independence condition in $x \in X$ and follows a Poisson distribution, $D_x \sim Pois\,(m_x E_x)$ for all $x \in X$, where m_x is the central death rate and E_x are the exposures. Let us denote the expected number of deaths estimated by a given stochastic mortality model j as d_x^j and let m_x^j be the corresponding central death rate. Following the framework in Deprez et al. (2017), the initial condition of the model is $m_x = m_x^j$ and

$$D_x \sim Pois\left(\psi_x d_x^j\right), with \quad \psi_x \equiv 1, d_x^j = m_x^j E_x$$

Note that the condition $\psi_x \equiv 1$ is equivalent to state that the mortality model completely fits the crude rates. This is an ideal condition as in the real world the model might overestimate ($\psi_x \leq 1$) or underestimate ($\psi_x \geq 1$) the crude rates. The aim of the approach used in Deprez et al. (2017), Levantesi and Pizzorusso (2019), and Levantesi and Nigri (2020) is essentially to calibrate the parameter ψ_x according to an ML algorithm in order to improve the fitting accuracy of the mortality model. The estimator ψ_x is a solution of a tree-based algorithm applied to the ratio between the death observations and the corresponding value estimated by the specified mortality model:

$$\frac{D_x}{d_x^j} \sim gender + age + year + cohort \qquad (3.6)$$

Let $\hat{\psi}_x^{j,ML}$ denote the ML estimator that is solution of equation (3), where j is the mortality model and ML the ML technique we refer to. In order to reach a better fit of the observed data, the central death rate of the mortality model, m_x^j, are adjusted through $\hat{\psi}_x^{j,ML}$ as follows:

$$m_x^{j,ML} = \hat{\psi}_x^{j,ML} m_x^j, \quad \forall x \in X \qquad (3.7)$$

The mortality improvement reached by the ML algorithm can be also measured through the relative changes of central death rates $\Delta m_x^{j,ML} = \hat{\psi}_x^{j,ML} - 1$. The values of $\hat{\psi}_x^{j,ML}$ are then obtained by applying an ML algorithm. As shown in Levantesi and Nigri (2020), this approach can be also used to diagnose the limits of the traditional mortality models.

The ML algorithms used in the application provided by the specific literature on mortality modeling belong to CART, Decision Tree (DT), Random Forest (RF), and Gradient Boosting Machine (GBM), and are summarized in the following. DT operates a partition of a predictor space by a sequence of binary splits, giving rise to a tree (Hastie et al., 2016). Following a hierarchical structure, the predictor space is recursively split into simple regions, and the response for a given observation is predicted by the mean of the training observations in the region to which that observation belongs (James et al., 2017).

Let $(X_\tau)_{\tau \in T}$ be the partition of X, where J is the number of distinct and non-overlapping regions. The DT estimator, given a set of variables x, is defined as $\hat{\psi}^{DT}(x) = \Sigma_{\tau \in T} \hat{\psi}_\tau \, 1_{\{x \in X_\tau\}}$, where $1_{\{.\}}$ is the indicator function. The regions $(X_\tau) \, \tau \in T$ are found by minimizing the residual sum of squares.

RF aggregates many DTs, obtained by generating bootstrap training samples from the original dataset (Breiman, 2001). The main characteristic of this algorithm is to select a random subset of predictors at each split, thus preventing the dominance of strong predictors in the splits of each tree (James et al., 2017). The RF estimator is calculated as $\hat{\psi}^{RF}(x) = \frac{1}{B} \sum_{b=1}^{B} \hat{\psi}^{(DT)}(x|b)$, where B is the number of bootstrap samples and $\hat{\psi}^{(DT)}(x|b)$ is the DT estimator on the sample b.

GBM considers a sequential approach in which each DT uses the information from the previous one in order to improve the current fit (Friedman, 2001). Given the current fit $\hat{\psi}(x_{i-1})$, at each stage i (for $i = 1, 2, .., N$), the GBM algorithm provides a new model adding an estimator h to improve the fit: $\hat{\psi}(x_i) = \hat{\psi}(x_{i-1}) + \lambda_i h_i(x)$, where $h_i \in H$ is a base learner function (H is the set of arbitrary differentiable functions) and λ is a multiplier obtained by solving the optimization problem.

Furthermore, going beyond the logic of ML, Levantesi and Pizzorusso (2019) propose to forecast the ML estimator using the same framework of the original mortality model. This approach is tested on the Lee-Carter model ($j = LC$), where the ML estimator is modeled as follows:

$$\log\left(\hat{\psi}_x^{LC,ML}\right) = \alpha_a^\psi + \beta_a^{(1,\psi)} \kappa_t^{(1,\psi)} \qquad (3.8)$$

where the parameters α_a^{ψ}, $\beta_a^{(1,\psi)}$, and $\kappa_t^{(1,\psi)}$ have the same meaning of α_a, $\beta_a^{(1)}$, and $\kappa_t^{(1)}$ in the traditional Lee-Carter model. From equations (4) and (5), we obtain the following model, which improved the Lee-Carter through ML:

$$\log\left(m_x^{LC,ML}\right) = \left(\alpha_a^{\psi} + \alpha_a\right) + \beta_a^{(1,\psi)}\kappa_t^{(1,\psi)} + \beta_a^{(1)}\kappa_t^{(1)} \tag{3.9}$$

The use of the same framework of the original mortality model to fit and forecast the ML estimators $\hat{\psi}_x$, as proposed by Levantesi and Nigri (2020), allows both to improve the mortality projections' accuracy and to analyze the effect of such improvements directly on the model's parameters.

The forecasting performance of the Lee-Carter model can be also improved by following the methodology suggested by Levantesi and Nigri (2020), which finds the ML estimator future values through the extrapolation of $\hat{\psi}_s$ previously smoothed with two-dimensional P-splines (Eilers and Marx, 1996). In this method, forecasting is a natural consequence of the smoothing process: future values are considered as missing values that are estimated by the two-dimensional P-splines (Currie et al., 2006). The form of the forecast is then determined by the penalty function that is more important in the extrapolation of future vales with respect to the smoothing of data.

3.4 Numerical application

In this section, we present a numerical application with the aim to highlight the longevity risk impact on life insurance products. The choice of a mortality projection model rather than another leads to different actuarial valuations in the pricing and reserving policies. The impact of longevity projections depends on the features of the insurance product involved. A realized mortality lower than projected increases insurer's profit when death benefits are concerned. On the contrary, the underestimation of the probabilities of survival impacts negatively on the profit when life benefit is offered.

The section is organized as follows. In Section 5.1, we implement different mortality models in order to show how some ML techniques improve the fitting and modify the forecasts, exploiting real mortality data of three European countries. In Section 5.2, we present an actuarial analysis of the impact of longevity projections on two life insurance products whose payoffs depend on the future realized lifetime. Some actuarial basics are described and the single and periodic prices and the time profile of the actuarial reserves are calculated.

3.4.1 Mortality models by comparison: an empirical analysis

We apply the models presented in Section 3.1 to the mortality data of three EU countries: France, Italy, and the UK. Data are downloaded from the Human Mortality Database (www.mortality.org) and refer to ages 40–100 and years 1947–2014. The aim of the numerical application is to test the difference among a canonical stochastic mortality model and its improvements through the ML estimator in the mortality forecasting. The models are tested on the Lee-Carter model according to the following procedure:

■ Step 1: fitting Lee-Carter model (denoted by "*LC*") with *StMoMo* package (Villegas et al., 2015);

- Step 2: fitting the ML estimator $\psi_x^{LC,ML}$, which is the solution of equation (3), using the random forest algorithm then obtaining $\hat{\psi}_x^{LC,RF}$;
- Step 3: adjusting the central death rate of the Lee-Carter model through the RF estimator (see equation (4)): $m_x^{LC,RF} = \hat{\psi}_x^{LC,RF} m_x^{LC}$;
- Step 4: modeling the RF estimator with two different approaches: the first one proposed by Levantesi and Pizzorusso (2019) (denoted by "*LC-ψ*"), while the second one by Levantesi and Nigri (2020) (denoted by "*LC-ψ-spl*"):

  - *LC-ψ* model: the RF estimator is modeled with the Lee-Carter model as described in equation (5),
  - *LC-ψ-spl* model: the RF estimator is smoothed using two-dimensional (age and time) P-splines;

- Step 5: forecasting *LC* and *LC-ψ* models, and extrapolating *LC-ψ-spl* model. The forecast period is set to 2015–2074.

The goodness of fit is measured by the MAPE. The results are shown in Table 3.1 and evidence a high improvement in the Lee-Carter model fitting provided by the RF estimator in all the countries considered and for both gender.

To test the ability of the models we develop an out-of-sample test splitting the dataset in two parts: data from 1947 to 1998 (fitting period) and data from 1999 to 2014 (forecasting period). The goodness of the out-of-sample test is evaluated by the RMSE. The results reported in Table 3.2 show that the RF estimator provides strong improvements of the canonical Lee-Carter model. The LC-ψ results the best one.

Table 3.1 MAPE. Ages 40–100 and years 1947–2014

Model	FRA		ITA		UK	
	M	F	M	F	M	F
LC (%)	9.23	8.30	9.40	7.86	10.06	7.81
LC-ψ (%)	2.27	2.19	2.76	2.41	2.34	2.07

Table 3.2 Out-of-sample test results: RMSE for the models LC, LC-ψ, and LC-ψ-spl. Ages 40–100 and years 1999–2014

Model	FRA		ITA		UK	
	M	F	M	F	M	F
LC	0.0444	0.0352	0.0410	0.0272	0.0364	0.0222
LC-ψ	0.0159	0.0142	0.0148	0.0085	0.0123	0.0077
LC-ψ-spl	0.0232	0.0199	0.0403	0.0164	0.0129	0.0103

Now, we forecast the models over the period 2015–2074. To appreciate the model's difference, we show in Figure 3.1 the survival probabilities $_tp_x$ of a cohort of individuals aged 40 in 2015 over the years 2015–2074 for each model. Both LC$-\psi$ and LC-ψ-spl lower the LC model survival probabilities.

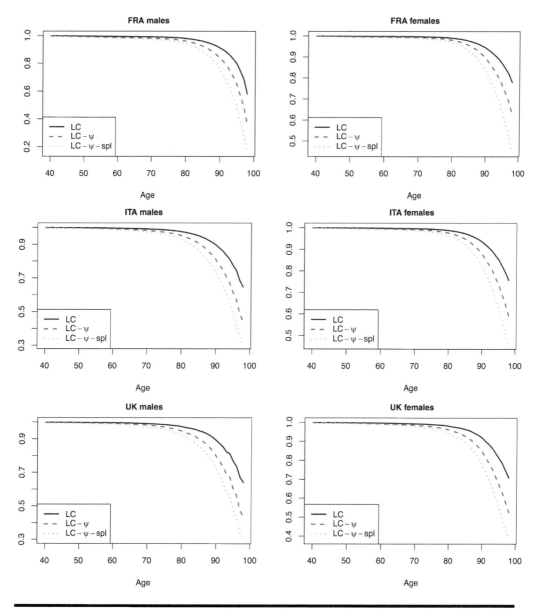

Figure 3.1 Survival probabilities $_tp_x$. Models LC-ψ and LC-ψ-spl. Ages 40–100 and years 2015–2074.

3.4.2 Longevity management for life insurance: sample cases

In this subsection, we use the forecasted probabilities previously derived to analyze two life insurance products: term insurance and pure endowment.

The term insurance pays the sum insured C at the end of the year of death if the insured dies prior to the expiration of the contract n. It is useful to face the financial distress of the family in the case of an early death of a member. The single premium the insured aged x has to pay, at the inception of the contract $t = 0$, to buy this product is given by

$$U = C \cdot {}_n A_x \tag{3.10}$$

where nA_x is the expected value at $t = 0$ of a random variable whose outcome is the discounted unitary sum at the technical rate i insured in the case of death:

$$ {}_n A_x = \sum_{h=0}^{n-1}(1+i)^{-(h+1)} \, {}_{h/}q_x \tag{3.11}$$

with ${}_{h/}q_x$ being the probability that an insurer aged x will die between ages $x + h$ and $x + h + 1$.

The pure endowment insurance provides the beneficiary with a lump sum benefit C at time n if the insured is still alive. The single premium is given by

$$U = C \cdot {}_n E_x = C(1+i)^{-n} \, {}_n p_x \tag{3.12}$$

where ${}_n p_x$ is the probability that the insured aged x at the inception of the contract will be alive at age $x + n$.

For both contracts the single premium can be converted in a sequence of m premiums P paid at the policy anniversaries through the following formula:

$$U = \sum_{h=1}^{m} P \cdot {}_m E_x$$

The mathematical reserve is a technical tool for assessing the insurer's debt during the period the contract is in force. The insurer has to register in the balance sheet the amount of the mathematical reserve to ensure the ability to meet the obligations assumed whenever the insured event occurs until the expiration date n. At time t the perspective reserve is defined as

$$V_t = E[Y(t, n)] - E[X(t, n)]$$

where $E[Y(t, n)]$ and $E[X(t, n)]$ at time t are respectively the expected actuarial present value of the benefits which fall due in the period (t, n) and the expected actuarial present value of the premiums paid in the same interval.

Let us consider an Italian male insured and set $C = 1000$, $x = 40$, $i = 2\%$, $n = m = 25$ for both the term insurance contract and the pure endowment. In Table 3.3, we report the single and the period premiums calculated projecting the probabilities in equations (13)–(14) according to the three models previously described LC, LC-ψ, and LC-ψ-spl. Figures 3.2 and 3.3 show the trends of the reserves for both contracts from the issue to the expiration.

Table 3.3 The single (U) and period (P) premium of the term life insurance and pure endowment for the models LC, LC-ψ, and LC-ψ-spl

	Term life insurance			Endowment insurance		
	LC	LC-ψ	LC-ψ-spl	LC	LC-ψ	LC-ψ-spl
U	290,8485	301,9316	311,2901	359,4046	350,4961	341,7526
P	16,30582	17,03309	17,59216	20,14928	19,77279	19,3137

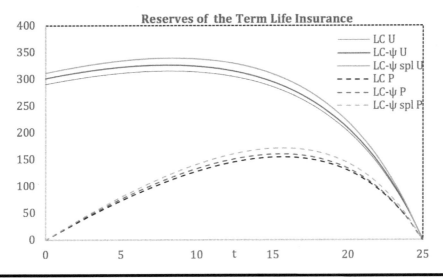

Figure 3.2 Reserves for term life insurance with single and periodic premium for the models LC, LC-ψ, and LC-ψ-spl.

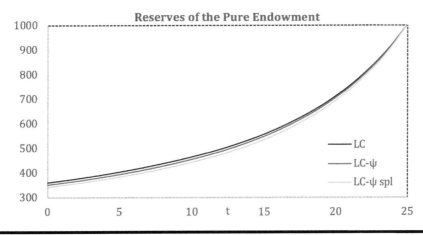

Figure 3.3 Reserves for pure endowment contract with single premium for the models LC, LC-ψ, and LC-ψ-spl.

As it is clear, the longevity projections impact on pricing and reserving policy. The traditional LC model produces lower projected probability of death and, speculatively, higher survival probabilities than those obtained applying ML models. Consequently, on one hand in the case of a death benefit the LC leads to lower prices and underestimated reserves with negative impact on the solvency of the insurance company. On the other hand, in the case of a life benefit it leads to overestimate prices and reserve with potential negative impact on the competitiveness and attractiveness of the products.

3.5 Conclusions

In this chapter, we have illustrated the potentialities of an ML model applied to the quantification of longevity risk in the management of real insurance products. The numerical application presented has aimed to highlight the longevity risk impact on two life insurance policies, the pure endowment and the term insurance, that are the basis for more complex portfolios. The choice of a mortality projection model rather than another leads to different actuarial valuations in the pricing and reserving policies. The impact of longevity projections depends on the features of the insurance product involved. A realized mortality lower than projected increases insurer's profit when death benefits are concerned.

As ML is largely changing the way in which the society operates and economy grows, in the insurance sector it can be used to manage and extract important information from very large available datasets, increase competitiveness, reduce risk exposures, and improve profits through automated and efficient pricing policies. An important aspect is that ML can reduce one point of weakness of the insurance business, the information asymmetry between insurer and policyholder, allowing for better understanding and quantification of the specific risk of each policyholder. This appears fundamental in the longevity risk management of life products with long-term duration as well as of some lifelong guaranteed options embedded in most insurance and pension contracts. The accurate assessment of the impact of longevity risk on the balance sheets of the insurance companies is until now based on the choice of the stochastic models and on scenario testing; the results of the projections and the strategies implemented are model dependent. Instead, ML techniques permit to integrate a stochastic model with a data-driven approach. These tools, improving the longevity risk quantification, can support also the risk transfer through both the reinsurance and the longevity capital market. As regards the first aspect, there is the perception that reinsurers are reluctant to take this "toxic" risk (Blake et al., 2006), but the perplexities could be resized thanks to a precise understanding of this risk deepening pieces of information extracted by large datasets. As regards the second aspect, longevity risk market plays a role in the risk management of longevity risk. Another crucial point is the improvement of longevity risk management, thanks to the opportune exploitation of the available medical and socio-economical data. Traditional risk models require very long time to process huge available datasets and often are incapable of deepen each information. The advances of the microeconomic models are favored by AI and the risk management is shifting from statistical methods such as principal component analysis to ML to select important variables on the basis of supervised tree algorithms, which automatically select variables of interest for building predictive models. A life insurance compartment where longevity risk is acting up its strong impact is represented by the health insurance and long-term care for elderly. Thanks to AI, smart sensor technologies are available for insurers to improve policyholders' health monitoring and encourage a healthier lifestyle; they are improving older people's quality of lives, reducing health costs at older ages. Finally, through ML the output from internal risk models can be more accurate and also the validation process can be improved running on a continuous basis. In the light of the improvements reached, we are convinced that ML can offer insurance companies and pension fund managers new tools and methods supporting actuaries in classifying longevity risks, offering accurate predictive pricing models, and reducing losses.

3.6 Appendix

```
rm(list=ls(all=TRUE))
library(demography)
library(StMoMo)
library(randomForest)
library(fields)
library(MortalitySmooth)

#-----------HMD function-----------#
hmd.mx <- function(country, username, password, label=country){
path <- paste("https://www.mortality.org/hmd/",country, "/STATS/",
"Mx_1x1.txt", sep = "")
userpwd <- paste(username, ":", password, sep = "")
txt <- RCurl::getURL(path, userpwd = userpwd)
con <- textConnection(txt)
mx <- try(utils::read.table(con, skip = 2,
header = TRUE, na.strings = "."),TRUE)
close(con)
if(class(mx)=="try-error")
stop("Connection error at www.mortality.org. Please check username,
password and country label.")
path <- paste("https://www.mortality.org/hmd/", country, "/STATS/",
"Exposures_1x1.txt", sep = "")
userpwd <- paste(username, ":", password, sep = "")
txt <- RCurl::getURL(path, userpwd = userpwd)
con <- textConnection(txt)
pop <- try(utils::read.table(con, skip = 2, header = TRUE,
na.strings = "."),TRUE)
close(con)
if(class(pop)=="try-error")
stop("Exposures file not found at www.mortality.org")
obj <- list(type="mortality",label=label,lambda=0)
obj$year <- sort(unique(mx[, 1]))
n <- length(obj$year)
m <- length(unique(mx[, 2]))
obj$age <- mx[1:m, 2]
mnames <- names(mx)[-c(1, 2)]
n.mort <- length(mnames)
obj$rate <- obj$pop <- list()
for (i in 1:n.mort){
obj$rate[[i]] <- matrix(mx[, i + 2], nrow = m, ncol = n)
obj$rate[[i]][obj$rate[[i]] < 0] <- NA
```

```
obj$pop[[i]] <- matrix(pop[, i + 2], nrow = m, ncol = n)
obj$pop[[i]][obj$pop[[i]] < 0] <- NA
dimnames(obj$rate[[i]]) <- dimnames(obj$pop[[i]])
   <- list(obj$age, obj$year)}
names(obj$pop) = names(obj$rate) <- tolower(mnames)
obj$age <- as.numeric(as.character(obj$age))
if (is.na(obj$age[m]))
obj$age[m] <- 2 * obj$age[m - 1] - obj$age[m - 2]
return(structure(obj, class = "demogdata"))
}


#------------DATA------------#
for(country in c("FRATNP","ITA","GBR_NP")){
Data= hmd.mx(country = country, username ="insert␣username",
password ="insert␣password" ,label = country)
Data.F=StMoMoData(Data, series = "female")
Data.M=StMoMoData(Data, series = "male")
Data.M$Dxt=round(Data.M$Dxt)
Data.M$Ext=round(Data.M$Ext)
Data.F$Dxt=round(Data.F$Dxt)
Data.F$Ext=round(Data.F$Ext)
ages=40:100
years0=1947:2014
years=years0
lim1.y = years[1]+1-Data.M$years[1]
limn.y = tail(years,1)+1-Data.M$years[1]
lim1.a = ages[1]+1
limn.a = tail(ages,1)+1
n.data = length(years)*length(ages)
Years = rep(rep(years[1]:tail(years,1), each=length(ages)),2)
Ages = rep(rep(ages,length(years)), 2)
Cohort = Years-Ages
Gender = c(rep("F",length(years)*length(ages)),
rep("M",length(years)*length(ages)))
Dxt.C = c(as.vector(Data.F$Dxt[lim1.a:limn.a,lim1.y:limn.y]),
as.vector(Data.M$Dxt[lim1.a:limn.a,lim1.y:limn.y]))
Ext.C = c(as.vector(Data.F$Ext[lim1.a:limn.a,lim1.y:limn.y]) ,
as.vector(Data.M$Ext[lim1.a:limn.a,lim1.y:limn.y]))
Data.ML.C = data.frame(Year=Years, Age=Ages, Cohort=Cohort,
Gender=Gender, Dxt=Dxt.C, Ext=Ext.C)
# crude mortality rates
CR.M = Data.M$Dxt[ages[2]:(tail(ages,1)+1),lim1.y:limn.y]/
Data.M$Ext[ages[2]:(tail(ages,1)+1),lim1.y:limn.y]
CR.F = Data.F$Dxt[ages[2]:(tail(ages,1)+1),lim1.y:limn.y]/
Data.F$Ext[ages[2]:(tail(ages,1)+1),lim1.y:limn.y]
write.table(CR.M,file=paste("CR.M","_",country,".txt",sep=""))
write.table(CR.F,file=paste("CR.F","_",country,".txt",sep=""))
log.CR.F=log(CR.F)
log.CR.M=log(CR.M)

#------------Lee-carter model------------#
```

```
wxt= genWeightMat(ages = ages,years = years, clip=0)
  #matrix of weights
LC.M = fit(lc(link="log"), data=Data.M, ages.fit = ages,
years.fit = years)  # males
LC.F = fit(lc(link="log"), data=Data.F, ages.fit = ages,
years.fit = years)  # females
q.LC.M = fitted(LC.M, type="rates")
q.LC.F = fitted(LC.F, type="rates")
m.LC.M = - log(1-q.LC.M)
m.LC.F = - log(1-q.LC.F)
log.q.LC.M <- log(q.LC.M)
log.q.LC.F <- log(q.LC.F)


#------------RANDOM FOREST algorithm------------#
model0 = "LC"
obj.mxM <- m.LC.M
obj.mxF <- m.LC.F
vol.mdl.F=Data.F$Ext[ages[2]:(tail(ages,1)+1),lim1.y:limn.y]* obj.mxF
vol.mdl.M=Data.M$Ext[ages[2]:(tail(ages,1)+1),lim1.y:limn.y]* obj.mxM
volF=as.vector(vol.mdl.F)
volM=as.vector(vol.mdl.M)
vol.mdl = c(volF, volM)
Data.ML.mdl=cbind(Data.ML.C,vol.mdl)
rap.mdl=Data.ML.mdl$Dxt/Data.ML.mdl$vol.mdl
Data.ML.mdl=cbind(Data.ML.mdl,rap.mdl)
set.seed(3)
rf.mdl = randomForest(rap.mdl~Year+Age+Cohort+Gender,
data =Data.ML.mdl, ntree=200, mtry = 2,
importance=TRUE, na.action=na.roughfix)
rf.mdl
corrf.mdl=predict(rf.mdl)
importance(rf.mdl)
write.table(importance(rf.mdl),file=
paste("rf_imp","_",model0,"_",country,".txt",sep=""))
pdf(file=paste("IncNodePurity","_",model0,"_",
   country,".pdf",sep=""),
width=5, height=5)
par(mfrow=c(1,1), pty="m", mar=c(4,2,2,2), oma=c(0,0,0,0))
varImpPlot(rf.mdl, pch=19, col="blue", cex=1.3, lwd=2,
main = "", type=2)
dev.off()
v.F=c()
v.M=c()
for(i in 1:n.data){
v.F[i]=corrf.mdl[i]
v.M[i]=corrf.mdl[i+n.data]
}
corrf.mdl.F=matrix(v.F, nrow = length(c(ages[2]:
(tail(ages,1)+1))),ncol=length(years),dimnames = list(ages,years))
corrf.mdl.M=matrix(v.M, nrow = length(c(ages[2]:
(tail(ages,1)+1))),ncol=length(years),dimnames = list(ages,years))
```

```
corrf.LC.F <- corrf.mdl.F
corrf.LC.M <- corrf.mdl.M
m.rf.LC.M = (corrf.LC.M)*m.LC.M
m.rf.LC.F= (corrf.LC.F)*m.LC.F
q.rf.LC.F=1-exp(-m.rf.LC.F)
q.rf.LC.M=1-exp(-m.rf.LC.M)
log.q.rf.LC.M = log(q.rf.LC.M)
log.q.rf.LC.F = log(q.rf.LC.F)
#-----------MAPE------------#
tab3M <- matrix(0, nrow=2, ncol=1)
tab3M[1,1] <- 100/length(CR.M)*sum(abs((CR.M-m.LC.M)/CR.M))
tab3M[2,1] <- 100/length(CR.M)*sum(abs((CR.M-m.rf.LC.M)/CR.M))
colnames(tab3M)=c("LC")
rownames(tab3M)=c("mdl","mdl-RF")
tab3F <- matrix(0, nrow=2, ncol=1)
tab3F[1,1] <- 100/length(CR.F)*sum(abs((CR.F-m.LC.F)/CR.F))
tab3F[2,1] <- 100/length(CR.F)*sum(abs((CR.F-m.rf.LC.F)/CR.F))
colnames(tab3F)=c("LC")
rownames(tab3F)=c("mdl","mdl-RF")
MAPE <- cbind(round(tab3M, 2),round(tab3F, 2))
write.table(MAPE,file=paste("MAPE","_",country,"_",
years0[1],".txt",sep=""))
#-----------forecasting------------#
years.for <- c(2015:2074)
ny.for <- length(years.for)
kt.lb <- 40
lim.oos <- lim1.y+length(years)
LCfor.M <- forecast(LC.M, h= ny.for, kt.lookback = kt.lb)
LCfor.F <- forecast(LC.F, h= ny.for, kt.lookback = kt.lb)
LC.fore.mM <- - log(1-LCfor.M$rates)
LC.fore.mF <- - log(1-LCfor.F$rates)
colnames(LC.fore.mF)=years.for
row.names(LC.fore.mF)=ages
colnames(LC.fore.mM)=years.for
row.names(LC.fore.mM)=ages
write.table(LC.fore.mM,file=paste("LC.fore.mM","_",
country,".txt",sep=""))
write.table(LC.fore.mF,file=paste("LC.fore.mF","_",
country,".txt",sep=""))
#-----------smoothing psi------------#
y.new <- years.for
df.fix <- 3
subst <- 1
y.tot <- c(years, y.new)
W <- matrix(1, nrow=length(ages), ncol=(length(y.tot)-
length(y.new)))
E <- matrix(0, nrow=length(ages), ncol=length(y.new))
W.new <- cbind(W, E)
rownames(W.new) <- ages
colnames(W.new) <- c(years[1]:tail(years.for,1))
arg.ext.M <- cbind(Data.M$Ext[ages[2]:(tail(ages,1)+1),
```

```
lim1.y:(lim.oos-1)],E)
arg.ext.F <- cbind(Data.F$Ext[ages[2]:(tail(ages,1)+1),
lim1.y:(lim.oos-1)],E)
colnames(arg.ext.M) <- c(years[1]:tail(years.for,1))
colnames(arg.ext.F) <- colnames(arg.ext.M)
for(sex0 in c("M","F")){
if(sex0=="M"){
name <- "corrf_LC_M"
obj.cor <- corrf.LC.M
obj.ext <- arg.ext.M
fitcor = fit(lc(link="log"), Dxt= obj.cor*obj.ext[,1:ncol(W)],
Ext=obj.ext[,1:ncol(W)], ages = ages, years = years)
cor.fit <- forecast(fitcor, h= ny.for, kt.lookback = kt.lb)
pdf(file=paste("k1","_",name,".pdf",sep=""),width=8, height=6)
par(mfrow=c(1,1), pty="m", mar=c(4,4,3,2), oma=c(0,0,0,0))
plot(cor.fit,only.kt=TRUE)
dev.off()
fit2D <- Mort2Dsmooth(x=ages, y=y.tot, Z=cbind(obj.cor,E),
W=W.new, method=3, lambdas=c(0.1,0.1))
cor.fit2D <- exp(fit2D$logmortality)[,(ncol(W)+1):length(y.tot)]
pdf(file=paste("fit2D_ext","_",name,"_",country,".pdf",sep=""),
width=7, height=5.8)
par(mfrow=c(1,1), pty="m", mar=c(4,4,2,6), oma=c(0,0,0,0))
image(ages,y.tot,exp(fit2D$logmortality),breaks=c(0,seq(0.5,
round(max(obj.cor),1), length.out=20)),
col=designer.colors(20, c("blue", "white", "red")),
axes=T, ylab="",xlab="", cex=0.6)
abline(v=(seq(0,105,5)), col="lightgray", lty=3)
abline(h=(c(seq(y.tot[1],2014,10),2014)), col="lightgray", lty=3)
image.plot(ages, y.tot, exp(fit2D$logmortality), legend.only=TRUE,
breaks=c(0,seq(0.5, round(max(obj.cor),1), length.out=20)),
col=designer.colors(20, c("blue", "white", "red")),
    ylab="",xlab="",cex=0.6)
dev.off()
write.table(cor.fit$rates,file=paste("corfit","_",name,"_",
country,".txt",sep=""))
write.table(cor.fit2D,file=paste("fit2D","_",name,"_",
country,".txt",sep=""))
}
if(sex0=="F"){
name <- "corrf_LC_F"
obj.cor <- corrf.LC.F
obj.ext <- arg.ext.F
fitcor = fit(lc(link="log"), Dxt= obj.cor*obj.ext[,1:ncol(W)],
Ext=obj.ext[,1:ncol(W)], ages = ages, years = years)
cor.fit <- forecast(fitcor, h= ny.for, kt.lookback = kt.lb)
pdf(file=paste("k1","_",name,".pdf",sep=""),width=8, height=6)
par(mfrow=c(1,1), pty="m", mar=c(4,4,3,2), oma=c(0,0,0,0))
plot(cor.fit,only.kt=TRUE)
dev.off()
fit2D <- Mort2Dsmooth(x=ages, y=y.tot, Z=cbind(obj.cor,E),
```

```
W=W.new, method=3, lambdas=c(0.1,0.1))
cor.fit2D <- exp(fit2D$logmortality)[,(ncol(W)+1):length(y.tot)]
pdf(file=paste("fit2D_ext","_",name,"_",country,".pdf",sep=""),
width=7, height=5.8)
par(mfrow=c(1,1), pty="m", mar=c(4,4,2,6), oma=c(0,0,0,0))
image(ages,y.tot,exp(fit2D$logmortality),
breaks=c(0,seq(0.5, round(max(obj.cor),1), length.out=20)),
col=designer.colors(20, c("blue", "white", "red")),
axes=T, ylab="",xlab="", cex=0.6)
abline(v=(seq(0,105,5)), col="lightgray", lty=3)
abline(h=(c(seq(y.tot[1],2014,10),2014)), col="lightgray", lty=3)
image.plot(ages, y.tot, exp(fit2D$logmortality),
legend.only=TRUE,breaks=c(0,seq(0.5, round(max(obj.cor),1),
length.out=20)),
col=designer.colors(20, c("blue", "white", "red")),
ylab="",xlab="",cex=0.6)
dev.off()
write.table(cor.fit$rates,file=paste("corfit","_",name,"_",
country,".txt",sep=""))
write.table(cor.fit2D,file=paste("fit2D","_",name,"_",
country,".txt",sep=""))
}}}

for(country in c("FRATNP","ITA","GBR_NP")){
for(sex0 in c("M","F")){
if(sex0=="M"){
qx <- as.matrix(read.table(paste("LC.fore.mM","_",
country,".txt",sep="")))
psi_LP <- as.matrix(read.table(paste("corfit","_",name,"_",
country,".txt",sep="")))
psi_LN <- as.matrix(read.table(paste("fit2D_corrf_LC_M","_",
country,".txt",sep="")))
qxcor.LC <- qx*psi_LP
qxcor <- qx*psi_LN
write.table(qx,file=paste("qx","_",sex0,"_",country,".txt",sep=""))
write.table(qxcor.LC,file=paste("qxcor.LC","_",sex0,"_",
country,".txt",sep=""))
write.table(qxcor,file=paste("qxcor","_",sex0,"_",
country,".txt",sep=""))
write.table(cbind(diag(qx),diag(qxcor.LC),diag(qxcor)),
file=paste("qx.coh","_",sex0,"_",country,".txt",sep=""))
}
if(sex0=="F"){
qx <- as.matrix(read.table(paste("LC.fore.mF","_",
country,".txt",sep="")))
psi_LP <- as.matrix(read.table(paste("corfit","_",name,"_",
country,".txt",sep="")))
psi_LN <- as.matrix(read.table(paste("fit2D_corrf_LC_F","_",
country,".txt",sep="")))
qxcor.LC <- qx*psi_LP
qxcor <- qx*psi_LN
```

```
cbind(diag(qx),diag(qxcor.LC),diag(qxcor))
write.table(qx,file=paste("qx","_",sex0,"_",country,".txt",sep=""))
write.table(qxcor.LC,file=paste("qxcor.LC","_",sex0,"_",
country,".txt",sep=""))
write.table(qxcor,file=paste("qxcor","_",sex0,"_",
country,".txt",sep=""))
write.table(cbind(diag(qx),diag(qxcor.LC),diag(qxcor)),
file=paste("qx.coh","_",sex0,"_",country,".txt",sep=""))}}}
```

Note

1 The setting has been proposed by Haberman and Renshaw (2011) for reaching a better stability with respect to the original version.

References

Breiman, L. (2001). Random forests. *Machine Learning, 45*, 5–32.

Brouhns, N., Denuit, M., & van Keilegom, I. (2005). Bootstrapping the Poisson logbilinear model for mortality forecasting. *Scandinavian Actuarial Journal, 3*, 212–224.

Carracedo, P., DebÃşn, A., Iftimi, A. et al. (2018). Detecting spatio-temporal mortality clusters of European countries by sex and age. *International Journal for Equity in Health, 17*, 38.

Currie, I. D., Durban, M., & Eilers P. H. C. (2004). Smoothing and forecasting mortality rates. *Statistical Modelling, 4*, 279–298.

Currie, I. D., Durban, M., & Eilers, P. H. C. (2006). Generalized linear array models with applications to multidimentional smoothing. *Journal of the Royal Statistical Society B, 68*, 259–280.

Deprez, P., Shevchenko, P. V., & Wüthrich, M. (2017). Machine learning techniques for mortality modeling. *European Actuarial Journal, 7*(2), 337–352.

Eilers, P. H. C., & Marx, B. D. (1996). Flexible smoothing with B-splines and penalties. *Statistical Science, 11*, 89–102.

Friedman, J. H. (2001). Greedy function approximation: A gradient boosting machine. *Annals of Statistics, 29*, 1189–1232.

Hainaut, D. (2018). A neural-network analyzer for mortality forecast. *Astin Bulletin, 48*, 481–508.

Hastie, J., Hastie, T., & Tibshirani, R. (2016). *The elements of statistical learning* (2nd ed.). Data Mining, Inference, and Prediction. New York: Springer.

James, G., Witten, D., Hastie, T., & Tibshirani, R. (2017). *An introduction to statistical learning: with applications in R.* New York: Springer.

Lee, R. D., & Carter, L. R. (1992). Modeling and forecasting US mortality. *Journal of the American Statistical Association, 87*, 659–671.

Levantesi, S., & Nigri, A. (2020). A random forest algorithm to improve the Lee-Carter mortality forecasting: Impact on q-forward. *Soft Computing, 24*, 8553–8567.

Levantesi, S., & Pizzorusso, V. (2019). Application of machine learning to mortality modeling and forecasting. *Risks, 7*(1), 26.

Li, N., Lee, R., & Gerland, P. (2013). Extending the Lee-Carter method to model the rotation of age patterns of mortality decline for long-term projections. *Demography, 50*(6), 2037–2051.

Nigri, A., Levantesi, S., Marino, M., Scognamiglio, S., & Perla, F. (2019). A deep learning integrated Lee-Carter model. *Risks, 7*(1), 33.

Piscopo, G., & Resta, M.(2017). Applying spectral biclustering to mortality data. *Risks, 5*, 24.

Renshaw A. E., & Haberman S. (2003). On the forecasting of mortality reduction factors. *Insurance: Mathematics and Economics, 32*(3), 379–401.

Renshaw, A. E., & Haberman, S. (2006). A cohort-based extension to the Lee-Carter model for mortality reduction factors. *Insurance: Mathematics and Economics, 38*, 556–570.

Richman, R., & Wüthrich, M. (2018). A neural network extension of the Lee-Carter model to multiple populations. *SSRN manuscript*, id 3270877.

Villegas, A. M., Kaishev, V. K., & Millossovich, P. (2015). *Stmomo: An r package for stochastic mortality modelling.* Available at: https://cran.r-project.org/web/packages/StMoMo/vignettes/StMoMoVignette.pdf.

Chapter 4

Kernel switching ridge regression in business intelligence systems

Md. Ashad Alam, Osamu Komori, and Md. Ferdush Rahman

4.1 Introduction

Business intelligence measurements depend on a variety of statistical advanced technologies used to enable the collection, analysis, and dissemination of internal and external business information. The key goal of business intelligence is to draw a well-informed business decision. Statistical machine learning-based business intelligence systems (e.g., supervised learning) prioritize a comprehensive analysis to empower businesses (Brannon, 2010). Many supervised learning algorithms have been developed to improve business decisions. The most effective algorithms are support vector machines (SVM) and support vector regression with a positive-definite kernel (Wang et al., 2005). Regression analysis is a classical but the most useful approach in supervised learning to identify trends and establish relationships of business data (Duan and Xu, 2012).

Regression techniques tell us the degree of change of a response variable by one or more predictor variables using the conditional mean of a response variable given the predictor variables instead of the mean of the response variable. Let us consider Y to be a response variable and X to be a vector of predictor variables having a mean, the conditional mean of a random variable given that the other variable is equal to the mean of the random variable, i.e., $E_X[E_Y(Y|X)] = E_Y(Y)$. The regression analysis deals with the conditional mean of Y given X, $E(Y = y|X = x)$ and the data are assumed to come from a single class or regime such that the mean or the conditional mean works well. But neither the mean nor the conditional mean works properly for the data collected from different and mixed classes. For example, to fit a nonlinear data set with two classes, we apply two nonlinear regression approaches: kernel ridge regression (KRR) and support vector regression (SVR) (Saunders and Gammerman, 1998; Shawe-Taylor and Cristianini, 2004). Figure 4.1 presents a scatter plot of the original data and the fitted curves of the booth methods. It is clearly shown that both methods are failed to fit the data properly. To overcome the problem, the switching regression model is appropriate to study (Quandt, 1972). The switching regression model forms a suitable model class for the regression problems with unknown heterogeneity.

In supervised learning, switching regression approach has become a well-known tool to deal more than one regimes at known or unknown points (Dannemann and Holzmann, 2010; Liu and Lin, 2013; Malikov and Kumbhakar, 2014; Souza and Heckman, 2014). However, with a number of explanatory variables, switching regression is shown that parameter estimates have a high probability of producing unsatisfactory results for non-orthogonal prediction vectors. The ridge trace-based estimation has been found to be a procedure that can be used to overcome the difficulties of estimation in supervised learning.

Ridge regression is a standard statistical technique that aims to address the bias variance trade-off in the design of linear regression model. This procedure plays a central role in supervised learning and has become a very popular approach to estimating complex functions as the solution to a minimization problem (Cawley and Talbot, 2003; Hastie et al., 2009). This problem is also a dual-form problem. In the dual ridge regression model, the original input data are mapped into some high-dimensional space called a "feature space." To represent a nonlinear regression, the algorithms are used to construct a linear regression function in the feature space. We look at several complex data sets with a large number of parameters, and this leads to serious computational complexity that can be unbearable to overcome. To this end, we can deal with a dual version of the ridge regression algorithms based on a positive-definite kernel function as a kernel method (Alam, 2014; Alam and Fukumizu, 2013; Ham et al., 2004; Saunders and Gammerman, 1998).

Since the beginning of the 21st century, positive-definite kernels have a rich history with successful applications in the area of nonlinear data analysis. A number of methods have been proposed based on reproducing kernel Hilbert space (RKHS) using positive-definite kernels, including kernel supervised as well as unsupervised dimensional reduction techniques, support vector machine (SVM), kernel ridge regression, kernel Fisher's discriminant analysis, and kernel canonical correlation analysis (Akaho, 2001; Alam, 2014, Alam and Fukumizu, 2013; Alam et al., 2019; Bach and Jordan, 2002; Fukumizu et al., 2009; Hofmann et al., 2008). Kernel ridge regression

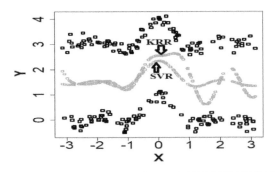

Figure 4.1 Scatter plots of original data and fitted curves of kernel ridge regression, KRR and support vector regression, SVR (green curve is for the KRR and orange curve is for the SVR).

or support vector regression does not consider any regime of the data; they are not sufficient for two or more regime data in the area of statistical machine learning. However, to the best of our knowledge, few well-founded methods have been established in general for penalized and nonlinear switching regression in RKHS (Alam, 2014; Richfield et al., 2017).

The goal of this chapter is to propose a method called "kernel switching ridge regression" (KSRR) to a comprehensive analysis of business data. The proposed method is able to overcome the unstable solution and curse of dimensionality. We can use a large number even an infinite number of explanatory variables by the proposed method. The experimental results on synthesized data sets demonstrate that the proposed method shows better performance than the state-of-the-art methods in supervised machine learning.

The rest of the chapter is structured as follows. In Section 2, we discuss a brief notion of switching regression, switching ridge regression, dual form of ridge regression, basic notion of kernel methods, ridge regression in the feature space, kernel ridge regression, duality of kernel ridge regression, and kernel switching ridge regression. Experimental results with different synthetic data to measure the performance of the proposed method are presented in Section 3. Section 4 presents a discussion of the results. We draw conclusions on our work with a direction of the future in Section 5. An R code of the proposed can be found in Appendix A.

4.2 Method

In the following subsections, we present the notion of switching regression, switching ridge regression, dual form of ridge regression, basic notion of kernel methods, ridge regression in the feature space, kernel ridge regression, duality of kernel ridge regression, and kernel switching ridge regression.

4.2.1 Switching regression

In switching regression, it is assumed that the dependent variable is generated by one of the following two equations:

$$y_i = \beta_{10} + \mathbf{x}_i^T \beta_1 + \epsilon_{1i},$$

with probability λ and

$$y_i = \beta_{20} + \mathbf{x}_i^T \beta_2 + \epsilon_{2i},$$

with probability $1 - \lambda$ in regime 1 and regime 2, respectively, where $\mathbf{x}_i \in \mathbb{R}^d$ is the independent variables. The β_j are the regression coefficients with $j = 1, 2$. The ϵ_{ji} are distributed as normal with mean zero and variances σ_j^2. The coconditional density of the ith value of y_i on $x_{1i}, x_{2i}, \dots, x_{di}$ is given by

$$g(y_i|x_{1i}, x_{2i}, \dots, x_{di}) = \frac{\lambda}{\sqrt{z\pi\sigma_1^2}} \exp\left\{ -\frac{1}{2\sigma_1^2}(y_i - \beta_{10} - \sum_{j=1}^{d}\beta_{1j}x_{ij})^2 \right\}$$

$$+ \frac{1-\lambda}{\sqrt{2\pi\sigma_2^2}} \exp\left\{ -\frac{1}{2\sigma_2^2}(y_i - \beta_{20} - \sum_{j=1}^{d}\beta_{2j}x_{ij})^2 \right\}. \quad (4.1)$$

The log-likelihood function of Eq. (4.1) over $i = 1, 2, \ldots, n$ is defined as

$$
L = \sum_{i=1}^{n} \log \left[\frac{\lambda}{\sqrt{2\pi\sigma_1^2}} \exp \left\{ -\frac{1}{2\sigma_1^2} (y_i - \sum_{j=0}^{d} \beta_{1j} x_{ij})^2 \right\} \right.
$$
$$
\left. + \frac{1-\lambda}{\sqrt{2\pi\sigma_2^2}} \exp \left\{ -\frac{1}{2\sigma_2^2} (y_i - \sum_{j=0}^{d} \beta_{2j} x_{ij})^2 \right\} \right], \tag{4.2}
$$

where $x_{i0} = 1$. We need to maximize the above nonlinear function with respect to β_{1j}, β_{2j}, $\sigma_1^2 > 0$, $\sigma_2^2 > 0$, and $0 \le \lambda \le 1$.

4.2.2 Switching ridge regression

In multiple regression, it is shown that parameter estimates based on minimum residual sum of squares have a high probability of producing unsatisfactory for the non-orthogonal vectors. The log-likelihood function of Eq. (4.2) becomes

$$
L = \sum_{i=1}^{n} \log \left[\frac{\lambda}{\sqrt{2\pi\sigma_1^2}} \exp \left\{ -\frac{1}{2\sigma_1^2} (y_i - \sum_{j=1}^{d} \beta_{1j} x_{ij})^2 \right\} \right.
$$
$$
\left. + \frac{1-\lambda}{\sqrt{2\pi\sigma_2^2}} \exp \left\{ -\frac{1}{2\sigma_2^2} (y_i - \sum_{j=1}^{d} \beta_{2j} x_{ij})^2 \right\} \right] + \eta_1 \|\beta_1\| + \eta_2 \|\beta_2\|.
$$

For simplicity, we can consider $\eta_1 = \eta_2$.

4.2.3 Dual form of the ridge regression

Using a matrix identity, $\mathbf{A}[\mathbf{A}^T\mathbf{A}]^{-1} = [\mathbf{A}\mathbf{A}^T]^{-1}\mathbf{A}$. The solution of ridge regression is then rewrite as

$$
\hat{\beta} = [\mathbf{X}^T\mathbf{X} + \lambda \mathbf{I}_m]^{-1}\mathbf{X}^T\mathbf{y}
$$
$$
\Rightarrow (\mathbf{X}^T\mathbf{X} + \lambda \mathbf{I})\hat{\beta} = \mathbf{y}
$$
$$
\Rightarrow \hat{\beta} = \lambda^{-1}(\mathbf{X}^T\mathbf{y} - \mathbf{X}^T\mathbf{X}\beta)
$$
$$
\Rightarrow \hat{\beta} = \lambda^{-1}\mathbf{X}^T(\mathbf{y} - \mathbf{X}\beta) = \mathbf{X}^T\alpha. \tag{4.3}
$$

Now, using Eq. (4.3)

$$
\alpha = \lambda^{-1}(\mathbf{y} - \mathbf{X}\hat{\beta})
$$
$$
\Rightarrow \alpha\lambda = [\mathbf{y} - \mathbf{X}\hat{\beta}] = [\mathbf{y} - \mathbf{X}\mathbf{X}^T\alpha]
$$
$$
\Rightarrow \mathbf{X}\mathbf{X}^T\alpha + \alpha\lambda = \mathbf{y}.
$$

By solving $n \times n$ equation, the solution is

$$\alpha = [\mathbf{G} + \lambda \mathbf{I}_n]^{-1} \mathbf{y},$$

where $\mathbf{G} = \mathbf{XX}^T$. To predict new point:

$$f_\ell(\mathbf{x}) = \left\langle \hat{\beta}, \mathbf{x} \right\rangle = \left\langle \sum_{i=1}^{n} \alpha_i \mathbf{x}_i, \mathbf{x} \right\rangle = \mathbf{y}^T [\mathbf{G} + \lambda \mathbf{I}]^{-1} \langle \mathbf{x}_i, \mathbf{x} \rangle. \tag{4.4}$$

We need to compute the gram matrix $\mathbf{G} = \mathbf{XX}^T$ in Eq. (4.4), where $G_{ij} = \langle \mathbf{x}_i, \mathbf{x}_j \rangle$. Ridge regression requires only inner products between data points.

4.2.4 Basic notion of kernel methods

In kernel methods, the nonlinear feature map is given by a *positive-definite kernel*, which provides nonlinear methods for data analysis with efficient computation. A symmetric kernel $k(\cdot, \cdot)$ defined on a space $\mathcal{X}$ is called *positive definite* if for arbitrary number of points $x_1, \dots, x_n \in \mathcal{X}$ the Gram matrix $(k(x_i, x_j))_{ij}$ is positive semi-definite (Alam et al., 2018; Aronszajn, 1950; Huang et al., 2009). As Aronszajn (1950) noted, it is known that a positive-definite kernel k is associated with a Hilbert space $\mathcal{H}$ called *reproducing kernel Hilbert space*, consisting of functions on $\mathcal{X}$ so that the function value is reproduced by the kernel (Alam, 2014; Ham et al., 2004); namely, for any function $f \in \mathcal{H}$ and point $\mathbf{x} \in \mathcal{X}$, the function value $f(\mathbf{x})$ is given by

$$f(\mathbf{x}) = \langle f(\cdot), k(\cdot, \mathbf{x}) \rangle_{\mathcal{H}}, \tag{4.5}$$

where $\langle, \rangle_{\mathcal{H}}$ in the inner product of $\mathcal{H}$. Eq. (4.5) is called the "reproducing property." Replacing f with $k(\cdot, \tilde{\mathbf{x}})$ yields $k(\mathbf{x}, \tilde{\mathbf{x}}) = \langle k(\cdot, \mathbf{x}), k(\cdot, \tilde{\mathbf{x}}) \rangle_{\mathcal{H}}$ for any $\mathbf{x}, \tilde{\mathbf{x}} \in \mathcal{X}$.

To transform data for extracting nonlinear features, the mapping $\Phi : \mathcal{X} \to \mathcal{H}$ is defined by

$$\Phi(\mathbf{x}) = k(\cdot, \mathbf{x}),$$

which is regarded as a function of the first argument. This map is called *feature map*, and the vector $\Phi(\mathbf{x})$ in $\mathcal{H}$ is called *feature vector*. The inner product of two feature vectors is then given by

$$\langle \Phi(\mathbf{x}), \Phi(\tilde{\mathbf{x}}) \rangle_{\mathcal{H}} = k(\mathbf{x}, \tilde{\mathbf{x}}).$$

This is known as the *kernel trick*, serving as a central equation in kernel methods. By this trick the kernel can evaluate the inner product of any two feature vectors efficiently without knowing an explicit form of either $\Phi(\cdot)$ or $\mathcal{H}$. With this computation of inner product, many linear methods of classical data analysis can be extended to nonlinear ones with efficient computation based on Gram matrices. Once Gram matrices are computed, the computational cost does not depend on the dimensionality of the original space (Bach and Jordan, 2002).

4.2.5 Alternative derivation to use ridge regression in the feature space

We know $\mathbf{X}^T\mathbf{X} = \sum_{i=1}^{n} \mathbf{x}_i \mathbf{x}_i^T$, where $\mathbf{x}_i$ is a column vector of the ith row of $\mathbf{X}$. Possibly the most elementary algorithm that can be kernelized is ridge regression. Here our task is to find a linear function that models the dependencies between response and predictor variables. The classical way to do that is to minimize the quadratic cost,

$$L(\beta) = \frac{1}{2} \sum_{i=1}^{n} \left(y_i - \beta^T \mathbf{x}_i \right)^2 .$$

However, if we are going to work in feature space, where we replace $\mathbf{x}_i \to \Phi(\mathbf{x}_i)$, there is a clear danger that we overfit. Hence, we need to regularize. A simple yet effective way to regularize is to penalize the norm of β. This is sometime called "weight-decay." It remains to be determined how to choose λ. The most used algorithm is to use cross-validation or leave-one-out estimates. The total cost function hence becomes

$$L = \frac{1}{2} \sum_{i=1}^{n} \left(y_i - \beta^T \mathbf{x}_i \right)^2 + \frac{1}{2} \lambda \|\beta\|^2, \tag{4.6}$$

which needs to be minimized. Taking derivatives of Eq. (4.6) and equating them to zero gives

$$\sum_{i=1}^{n} \left(y_i - \beta^T \mathbf{x}_i \right) \mathbf{x}_i = \lambda \beta \Rightarrow \hat{\beta} = \left[\lambda \mathbf{I} + \sum_{i=1}^{n} \mathbf{x}_i \mathbf{x}^T \right]^{-1} \left[\sum_{i=1}^{n} y_i \mathbf{x}_i \right].$$

We see that the regularization term helps to stabilize the inverse numerically by bounding the smallest eigenvalues away from zero.

4.2.6 *Kernel ridge regression*

In order to construct a kernel ridge regression model, we have to replace all data points with their feature vector (Saunders and Gammerman, 1998), $\mathbf{x}_i \to \Phi(\mathbf{x}_i) \in \mathcal{F}$. The space $\mathcal{F}$ is called "feature space." The number of dimensions in this space can be much higher, or even infinitely higher than the number of data points. There is a trick that allows us to perform the inverse in Eq. (4.2.5) in smallest space of the two possibilities, either the dimension of the feature space or the number of data points. The trick is given by the following identity of matrices $\mathbf{A}$, $\mathbf{C}$, and $\mathbf{G}$:

$$\left(\mathbf{A}^{-1} + \mathbf{C}^T \mathbf{G}^{-1} \mathbf{C} \right)^{-1} = \mathbf{A} \mathbf{C}^T \left(\mathbf{C} \mathbf{A} \mathbf{C}^T + \mathbf{G}^{-1} \right) .$$

The inverse is performed in spaces of different dimensionality if $\mathbf{C}$ is not square. Consider a feature space ϕ_a such that $\Phi = \phi_{ai}$ and $\mathbf{y} = y_i$. The solution is then given by

$$\hat{\beta} = \left[\lambda \mathbf{I}_d + \Phi \Phi^T \right]^{-1} \Phi \mathbf{y} = \Phi \left[\Phi^T \Phi + \lambda, \mathbf{I}_n \right]^{-1} \mathbf{y}, \tag{4.7}$$

where d is the number of dimension in the feature space and n is the number of data points. Using Eq. (4.7), we can write

$$\hat{\beta} = \sum_{i=1}^{n} \alpha_i \phi(x_i),$$

with $\alpha = \left[\Phi^T \Phi + \lambda \mathbf{I}_n \right]^{-1} \mathbf{y}$. This is an equation that will be a recurrent theme and it can be interpreted as: the solution $\hat{\beta}$ must lie in the span of the data points, even if the dimensionality of the feature space is much larger than the number of data points. This seems intuitively clear, since the algorithm is linear in feature space.

We finally need to show that we never actually need to access the feature vectors, which could be infinitely long. This is computed by projecting it onto the solution $\hat{\beta}$,

$$y = \hat{\beta}^T \phi(x) = \mathbf{y} \left[\Phi^T \Phi + \lambda \mathbf{I}_n \right]^{-1} \Phi^T \Phi(x) = \mathbf{y} \left(\mathbf{K} + \lambda \mathbf{I}_n \right)^{-1} \mathbf{k}(\mathbf{x}), \tag{4.8}$$

where $K(\mathbf{x}_i, \mathbf{x}_j) = \Phi(x_i)^T \Phi(x_j)$ and $\mathbf{k}(\mathbf{x}) = K(\mathbf{x}_i, \mathbf{x})$. The important message here is of course that we only need to access the kernel $\mathbf{K}$.

We can now add bias to the whole story by adding one more constant feature to $\Phi : \phi_0 = 1$. The value of β_0 then represents the bias since

$$\hat{\beta}^T \Phi = \sum_a \hat{\beta}_a \phi_{ai} + \hat{\beta}_0. \tag{4.9}$$

Hence, the story goes through unchanged.

4.2.7 Kernel ridge regression: duality

The problem is to minimize (using Eq. (4.6))

$$\sum_{i=1}^{n} \left(y_i - \beta^T \mathbf{x}_i \right)^2 + \lambda \|\beta\|^2.$$

Taking derivatives and equating set to zero gives

$$\mathbf{0} = \sum_{i=1}^{n} 2 \left(y_i - \beta^T \mathbf{x}_i \right) + 2\lambda\beta$$

$$\hat{\beta} = \left(\sum_{i=1}^{n} \mathbf{x}_i \mathbf{x}_i^T + \lambda \mathbf{I}_n \right)^{-1} \sum_{i=1}^{n} \mathbf{x}_i y_i.$$

Now let us consider a different derivation, making use of some Lagrange duality. If we introduce a new variable w_i and constrain it to be the difference between $\beta^T \mathbf{x}_i$ and y_i, we have

$$\min_{\beta, \mathbf{w}} \quad \frac{1}{2} \mathbf{w}^T \mathbf{w} + \frac{1}{2} \lambda \beta^T \beta$$

$$s.t. \quad w_i = y_i - \mathbf{x}_i^T \beta. \tag{4.10}$$

Using α_i to denote the Lagrange multipliers, this has the Lagrangian

$$\mathcal{L} = \frac{1}{2} \mathbf{w}^T \mathbf{w} + \frac{1}{2} \lambda \beta^T \beta + \sum_{i=1}^{n} \alpha_i \left(y_i - \mathbf{x}_i^T \beta - w_i \right).$$

Recall the foray into Lagrange duality. We can solve the original problem by doing

$$\max_{\alpha} \min_{\beta, \mathbf{w}} \mathcal{L}(\beta, \mathbf{w}, \alpha).$$

First, we will take the inner minimization: by fixing α, we would like to solve for the minimizing β and $\mathbf{w}$. We can do this by setting the derivatives of $\mathcal{L}$ with respect to z_i and β. We can do this by setting the derivatives of $\mathcal{L}$ with respect to w_i and β to be zero. Doing this, we have

$$0 = \frac{\partial \mathcal{L}}{\partial w_i} = w_i - \alpha_i$$
$$\Rightarrow \hat{w}_i = \alpha_i$$

and

$$0 = \frac{\partial \mathcal{L}}{\partial \beta} = \lambda \beta - \sum_{i=1}^{n} \alpha_i \mathbf{x}_i$$
$$\Rightarrow \hat{\beta} = \frac{1}{\lambda} \sum_{i=1}^{n} \alpha_i \mathbf{x}_i.$$

So, we can solve the problem by maximizing the Lagrangian with respect to β, where we substitute the above expressions for z_i and β. Thus, we have an unconstrained maximization

$$\max_{\alpha} \mathcal{L}(\hat{\beta})(\alpha), \hat{\mathbf{w}}(\alpha), \alpha).$$

Thus, we obtain

$$\max_{\alpha} \min_{\beta, \mathbf{w}} \mathcal{L}(\beta, \mathbf{w}, \alpha)$$

$$= \max_{\alpha} \frac{1}{2} \sum_{i} \alpha_i^2 + \frac{1}{2} \lambda \left(\frac{1}{\lambda} \sum_{i=1}^{n} \alpha_i \mathbf{x}_i \right) \cdot \left(\frac{1}{\lambda} \sum_{j=1}^{n} \alpha_j \mathbf{x}_j \right) + \sum_{i=1}^{n} \alpha_i \left(y_i - \mathbf{x}_i \cdot \frac{1}{\lambda} \sum_{i=1}^{n} \alpha_i \mathbf{x}_i - \alpha_i \right)$$

$$= \max_{\alpha} \frac{1}{2} \sum_{i} \alpha_i^2 + \frac{1}{2\lambda} \sum_{i=1}^{n} \sum_{j=1}^{n} \alpha_i \alpha_j \langle \mathbf{x}_i, \mathbf{x}_j \rangle - \frac{1}{\lambda} \sum_{i=1}^{n} \sum_{j=1}^{n} \alpha_i \alpha_j \langle \mathbf{x}_i, \mathbf{x}_j \rangle + \sum_{i=1}^{n} \alpha_i(y_i - \alpha_i)$$

$$= \max_{\alpha} -\frac{1}{2} \sum_{i} \alpha_i^2 - \frac{1}{2\lambda} \sum_{i=1}^{n} \sum_{j=1}^{n} \alpha_i \alpha_j \langle \mathbf{x}_i, \mathbf{x}_j \rangle + \sum_{i=1}^{n} \alpha_i y_i$$

$$= \max_{\alpha} -\frac{1}{2} \sum_{i} \alpha_i^2 - \frac{1}{2\lambda} \sum_{i=1}^{n} \sum_{j=1}^{n} \alpha_i \alpha_j k(\mathbf{x}_i, \mathbf{x}_j) + \sum_{i=1}^{n} \alpha_i y_i,$$

where $k(\mathbf{x}_i, \mathbf{x}_j)$ is the kernel function. Again, we only need inner products. If we define the matrix $\mathbf{K}$ by $K_{ij} = k(\mathbf{x}_i, \mathbf{x}_j)$, then we can rewrite this in a punchier vector notation as

$$\max_{\alpha} \min_{\beta, \mathbf{w}} \mathcal{L}(\beta, \mathbf{w}, \alpha) = \max_{\alpha} -\frac{1}{2} \alpha^T \alpha - \frac{1}{2\lambda} \alpha^T \mathbf{K} \alpha + \alpha^T \mathbf{y}.$$

Thing on the right is just a quadratic in α. As such, we can find the optimum as the solution of a linear system. What is important is the observation that again we only need the inner products of the data $k(\mathbf{x}_i, \mathbf{x}_j) = \langle \mathbf{x}_i, \mathbf{x}_j \rangle$ to do the optimization over α. Then, once we have solve for α we can predict $f_\ell(\mathbf{x})$ for new $\mathbf{x}$ using only inner products. If someone tells us all the inner products, we do not need the original data $\mathbf{x}_i$ at all,

$$\mathbf{0} = \frac{d\mathcal{L}}{d\alpha} = -\alpha - \frac{1}{\lambda}\mathbf{K}\alpha + \mathbf{y}.$$

Thus,

$$\hat{\alpha} = (\mathbf{K} + \lambda\mathbf{I}_n)^{-1}\mathbf{y}.$$

Since β is given by sum of the input vectors $\mathbf{x}_i$, weighted by $\frac{\alpha_i}{\lambda}$. If we were so inclined, we could avoid explicitly computing β and predict a new point $\mathbf{x}$ directly from the data as

$$f_\ell(\mathbf{x}) = \langle \mathbf{x}, \beta \rangle = \frac{1}{\lambda}\sum_{i=1}^{n}\alpha_i\langle \mathbf{x}_i, \mathbf{x} \rangle. \tag{4.11}$$

We can write the kernel ridge regression predictions as

$$f_\ell(\mathbf{x}) = \langle \mathbf{x}, \beta \rangle = \frac{1}{\lambda}\sum_{i=1}^{n}\alpha_i k(\mathbf{x}_i, \mathbf{x}).$$

4.2.8 Kernel switching ridge regression

We assume that the dependent variable is generated by one of the following two models in RKHS:

$$y_i = f_1(\mathbf{x}_i) + \epsilon_{1i} = \alpha_{10} + \sum_{i=1}^{n}\alpha_i k(\cdot, \mathbf{x}_i) + \epsilon_{1i}$$

with probability λ and

$$y_i = f_2(\mathbf{x}_i) + \epsilon_{1i} = \alpha_{20} + \sum_{i=1}^{n}\alpha_i k(\cdot, \mathbf{x}_i) + \epsilon_{1i}$$

with probability $1 - \lambda$ in regime 1 and regime 2, respectively, where $f_1, f_2 \in \mathcal{H}$ with positive-definite kernel $k(\cdot, \cdot)$ and kernel matrix K, $K_{ij} = k(\mathbf{x}_i, \mathbf{x}_j)$. The assumption of ϵ_{ji} is the same as the switching regression. The conditional density is then defined as

$$g(y_i | k(\cdot, x_{1i}), k(\cdot, x_{2i}), \ldots, k(\cdot x_{di})) = \frac{\lambda}{\sqrt{z\pi\sigma_1^2}}\exp\left\{-\frac{1}{2\sigma_1^2}(y_i - \sum_{j=0}^{n}\alpha_{1j}k(\mathbf{x}_i, \mathbf{x}_j)^2\right\}$$

$$+ \frac{1-\lambda}{\sqrt{2\pi\sigma_2^2}}\exp\left\{-\frac{1}{2\sigma_2^2}(y_i - \sum_{j=0}^{n}\alpha_{2j}k(\mathbf{x}_i, \mathbf{x}_j)^2\right\}.$$

The log-likehood function over $i = 1, 2, \ldots, n$ is defined as

$$
L = \sum_{i=1}^{n} log \left[\frac{\lambda}{\sqrt{z\pi\sigma_1^2}} \exp\left\{ -\frac{1}{2\sigma_1^2}(y_i - f_1(\mathbf{x}_i))^2 \right\} + \frac{1-\lambda}{\sqrt{2\pi\sigma_2^2}} \exp\left\{ -\frac{1}{2\sigma_2^2}(y_i - f_1(\mathbf{x}_i))^2 \right\} \right]
$$

$$
+ \frac{\eta_1}{2} \|f_1\|_{\mathcal{H}}^2 + \frac{\eta_2}{2} \|f_1\|_{\mathcal{H}}^2
$$

$$
= \sum_{i=1}^{n} log \left[\frac{\lambda}{\sqrt{z\pi\sigma_1^2}} \exp\left\{ -\frac{1}{2\sigma_1^2}(y_i - \sum_{j=0}^{n} \alpha_{1j}k(\mathbf{x}_i, \mathbf{x}_j)^2 \right\} \right.
$$

$$
\left. + \frac{1-\lambda}{\sqrt{2\pi\sigma_2^2}} \exp\left\{ -\frac{1}{2\sigma_2^2}(y_i - \sum_{j=0}^{n} \alpha_{2j}k(\mathbf{x}_i, \mathbf{x}_j)^2 \right\} \right] + \frac{\eta_1}{2}\alpha_1^T \mathbf{K}\alpha_1 + \frac{\eta_2}{2}\alpha_2^T \mathbf{K}\alpha_2, \quad (4.12)
$$

where $k(\mathbf{x}_i, \mathbf{x}_0) = 1$, and α_1 and α_2 are the vector of coefficients. For simplicity in our experiment, we consider $\eta_1 = \eta_2 = 10^{-4}$. We need to maximize the above nonlinear function with respect to free parameters.

4.3 Experimental results

To measure the performance of the proposed method, we have made empirical studies using synthetic examples and have consider two numerical optimization algorithms to estimate the parameters: the expectation-maximization (EM) algorithm and stochastic gradient descent (SGD) for classical switching regression. The performance of the proposed method using SGD is compared with the state of the art in supervised machine learning: KRR and SVR.

4.3.1 Simulation

Synthetic data-1 (SD-1): The dependent variable y_i is generated by one of the following two models with probability 0.5:

$$
y_i = 3 + 15x_i + \epsilon_{1i} \text{ and}
$$
$$
y_i = -3 + 1x_i + \epsilon_{1i},
$$

where $x_i \sim N(10, 1)$, $\epsilon_{1i} \sim N(0, 2)$, and $\epsilon_{2i} \sim N(0, 2.5)$.

Synthetic data-2 (SD-2): The dependent variable y_i is generated by one of the following two models with probability 0.5:

$$
y_i = 1 + 2x_i + \epsilon_{1i} \text{ and}
$$
$$
y_i = -1 + 1x_i + \epsilon_{1i},
$$

where $x_i \sim N(10, 1)$, $\epsilon_{1i} \sim N(0, 1.5)$, and $\epsilon_{2i} \sim N(0, 2)$.

Synthetic data-3 (SD-3): The dependent variable y_i is generated by one of the following two models with probability 0.5:

$$y_i = x_i \beta_1 + \epsilon_{1i} \text{ and}$$
$$y_i = x_i \beta_2 + \epsilon_{1i},$$

where $x_i \sim N(10, 1)$, $\epsilon_{1i} \sim N(0, 2)$, $\epsilon_{2i} \sim N(0, 2.5)$, and β_1 and $\beta_2 \sim U[-1, 1]$.

Synthetic data-4 (SD-4): The dependent variable y_i is generated by one of the following two models with probability 0.5:

$$y_i = \sin(4x_i)/x_i + 0.2\sin(30 * x) + \epsilon_{1i} \text{ and}$$
$$y_i = 3 + \sin(x_i)/x_i + 0.2\sin(30 * x) + \epsilon_{2i},$$

where $x_i \sim U(-\pi, \pi)$, $\epsilon_{1i} \sim N(0, 0.1)$, $\epsilon_{2i} \sim N(0, 0.01)$, $i = 1, 2, \ldots 400$.

First, we have compared the EM and SGD algorithms for the switching regression using different sizes of $n \in \{100, 250, 500, 750, 1000, 2500, 5000\}$ for the SD-1 and SD-2. For each size we have repeated the experiment 100 times. The mean error of the 100 samples is calculated. Table 4.1 presents the mean errors of intercept (β_1) and regression coefficient (β_2) of the switching regression for both algorithms. We observed that both algorithms have almost similar results, especially when the sample size is increased.

Second, we have compared the EM and SGD algorithms for the switching regression using different dimensions of $d \in \{2, 5, 10, 25, 50, 100\}$ for the SD-3. For each dimension, we have repeated the experiment 100 times. The mean error of the 100 samples is calculated. Table 4.2 presents the mean errors of intercept (β_1) and regression coefficient (β_2) of the switching regression for both algorithms. We observed that the EM algorithm does not work properly for the high-dimensional data but the SGD. We may conclude that the SGD algorithm is a good choice for the large dimensional data set.

Finally, the proposed method, KSRR via the SGD algorithm is applied for SD-4. To measure the performance of the proposed method over the KRR and SVR, training and ten-fold cross-validation test errors are used. For the stability check, we repeated the experiment over 100 samples, $n = 400$, using the Gaussian kernel with inverse bandwidth equal to 1 being considered. We also obtain standard errors for the proposed parameter estimators. Table 4.3 presents the training errors and ten-fold cross-validation test errors. Figure 4.2 shows the scatter plots of the original data and the fitted curve of the proposed method, KSRR, KRR, and SVR (blue curve and red curve for the KSSR, green curve for the KRR, and orange curve for the SVR). By this figure it is clear that in two-group data the KSRR is fitted to the data separately properly in two groups. But both methods KRR and SVR are not fitted to the date properly. They are fitted to the curve inside of the two groups.

4.3.2 Application in business intelligence

The standard industrial informatics are facing the challenges of processing complex business data. To overcome the challenge, we can use the business intelligence technology including classifiers and regressors (Duan and Xu, 2012). Business intelligence plays an important role to bridge the gap between enterprise systems and industrial informatics. These techniques are required not only to describe training data but also to be able to predict new data points. Many supervised approaches have been proposed to improve the prediction accuracy.

Table 4.1 The mean error of 100 samples of two data sets: SD-1 and SD-2

n		100		250		500		750	
		β_1	β_2	β_1	β_2	β_1	β_2	β_1	β_2
SD-1	EM	2.154 ± 1.755	2.829 ± 2.218	1.444 ± 1.047	1.9 ± 1.337	1.082 ± 0.896	1.334 ± 1.047	0.893 ± 0.675	1.013 ± 0.867
	SGD	1.628 ± 1.110	1.525 ± 1.128	1.027 ± 0.796	0.932 ± 0.683	0.732 ± 0.492	0.862 ± 0.534	0.546 ± 0.448	0.578 ± 0.4415
SD-2	EM	1.573 ± 1.000	1.708 ± 1.177	1.095 ± 0.759	1.174 ± 0.759	0.683 ± 0.475	0.959 ± 0.615	0.612 ± 0.399	0.822 ± 0.574
	SGD	1.235 ± 0.825	1.255 ± 0.783	0.919 ± 0.681	0.934 ± 0.715	0.669 ± 0.465	0.715 ± 0.479	0.543 ± 0.421	0.543 ± 0.406

n		1000		2500		5000	
		β_1	β_2	β_1	β_2	β_1	β_2
SD-1	EM	0.697 ± 0.550	0.927 ± 0.699	0.423 ± 0.309	0.524 ± 0.379	0.305 ± 0.264	0.441 ± 0.328
	SGD	0.468 ± 0.333	0.472 ± 0.305	0.271 ± 0.192	0.344 ± 0.239	0.227 ± 0.17	0.211 ± 0.124
SD-2	EM	0.546 ± 0.415	0.794 ± 0.591	0.296 ± 0.227	0.431 ± 0.329	0.229 ± 0.1781	0.331 ± 0.242
	SGD	0.453 ± 0.335	0.428 ± 0.329	0.297 ± 0.195	0.322 ± 0.192	0.229 ± 0.146	0.242 ± 0.141

Table 4.2 The mean error of 100 samples of the synthetic data sets (SD-3)

d	2	5	10	25	50	100
EM	3.4059 ± 0.699	4.279 ± 0.777	4.0662 ± 0.527	3.526 ± 0.586	2.268 ± 315	–
SGD	4.974 ± 0.628	4.3938 ± 0.924	4.798 ± 0.844	5.725 ± 1.392	5.708 ± 0.923	5.419 ± 0.605

Table 4.3 Training and test error over 100 samples, $n = 400$, the proposed method KSRR, kernel ridge regression, KRR, and support vector regression, SVR

	KSRR	KRR	SVR
Training error	1.475 ± 0.666	2.201 ± 0.036	2.273 ± 0.024
10-CV error	1.587 ± 0.749	2.362 ± 0.049	2.362 ± 0.049

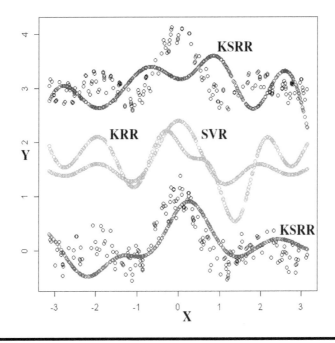

Figure 4.2 Scatter plots of the original data and fitted curves of the proposed method, KSRR, kernel ridge regression, KRR, and support vector regression, SVR (blue and red curves are for the KSSR, green curve is for the KRR, and orange curve is for the SVR).

In order to verify the applicability of the proposed method in a real-world problem, we use the motorcycle data set. The motorcycle data set is a well-known and widely used data set, especially throughout the areas of statistical machine learning, data mining, and nonparametric regression analysis. The data set consists of $n = 133$ measurements of head acceleration (in g) taken through time (in milliseconds) after impact in simulated motorcycle accidents. The data are available in the

Table 4.4 Perdition errors of the different methods

	KSRR	KRR	SVR
Five-fold	15.263 ± 1.256	18.325 ± 01.563	21.865 ± 1.905
Ten-fold	17.249 ± 1.056	21.672 ± 1.257	25.693 ± 1.459

R "switchnpreg" package and many different methodologies have been applied to the motorcycle data (de Souza et al., 2014).

More recently, the motorcycle data set has become a benchmark data set for machine learning techniques involving mixtures of Gaussian processes. In this section, we have used our proposed method along with state-of-the-art methods to discover the average prediction error. We have conducted five-fold and ten-fold cross-validation approaches to discover the average prediction error of the response variable. Table 4.4 presents the perdition error using the cross-validation (five-fold and ten-fold). From these results, it is evident that the proposed method-based prediction is significantly more accurate than using two different state of the art in supervised learning methods (KRR and SVR).

4.4 Discussion

In supervised machine learning tasks, switching regression is becoming an increasingly common component in the age of big business data. The state-of-the-art regression approaches including kernel ridge regression or support vector regression only work for a single regime of the data. In order to make a comprehensive prediction for two or more regimes of data set, we can use switching regression for the business intelligence system. The standard switching regression approach suffers from the curse of dimensionality as well as non-linearity of the data.

In this chapter, we have proposed a kernel-based switching regression model to study the effect of explanatory variables on two regimes' outcomes of interest. The performance of the proposed method has been compared over the state-of-the-art methods in supervised machine learning: KRR and SVR. To the end, we have made different experiments using synthetic examples and a real-world problem. By these experiments, we have observed that parameter estimation via EM algorithm has failed for the large dimensional data sets. In addition, for the sample dimensional data set, parameter estimation via EM and SGD algorithms has similar performance. The parameter estimation via the SGD algorithm is applied for the proposed method instead of the EM algorithm. By the experimental results, we observed that the KRR and SVR methods have failed to estimate the data properly when data have two classes or regimes. They are fitted to the curves inside of the two groups in the palace of the original data. However, it is clear that the KSRR is fitted to the data properly in two groups (see Figure 4.2).

4.5 Conclusion and future research

In this chapter, for switching regression, we have discussed the performance of the EM and SGD algorithms over different sample sizes and dimensions. The parameter estimation via the EM algorithm highly depends on sample size as well as dimension of the data. Finally, we have proposed a nonlinear extension of switching regression in RKHS using positive-definite kernel, which is called the "kernel switching ridge regression model." Extensive experiments on synthesized data and a real-world business data show that the performance of the proposed method is better than that of the state-of-the-art method in supervised machine learning. The proposed method should improve the integrity of analytics of the business intelligence system.

Statistical properties such as consistency, asymptotic analysis, and application in more real data sets are important future directions of the research.

4.6 Appendix: Kernel switching ridge regression: an R code

```
KSRR_SGD < − function (X, y, beta1, beta2, sigma1, sigma2, lam1, eta, nmax)
{
n < −nrow(X)
d < − ncol(X)
lam2 < − 1-lam1
ctr < − 0
beta1.new < − beta1
beta2.new < − beta2
sigma1.new < − sigma1
sigma2.new < − sigma2
lam1.new < − lam1
lam2.new < − 1-lam1.new
while(ctr < nmax)
{
rv < − sample(n, 1)
for (i in rv)
{
beta1.old < − beta1.new
beta2.old < − beta2.new
sigma1.old < − sigma1.new
sigma2.old < − sigma2.new
lam1.old < − lam1.new
lam2.old < − 1-lam1.new
q1 < − (lam1.old/sqrt(2*pi*sigma1.old))*exp(-(y[i]-X[i,]%*%beta1.old)^2/(2*sigma1.old))
q2 < − (lam2.old/sqrt(2*pi*sigma2.old))*exp(-(y[i]-X[i,]%*%beta2.old)^2/(2*sigma2.old))
Q1 < − as.vector(q1/(q1+q2))
Q2 < − as.vector(q2/(q1+q2))
beta1.new < − beta1.old +
eta*Q1*(as.vector((y[i]-t(X[i,])%*%beta1.old)%*%X[i, ])/sigma1.old +0.0001*beta1.old)
beta2.new < − beta2.old+
eta*Q2*(as.vector((y[i]-t(X[i,])%*%beta2.old)%*%X[i, ])/sigma2.old+0.0001*beta2.old)
lam1.new < − lam1.old+ eta*((Q1)/lam1.old - 1)
lam2.new < − 1-lam1.new
```

```
sigma1.new < − sigma1.old +
eta *Q1/2*(as.vector(( y[i]-X[i,]%*%beta1.old)²)*(1/sigma1.old²)-1/(sigma1.old))
sigma2.new < − sigma2.old +
eta *Q2/2*(as.vector(( y[i]-X[i,]%*%beta2.old)²)*(1/sigma2.old²)-1/(sigma2.old))
}
q1 < − (lam1.new/sqrt(2*pi*sigma1.new))*exp(-(y-X%*%beta1.new)²/(2*sigma1.new))
q2 < − (lam2.new/sqrt(2*pi*sigma2.new))*exp(-(y-X%*%beta2.new)²/(2*sigma2.new))
logL < − sum(log(q1+q2))
cat("ctr =", ctr, " ")
cat("Log L =", logL, " ")        cat("Beta1 =", beta1.new, " ", "Beta2=", beta2.new, " ")
cat("lam1 =", lam1.new, " ", "lam2=", lam2.new, " ")
cat("Sigma1 =", sigma1.new, " ", "Sigma2=", sigma2.new, " ")
ctr < − ctr+1
}
yhat12 < − cbind((y-X%*% beta1.new)², (y-X%*% beta2.new)²)
yhat < − apply(yhat12, 1, min)
MSE < − mean(yhat)
return(list(error = MSE, log-likelihood = logL, Beta1 = beta1.new, Beta2 = beta2.new,
Par1 = lam1.new, Par2 = lam2.new, Var1= sigma1.new, Var2 = sigma2.new))
}
```

References

Akaho, S. (2001). A kernel method for canonical correlation analysis, *in Proceedings of the International Meeting of Psychometric Society, Japan*, *35*, 321–377.

Alam, M. A. (2014). *Kernel Choice for Unsupervised Kernel Methods*, Ph.D. Dissertation, The Graduate University for Advanced Studies, Japan.

Alam, M. A., Calhoun, V., and Wang, Y. P. (2018). Identifying outliers using multiple kernel canonical correlation analysis with application to imaging genetics, *Computational Statistics and Data Analysis*, *125*, 70–85.

Alam M. A. and Fukumizu, K. (2013). Higher-order regularized kernel CCA. *12th International Conference on Machine Learning and Applications, Miami, Florida, USA*, 374–377.

Alam M. A., Komori, O. Deng H-W. Calhoun V. D. and Wang Y-P. (2020). Robust kernel canonical correlation analysis to detect gene-gene co-associations: A case study in genetics. *Journal of Bioinformatics and Computational Biology* , *17*(4), 1950028.

Aronszajn, N. (1950). Theory of reproducing kernels. *Transactions of the American Mathematical Society*, 337–404.

Bach, F. R. and Jordan, M. I. (2002). Kernel independent component analysis. *Journal of Machine Learning Research*, *3*, 1–48.

Brannon, N (2010), Business intelligence and E-discovery. *Intellectual Property & Technology Law Journal*. *22*(7), 1–5.

Cawley, G. C. and Talbot, N. L. C. (2003). Reduced rank kernel ridge regression. *Neural Processing Letters*, *16*, 293–302.

Dannemann, J. and Holzmann, H. (2010). Testing for two components in a switching regression model. *Computation Statistics and Data Analysis*, *54*, 1592–1604.

Duan, L. and Xu, L. D. (2011). Business intelligence for enterprise systems: A survey. *IEEE Transactions on Industrial Informatics*, *8*, 679–687.

Fukumizu, K. Bach, F. R., and Jordan, M. I. (2009). Kernel dimension reduction in regression. *Annals of Statistics*, *37*, 1871–1905.

Ham, J. Lee, D. D. and Mika, S. (2001). Schölkopf, B. A kernel view of the dimensionality reduction of manifolds. *Proceedings of the 21st International Conference on Machine Learning. 47.*

Hastie, T, Tibshirani, R. and Friedman, J. (2009). *The Elements of Statistical Learning*. Springer, New York, 2nd ed.

Hofmann, T., Schölkopf, B. and Smola J. A. (2008). Kernel methods in machine learning. *Annals of Statistics*, *36*, 1171–1220.

Huang, S. Y., Yeh, Y. R. and Eguchi, S. (2009). Robust kernel principal component analysis. *Neural Computation*, *21*(11), 3179–3213.

Liu M. and Lin, T. (2013). A skew-normal mixture regression model. *Educational and Psychological Measurement*, *XX*(X), 1–24.

Malikov, E. and Kumbhakar, S. C. (2014). A generalized panel data switching regression model. *Economics Letters*, *124*, 353–357.

Quandt, R. E. (1972). A new approach to estimating switching regressions, *Journal of American Statistical Associating*, *67*(338), 306–310.

Richfield, O. Alam, M. A. Calhoun, V. and Wang, Y. P. (2017), Learning schizophrenia imaging genetics data via multiple kernel canonical correlation analysis. *Proceedings - 2016 IEEE International Conference on Bioinformatics and Biomedicine, Shenzhen, China*, *5*, 507–511.

Saunders, C. Gammerman, A. and Vovk, V. (1998). Ridge regression learning algorithm in dual variables. *Appears in Proceedings of the 15-th International Conference on Machine Learning, ICML'98, Madison, Wisconsin, USA*, 24–27.

Shawe-Taylor J. and Cristianini, N. (2004). *Kernel Methods for Pattern Analysis*. Cambridge University Press, Cambridge, 1st ed.

Souza, C. P. E. de. and Heckman, N. E. (2014). Switching nonparametric regression models. *Journal of Nonparametric Statistics*, *26*(4), 617–637.

Steinwart, I. and Christmann A. (2008). *Support Vector Machines*. Springer, New York, 1st ed.

Wang, J. Wu, X. and Zhang C. (2005). Support vector machines based on K-mean clustering for real-time business intelligence systems. *International Journal of Business Intelligence and Data Mining*, *1*(1), 54–64.

Chapter 5

Predicting stock return volatility using sentiment analysis of corporate annual reports

Petr Hajek, Renata Myskova, and Vladimir Olej

5.1 Introduction

It is well known that stock markets show certain periods of volatility caused by investors' reaction to economic and political changes. For this reason, monitoring and evaluation of volatility can be considered an integral part of the investment decision making.

In this chapter, we focus on the short-term volatility of corporate stocks and the causes that triggered it, and we derive implied (future) volatility based on historical volatility. As volatility increases, the flexibility of active investment can be very lucrative compared to passive investment, but it should also be noted that the risk increases with higher volatility. This is closely related to the expectations, behavior, and interactions of various market participants, which are not only informed investors but also noise traders. It is these investors who make their investment decisions without rational use of fundamental data and overreact to good or bad news. According to Staritz (2012), these investors may cause significant deviations in stock prices from their values obtained using fundamental analysis. In addition, analysts now point out that the capital markets are growing nervous and individual investors are very cautious about possible price slumps and react faster than usual.

Text mining tools for automated analysis of company-related documents (e.g., Internet postings, financial news, and corporate annual reports) have become increasingly important for stock market investors because information hidden in those documents may indicate future changes in stock prices (Hajek, 2018). In previous studies, it has been shown that investors' behavior is affected by the dissemination of those documents (Bicudo et al., 2019). The quality of financial reporting, including additional commentary, is associated with a reduction in information asymmetry among stakeholders, particularly between firm management and investors (Biddle et al., 2009). Therefore, the qualitative information disclosed by management is increasingly recognized as an essential supplement to accounting information (Kothari et al., 2009; Kumar and Vadlamani, 2016). According to Seng and Yang (2017), who examined the volatility of the capital market over the months, quarters, half-years, and year, positive (negative) reports are positively (negatively) correlated with positive stock returns. Chin et al. (2018) examined the links among stock market volatility, market sentiment, macroeconomic indicators, and spread volatility over the persisting long-term component and the temporary short-term component. They found no empirical evidence of the link between the volatile component and macroeconomic indicators but found that the intermediate component was linked to variations in market sentiment.

Significant effects of financial news and social media on stock return volatility have been reported in earlier studies (Groth and Muntermann, 2011; Hajek, 2018; Oliveira et al., 2017). However, little attention has been paid to the effect of other important textual disclosures. Here, we aim to (1) propose a machine learning-based model for predicting short-term stock return volatility and (2) study the effect of annual report filing on abnormal changes in firms' stock returns using the proposed model. In summary, we demonstrate that mining corporate annual reports can be effective in predicting short-term stock return volatility using a three-day event window.

5.2 Related literature

Stock return volatility has been recognized as a crucial determinant of prices in the stock markets and, therefore, financial experts must always pay close attention to its changes (Carr and Wu, 2009). On the stock market, value of the asset and its volatility are negatively correlated, which is usually defined as the leverage effect (Black, 1976). Kaeck and Alexander (2013) report that investors' decision making is affected by time-varying and stochastic components of volatility to various degrees. This corresponds to financial theory and the conclusions of its proponents, ascribing increased volatility both to the fundamental aspects and to noise traders and investors implementing their business strategies mainly based on statistical methods linked to other areas of the financial markets (see Knittel and Pindyck (2016) and others). Indeed, this may cause a herd effect where individual investors tend to imitate the decisions of a large group of investors. Preventing this effect would be one of the priority interests of corporate managers, as the high volatility of corporate stocks raises distrust among investors. In this context, it is appropriate to monitor not only the historical but also implied volatility of individual stocks.

The historical volatility is influenced by the published corporate information, which is usually assessed in relation to the achieved economic results and subsequently also to the value of the relevant asset. The data considered are not only of a financial nature. But the tone of the text in these reports, which tends to influence not only analysts but also investors, is important (Bicudo et al., 2019). As noted above, the quality of financial reporting, including additional commentary, is associated with equalizing information availability between firms and their stakeholders (Biddle et al., 2009). Text mining has therefore found a number of applications in different domains, especially in the financial field, but also in the stock market prediction.

According to Seng and Yang (2017), who investigated the volatility of the capital market over the months, quarters, half-years, and year, positive (negative) reports and high (low) occurrence of scores in reporting are in positive (negative) correlations with stock returns. In terms of implied volatility, ex-ante information should also be considered, subject to different expected market scenarios and relating to different expected prices of financial instruments, including corporate shares (Kaeck, 2018).

Table 5.1 summarizes the key findings of previous studies on stock return volatility prediction using text mining. Different sources of text data have been reported as important indicators of stock return volatility. These sources include (a) Internet message postings, (b) financial news, (c) analyst reports, and (d) corporate annual reports. In other words, information extracted from both outsiders (investors' postings, news, and analyst reports) and insiders (managerial comments in annual reports) have shown to be effective in predicting future stock return volatility. Antweiler and Frank (2004) investigated the role of two different sources of text data, namely Internet message postings and news articles. They found that higher number of postings and news indicate greater market volatility on the next day. The authors also demonstrated the significant effects of other financial indicators, such as trading value and stock market index. Tetlock (2007) investigated the effect of word categories obtained from the General Inquirer lexicon on stock market volatility. From those word categories, pessimism was the most informative indicator of increased stock market volatility. Kothari et al. (2009) used the General Inquirer to identify favorable/unfavorable messages and demonstrated that favorable news decreased volatility whereas unfavorable news increased stock return volatility. Loughran and McDonald (2011) were the first who investigated the long-term impact of opinion in corporate annual reports on stock return volatility. Unlike earlier studies, these authors created specific financial word lists to evaluate various sentiment categories in financial texts, including uncertainty and word modality. Significant long-term effects were observed for the sentiment polarity and modality indicators. Groth and Muntermann (2011) used a different approach based on machine learning. First, frequent words and word sequences were extracted from the news corpus and then machine learning methods were used to perform the forecasting of abnormal stock return volatility. This approach was more accurate than those based on word lexicons but this is achieved at the cost of decreased model transparency. Kim and Kim (2014) investigated the effect of investor sentiment as expressed in message board postings on stock return volatility of 91 companies. The NB classification method was used to identify the overall sentiment polarity in the messages but no evidence was found for the existence of significant effect of the sentiment polarity on future stock return volatility. On the contrary, previous stock price performance was found to be important determinant of investor sentiment. A similar sentiment indicator was proposed by Seeto and Yang (2017) to analyze sentiment in Twitter postings. Using the Support Vector Regression (SVR) machine learning model, it was demonstrated that individual sentiment dispersion represents an informative measure of stock realized volatility. A more in-depth investigation was conducted by Shi et al. (2016) in order to investigate the news sentiment effect across different industries, firm size, and low-/high-volatility states. The news sentiment indicator appeared to be particularly important in the calm scenario of low volatility. Ensemble-based machine learning methods such as Bagging and Boosting were used by Myskova et al. (2018) to show that more negative sentiment and more frequent news imply abnormally high stock return volatility. Chen et al. (2018) examined how single-stock options respond to contemporaneous sentiment in news articles. The authors found that sentiment indicators provide additional information to stock return prediction. A different topic of overnight news seems to be the reason of their positive effect that goes beyond market volatility. A novel stock return volatility prediction model was employed by Xing et al. (2019) to demonstrate the dominance of deep recurrent neural networks over traditional machine learning methods. This is attributed to their capacity of capturing the bi-directional effects between stock price and market sentiment.

The above literature suggests that information obtained from financial markets and financial statements provides important support to manage financial risks and decrease a firm's exposure to such risk. However, it is generally accepted that this information is insufficient to provide accurate early warning signals of abnormal stock price volatility. In fact, most firm-related information pertaining to stock market risk comes in linguistic, rather than numerical form. Notably, corporate annual reports offer a detailed, linguistic communication of the financial risks the company faces. In these reports, management discusses the most important risks that apply to the company, including how the company plans to handle those risks. However, only long-term effects of linguistic variables in corporate annual reports on stock price volatility have been examined in prior studies (Loughran and McDonald, 2011). Indeed, the short-term effects have only been demonstrated for the information obtained from outsiders, not the insiders. In this chapter, we overcome this problem by developing a novel prediction model utilizing managerial sentiment extracted from corporate annual reports.

5.3 Research methodology

The proposed research methodology is summarized in Figure 5.1. Our prediction system integrates three different components: (1) the linguistic component obtained from the analysis of corporate annual reports (10-K filings), (2) financial indicators of stock return volatility obtained

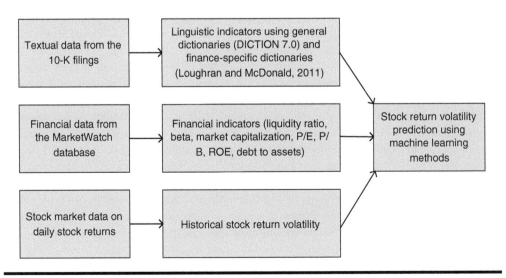

Figure 5.1 Research methodology.

from the MarketWatch database, and (3) historical stock return volatility. This research framework enables analysis of the effect of managerial comments in annual reports on stock return volatility by considering the effects of financial indicators. To achieve a high accuracy of the prediction system, several machine learning methods were examined, including REPTree, Bagging, Random Forest (RF), Multilayer Perceptron neural network (MLP), Support Vector Machine (SVM), and Deep Feed-Forward Neural Network (DFFNN).

5.3.1 Financial data and indicators

To obtain stock return volatility, we used standard deviation of daily stock returns, which is a commonly used risk indicator (Kothari et al., 2009). More precisely, the standard deviation was calculated for three consecutive days as follows:

$$\sigma_t(3) = \sqrt{\frac{1}{3-1} \sum_{t=-1}^{1} (R_t - \bar{R})^2},$$ (5.1)

where

$$R_t(3) = \frac{P_{t+1} - P_{t-1}}{P_{t-1}} \times 100,$$ (5.2)

with t being the filing day of annual report (10-K), P_t the closing stock price at time t, R_t stock return (rate of change) at time t, and $\bar{R}$ the mean value of stock price return for three consecutive days. This indicator was chosen because it represents the variance of stock return over a short period of time. Thus, the risk of the investment is taken into consideration. In general, more volatile stock returns indicate higher financial risk. Note that the three-day event window was adopted from previous related studies (Loughran and McDonald, 2011).

To reflect the systematic (market) risk, we also considered market return volatility in target variable calculation. Specifically, the standard deviation of stock return $\sigma_t(3)$ was compared with that of the stock market index and the instances were categorized into two classes: namely class 0 (negative abnormal volatility) was assigned to the less volatile stocks than the stock market index and class 1 (positive abnormal volatility) otherwise. To consider historical market and stock return volatilities as important indicators of future volatility, the standard deviations were also calculated for the three-day historical event window (t-4 to t-2).

In addition, we controlled for the effect of other factors of stock return volatility to avoid drawing erroneous conclusions. Therefore, we considered the following financial indicators adopted from previous research (Hajek, 2018):

1. company size (measured by market capitalization (MC), given as the market value of outstanding shares, i.e., MC = P × shares outstanding),

2. liquidity ratio (defined as the daily dollar volume of shares, calculated as trading volume per day/shares outstanding),

3. beta coefficient (sensitivity of a share to movements in the overall market, beta = cov(R_e, R_m)/var(R_m), where R_e denotes stock return and R_m is market return),

4. price-to-earnings ratio (stock price to earnings per share (EPS), price-to-earnings ratio P/E = P/EPS),

5. book-to-market ratio (firm's market capitalization to its book value, PBV = market price per share/book price per share),

6. return on equity (net income to shareholder's equity, ROE = net income/shareholder's equity), and

7. debt to equity (a measure of company's financial leverage, firm's total liabilities to shareholder's equity, D/E = total liabilities/shareholder's equity).

The data for the financial indicators were obtained from the freely available MarketWatch database. Those indicators reflect the risk effects of company size (small companies are more risky), market expectations (higher PBV and lower P/E indicate higher risk), and financial ratios (higher leverage and lower profitability indicate higher risk). Moreover, higher historical stock return volatility and beta coefficient also serve as risk indicators.

5.3.2 Textual data and linguistic indicators

In this study, we used 1,379 US companies from the New York Stock Exchange (NYSE) or Nasdaq. Stock price of 3 USD and MC of 100 million USD before the filing date was requested to limit the bid/ask bounce effect in response to the filing (Loughran and McDonald, 2011). The corresponding 10-K fillings were obtained from the Edgar database for the period 2016 that was chosen to reduce the effect of macroeconomic sentiment (we observed only limited fluctuations in the Dow Jones Economic Sentiment Indicator in this period). For text mining, we followed the prior studies (Hajek, 2018; Loughran and McDonald, 2011) and extracted only the Management's Discussion and Analysis (MD&A) section from the 10-Ks. The average number of word in the MD&A sections of the analyzed companies was 17,934. To reduce the size of documents, we used starting and ending phrases (delimiters) represented by section titles "Item 7." and "Item 8." respectively.

To calculate the linguistic indicators, two sets of dictionaries were applied: namely word lists from Diction 7.0, a general language dictionary, and those obtained from the finance-specific dictionary of Loughran and McDonald (2011). Indeed, previous related studies have demonstrated that the combination of these two types of dictionaries (general + finance-specific) improves the prediction performance of financial models (Hajek et al., 2014). Five general semantic indicators can be obtained from the Diction 7.0 word lists (Hart, 2001): activity, certainty, commonality, optimism, and realism:

$$
\begin{aligned}
activity = &(accomplishment + aggression + communication + motion) \\
&- (cognitive + embellishment + passivity),
\end{aligned} \tag{5.3}
$$

$$
\begin{aligned}
certainty = &(collectives + insistence + leveling + tenacity) \\
&- (ambivalence + numerical + self - reference + variety),
\end{aligned} \tag{5.4}
$$

$$
commonality = (centrality + cooperation + rapport) - (diversity + exclusion + liberation), \tag{5.5}
$$

$$optimism = (praise + inspiration + satisfaction) - (blame + denial + hardship), \qquad (5.6)$$

$$\begin{aligned} realism = &(concreteness + familiarity + humaninterest + presentconcern \\ &+ spatialawareness + temporalawareness) - (complexity + pastconcern). \qquad (5.7) \end{aligned}$$

The Diction 7.0 word lists can be downloaded from www.dictionsoftware.com.

The following word categories were obtained from the finance-specific dictionary: positive, negative, litigious, uncertainty, and modal (Loughran and McDonald, 2011). Similarly as for the Diction 7.0 word lists, the finance-specific word lists are freely available and can be downloaded from https://sraf.nd.edu/textual-analysis/resources/. When negation words were observed in positive statements, the words were considered negative. The raw term frequency of the ten linguistic categories was calculated and normalized to [0,1] by the lengths of the documents (Hajek, 2018; Hajek and Henriques, 2017). Both the data pre-processing and the calculation of linguistic indicators were conducted in Statistica 12 - Text & Document Mining software tool. To build the lexicons, we assigned each word in the lexicon with its corresponding label (e.g., positive: ACHIEVE) and then the labels of the lexicons were used as inclusion words. For more detailed information about the methods of text pre-processing and text mining used in this study, please refer to Feldman and Sanger (2007) and Manning (1999).

5.3.3 Machine learning methods

As noted above, predicting stock return volatility is represented by the two-class classification problem, where class 0 and class 1 denote negative and positive abnormal volatility, respectively. To perform the classification task, we used those machine learning methods that performed well in earlier research (Table 5.1). Specifically, the machine learning methods and their learning parameters were as follows:

1. REPTree (Quinlan, 1999). The REPTree (Reduced Error Pruning Tree) method generates a decision tree based on information gain with entropy and the pruning of the decision trees is performed using reduced-error pruning with backfitting. Thus, the error stemming from the variance is minimized. We opted for this decision tree classifier because traditional decision tree classifiers (C4.5, CART, ID3) may suffer from overfitting due to the generation of large decision trees. The pruning methods developed by Quinlan (1999) overcome the overfitting issue by replacing the internal nodes of the tree with the most frequent category. This pruning procedure is performed for the nodes in the tree only when the prediction accuracy is not affected. In our experiments, we used the REPTree implementation in the Weka 3.8.4 program environment. The REPTree classification model was trained using the following setting: the minimum total weight of instances per leaf was 2, the maximum depth of the decision tree was not limited, and the minimum proportion of variance at a tree node was set to 0.001. It should also be noted that this classifier is considered the fastest one among the methods used in this study.

2. Bagging (Breiman, 1996). It is an ensemble strategy based on generating multiple decision trees and aggregating their class predictions using a plurality vote. The multiple decision trees

Table 5.1 Summary of previous studies on predicting stock return volatility using text mining

Study	Source	Linguistic variables	Method	Key findings
Antweiler and Frank (2004)	Internet message postings from Yahoo!Finance Financial news from the *Wall Street Journal*	Number of messages, bullishness and agreement indexes	GARCH	Higher number of messages indicates greater next-day market volatility
Tetlock (2007)	Financial news from the *Wall Street Journal*	Pessimism, weak and negative word categories from the General Inquirer lexicon	OLS	Pessimism indicates increases in stock market volatility
Kothari et al. (2009)	Financial news from Factiva/Dow Jones, Interactive Company's 10K reports, Analyst disclosures from Factiva / Investext	Favorable and unfavorable word categories from the General Inquirer lexicon	Fama-MacBeth regression	Favorable and unfavorable words have respectively significantly negative and positive impact on stock return volatility
Loughran and McDonald (2011)	Company's 10K reports	Positive, negative, modal, litigious, and uncertainty word categories	Fama-MacBeth regression	Sentiment polarity and modal words in corporate reports indicate greater stock return volatility in the next year
Groth and Muntermann (2011)	Financial news from corporate disclosures	Bag-of-words with significant discriminative power	NB, k-NN, SVM, MLP	Bag-of-words improve the performance of financial risk prediction methods
Kim and Kim (2014)	Internet message postings from Yahoo!Finance	Overall investor sentiment	NB	Investor sentiment is not a significant predictor of stock return volatility

(Continued)

Table 5.1 (*Continued*) Summary of previous studies on predicting stock return volatility using text mining

Study	Source	Linguistic variables	Method	Key findings
Shi et al. (2016)	Financial news from RavenPack News Analytics Dow Jones Edition	News sentiment	Markov regime-switching GARCH	News sentiment is more important in low-volatility states
Seeto and Yang (2017)	Internet message postings from Twitter	Sentiment index calculated using NB from bag-of-words	OLS, SVR	Sentiment dispersion increases the realized volatility on the same day and decreases the realized volatility on the following several days
Oliveira et al. (2017)	Internet message postings from Twitter	Sentiment indicator from Twitter combined with sentiment indicators obtained from surveys	OLS, MLP, SVM, RF	The combined sentiment indicator significantly improves the prediction of DJIA realized volatility
Chen et al. (2018)	News articles from NASDAQ	Bullishness score	SVM	Overnight news are more informative than trading-time news, sentiment disagreement is a strong indicator of stock return volatility
Myskova et al. (2018)	Financial news from Yahoo!Finance	Sentiment score	Bagging, Boosting, Rotation forest	More negative sentiment and more frequent news indicate abnormally high stock return volatility

(*Continued*)

Table 5.1 (*Continued*)   Summary of previous studies on predicting stock return volatility using text mining

Study	Source	Linguistic variables	Method	Key findings
Zhao et al. (2019)	Oil-related news	Theme models	GIHS	Risk indicators from oil-related news can enhance the prediction performance of crude oil value-at-risk
Xing et al. (2019)	Internet message postings from StockTwits	SenticNet sentiment indicator	RNNs	Bi-directional interaction between movements of stock price and market sentiment produces a more accurate predictions

Legend: DJIA is Dow Jones Industrial Average, DRNN is deep recurrent neural network, GIHS is giant information history simulation, k-NN is k nearest neighbors, NB is Naïve Bayes, OLS is ordinary least square, MLP is multilayer perceptron neural network, RF is random forest, SVM is support vector machine, and SVR is support vector regression.

(base learners) are produced on different bootstrap replicates of the training set. Note that these replicates are produced randomly with replacement. Hence, each training sample may appear in the replicate training sets several times or not at all. In fact, bagging is effective only when the produced replicate training sets differ from each other (i.e., the bootstrap procedure is unstable). In our experiments, we used REPTree (with the same setting as presented above) as the base learners because it is prone to overfitting. Bagging was trained with ten iterations and bag size as 50% of the training set.

3. RF (Liaw and Wiener, 2002). It extends the Bagging algorithm by adding a random feature selection component into the ensemble learning. More precisely, a sub-set of predictors are randomly chosen at each node to improve the generalizability of the ensemble model. In contrast to standard decision trees, the split criterion is applied not to the best of all variables but only to the best predictor in the sub-set. As a result, the model is robust to overfitting and only two parameters are required to set, namely the number of trees to be generated (100 in our experiments) and the number of predictors used as candidates at each node (we used a heuristics $\log_2 (\#features) + 1$). In this study, this robustness feature is important also because no feature selection must be performed to decrease the dimensionality of the dataset. Again, the aggregation of the predictors was performed by using the majority vote. The same as for the above machine learning methods, the Weka 3.8.4 implementation was employed to train RF.

4. SVM (Keerthi et al., 2001). SVM is a kernel-based method based on the generation of the decision hyperplane separating classes in order to maximize the margin between the samples from different classes. In other words, in contrast to the remaining machine learning methods used here, SVM minimizes structural risk, rather than training error only (empirical risk). It is important to note that the optimal separating hyperplane is not produced in the input data space, but in the multidimensional space obtained using a non-linear projection. To find the optimal separating hyperplane in SVM, we used the sequential minimal optimization (SMO) algorithm that solves the large quadratic programming optimization problem by breaking it into a set of small quadratic programming problems. This method was used in this study due to its scalability, fast training, and effectiveness in handling sparse text datasets. SVM was trained with the following parameters: the complexity parameter was tested in the range of $C = \{2^{-2}, 2^{-1}, 2^0, 2^1, \ldots, 2^6\}$, polynomial kernel functions were employed to map the training instances from the input space into the new feature space of higher dimensionality. By controlling for the complexity of the SVM model, the risk of overfitting was reduced for the data used in this study. The SMO algorithm implemented in Weka 3.8.4 was used for predicting stock return volatility.

5. Neural networks MLP and DFFNN (Glorot and Bengio, 2010). The MLP model used here consisted of three layers of neurons, namely input layer representing the independent variables, hidden layer modeling the non-linear relationships between inputs and outputs, and output layer representing the predicted stock return volatility. In the DFFNN model, additional hidden layer was used to extract higher order features from the data. Both neural network models were trained using the gradient descent algorithm with mini batches, learning rate of 0.01 and 1,000 iterations. For MLP, we used the MultilayerPerceptron algorithm implemented in Weka 3.8.4, while for DFFNN, we employed the DeepLearning4J distributed deep learning library for Java and Scala. Distributed GPUs were used to perform

the prediction task. To find the optimal structures of the models, we tested different numbers of units in the hidden layer(s) in the range of $C = \{2^3, 2^4, \ldots, 2^7\}$. For MLP, we used one hidden layer, while two hidden layers were used for the DFFNN model. To avoid overfitting, we applied dropout for both input and hidden layer(s) with dropout rates of 0.2 and 0.4, respectively.

5.4 Experimental results

The basic statistics of the data used in this experimental study are presented in Table 5.2, together with the results from the Student's paired *t*-test. As can be seen from Table 5.2, significant differences between the two classes of negative and positive abnormal volatility were observed only for four variables, namely P/E, uncertainty, historical market, and stock return volatility. The differences for the remaining indicators were not statistically significant. Notably, a high historical stock return volatility indicates also its high future value, and higher frequency of uncertain words seems to be another significant determinant.

To predict stock return volatility, the machine learning methods were trained using ten-fold cross-validation, this is 10% randomly selected data were used as testing data and this procedure was repeated ten times to obtain reliable results. Table 5.3 shows the accuracy (Acc), area under Receiver Operating Characteristics curve (AUC), and true positive (TP) rate and true negative (TN) rate obtained using the input variables from Table 5.2. Note that AUC was used to reflect the imbalance of the classes in the dataset (386 vs. 993 instances) and TN and TP rates measure the accuracy on class 0 and class 1, respectively. The evaluation measures are given as follows:

$$Acc = \frac{(TP + TN)}{(P + N)}, \tag{5.8}$$

$$TPrate = \frac{TP}{P}, \tag{5.9}$$

$$TNrate = \frac{TN}{N}, \tag{5.10}$$

$$AUC = \int_0^1 TPR(T) \times \frac{d}{dT} FPR(T) dT, \tag{5.11}$$

where P and N are the numbers of samples classified as positive and negative abnormal volatility, respectively, TP and TN are the numbers of samples correctly classified as positive and negative abnormal volatility, respectively, and T is the cut-off point.

To further demonstrate the value of the proposed variables, we examined their merits using the Relief feature ranking algorithm (Kira and Rendell, 1992). In Table 5.3, the average worth of variables is presented over ten experiments (obtained using ten-fold cross-validation). In addition, the overall ranks are provided to show that historical stock and market volatilities represent the most important input variables in the data. However, linguistic variables ranked just after them, with commonality, certainty, and uncertainty ranked among top five variables. These results suggest that linguistic information is a relevant determinant of stock return volatility.

With respect to these evaluation measures, Bagging and RF achieved a more balanced performance, with acceptable accuracy on both classes (Table 5.4). By contrast, DFFNN and SVM

Table 5.2 Result of Student's paired *t*-test

Variable	Average for negative abnormal volatility (class 0, 386 instances)	Average for positive abnormal volatility (class 1, 993 instances)	t-value	p-value
Beta	1.179	1.260	−0.972	0.331
MC	9521.311	10855.913	−0.708	0.479
Liquid.	0.008	0.008	−0.625	0.532
D/E	0.885	0.985	−0.667	0.505
P/E	41.129	24.554	1.713*	0.087
PBV	7.926	5.956	0.745	0.456
ROE	0.122	0.164	−1.080	0.280
Positive	0.013	0.013	−0.261	0.794
Negative	0.027	0.027	−1.122	0.262
Uncertainty	0.013	0.014	−1.641*	0.099
Litigious	0.011	0.011	−0.333	0.739
Modal	0.001	0.001	1.109	0.268
Certainty	0.018	0.018	−0.170	0.450
Optimism	0.020	0.020	0.220	0.865
Realism	0.299	0.300	−0.857	0.392
Activity	0.023	0.023	−0.269	0.788
Commonality	0.027	0.028	−0.653	0.514
Histor. market volat.	0.005	0.003	9.204***	0.000
Histor. stock volat.	0.003	0.013	−14.448***	0.000

*** significant difference at $p = 0.01$, * significant difference at $p = 0.10$.

performed best on the majority class only (TP rate). However, DFFNN was not capable of detecting TN instances at all. In other words, the DFFNN model performed poorly for the imbalanced dataset. Overall, the ensemble algorithms outperformed the individual machine learning algorithms in terms of AUC. Regarding accuracy, REPTree performed best, with the balanced accuracy on both classes (84.7% and 86.7% for the negative and positive abnormal stock return volatility, respectively). To detect significant differences compared with the best performing machine method, Student's paired *t*-test was carried out, indicating that SVM and DFFNN were significantly outperformed in terms of both Acc and AUC.

In two further runs of experiments, sensitivity to linguistic indicators was tested. In Table 5.5, the results are presented for the experiment without the word categories from the general

Table 5.3 Worth of the variables obtained using the Relief feature selection method

Variable	Worth of a variable	Rank
Beta	0.00024	15
MC	0.00114	13
Liquid.	0.00168	12
D/E	0.00011	16
P/E	0.00031	17
PBV	0.00003	18
ROE	0.00001	19
Positive	0.00399	7
Negative	0.00398	8
Uncertainty	0.00460	5
Litigious	0.00404	6
Modal	0.00058	14
Certainty	0.00460	4
Optimism	0.00194	11
Realism	0.00291	10
Activity	0.00338	9
Commonality	0.00650	3
Histor. market volat.	0.00864	2
Histor. stock volat.	0.01356	1

dictionary, while Table 5.6 shows those obtained without the finance-specific dictionary. Most importantly, the performance of the prediction models improved in terms of Acc for most methods when the finance-specific dictionaries were removed, suggesting that the sentiment categories obtained using the general dictionaries were more informative for abnormal stock return volatility prediction. No other significant change was observed in the results presented in Tables 5.5 and 5.6 compared with those from Table 5.4, suggesting that general dictionaries may significantly enhance the balance in performance on both target classes. This provides investors with a more reliable prediction tool enabling them a wider range of investment strategies.

In the final run of experiments, only financial variables were employed for predicting abnormal stock return volatility. From the results presented in Table 5.7, it can be observed that the machine learning models were outperformed by their counterparts reported in previous experiments, indicating that linguistic information extracted from annual reports increases prediction performance regardless of the machine learning method used. Although Student's paired *t*-tests

Table 5.4   Prediction performance for all variables

	REPTree	Bagging	RF	SVM	MLP	DFFNN
Acc [%]	**86.15** ± 2.54	86.00 ± 2.24*	85.35 ± 1.91*	82.74 ± 2.06	83.83 ± 3.63*	72.01 ± 0.35
AUC	0.906 ± 0.024*	**0.925** ± 0.019	0.924 ± 0.018*	0.730 ± 0.043	0.899 ± 0.034*	0.485 ± 0.095
TN rate	**0.847** ± 0.107	0.783 ± 0.040	0.757 ± 0.063	0.507 ± 0.101	0.662 ± 0.222	0.000 ± 0.000
TP rate	0.867 ± 0.031	0.890 ± 0.019	0.891 ± 0.025	0.952 ± 0.024	0.906 ± 0.046	**1.000** ± 0.000

* significant difference at $p = 0.05$.

Table 5.5 Prediction performance without general dictionaries

	REPTree	Bagging	RF	SVM	MLP	DFFNN
Acc [%]	**85.93** ± 2.64	85.35 ± 1.91*	85.64 ± 1.93*	82.96 ± 2.86	83.18 ± 2.82*	72.01 ± 0.35
AUC	0.909 ± 0.022*	0.924 ± 0.015*	**0.925** ± 0.015	0.730 ± m0.050	0.913 ± 0.024*	0.515 ± 0.091
TN rate	**0.839** ± 0.100	0.788 ± 0.038	0.764 ± 0.039	0.505 ± 0.103	0.694 ± 0.168	0.000 ± 0.000
TP rate	0.867 ± 0.037	0.879 ± 0.018	0.892 ± 0.028	0.956 ± 0.024	0.885 ± 0.069	**1.000** ± 0.000

* significant difference at $p = 0.05$.

Table 5.6 Prediction performance without finance-specific dictionaries

	REPTree	Bagging	RF	SVM	MLP	DFFNN
Acc [%]	86.22 ± 2.07*	86.30 ± 2.51*	**86.73 ± 2.64***	83.39 ± 2.15	83.76 ± 3.03*	72.01 ± 0.35
AUC	0.901 ± 0.024*	0.925 ± 0.016*	**0.926 ± 0.020**	0.741 ± 0.047	0.909 ± 0.030*	0.508 ± 0.096
TN rate	**0.836 ± 0.101**	0.793 ± 0.049	0.793 ± 0.063	0.530 ± 0.109	0.688 ± 0.184	0.000 ± 0.000
TP rate	0.872 ± 0.030	0.890 ± 0.023	0.896 ± 0.028	0.952 ± 0.024	0.895 ± 0.049	**1.000 ± 0.000**

* significant difference at $p = 0.05$.

Table 5.7 Prediction performance with financial indicators only

	REPTree	Bagging	RF	SVM.	MLP	DFFNN
Acc [%]	85.21 ± 1.11*	85.50 ± 1.16*	**86.37** ± 0.75*	80.28 ± 4.40	82.82 ± 3.96*	72.01 ± 0.16
AUC	0.898 ± 0.014	0.921 ± 0.016*	**0.925** ± 0.008	0.672 ± 0.086	0.918 ± 0.016*	0.525 ± 0.230
TN rate	**0.829** ± 0.073	0.785 ± 0.039	0.795 ± 0.039	0.376 ± 0.184	0.582 ± 0.235	0.000 ± 0.000
TP rate	0.861 ± 0.026	0.882 ± 0.015	0.890 ± 0.011	0.969 ± 0.019	0.923 ± 0.060	**1.000** ± 0.000

* significant difference at $p = 0.05$.

performed to compare these approaches did not indicate significant differences, note that the potential reduction in investors' financial risk may have huge financial impact on the value of their portfolios.

5.5 Conclusions

This study has shown that a more balanced performance of the prediction methods can be achieved when incorporating the linguistic indicators from annual reports into the volatility prediction models. More precisely, our results indicate that general dictionaries are more discriminative than their finance-specific counterparts. Slightly more accurate machine learning models were obtained using the linguistic indicators compared with the models trained using only financial indicators. From the theoretical point of view, the current findings add substantially to our understanding of the effect of annual reports' release on short-term stock return volatility. An important practical implication is that investors can use the proposed tool to reduce their financial risk. Notably, we found that uncertainty in managerial comments indicates higher future stock return volatility.

The main limitation of the current investigation is that it has only examined one-year period. To further our research we intend to extend the monitored period. Future trials should also assess the model for predicting stock return volatility for different prediction horizons and focus on specific industries. Additional linguistic indicators can also be incorporated, such as those based on semantic and syntactic features of words and phrases.

Acknowledgments

We gratefully acknowledge the support of the Czech Sciences Foundation under Grant No. 19-15498S. We also appreciate the comments and suggestions of reviewers and ICABL 2019 conference discussants on research methodology for this chapter.

References

Antweiler, W., & Frank, M. Z. (2004). Is all that talk just noise? The information content of Internet stock message boards. *The Journal of Finance, 59*(3), 1259–1294.

Bicudo de Castro, V. Gul, F. A. Muttakin, M. B., & Mihret, D. G. (2019). Optimistic tone and audit fees: Some Australian evidence. *International Journal of Auditing, 23*(2), 352–364.

Biddle, G. C., Hilary, G., & Verdi, R. S. (2009). How does financial reporting quality relate to investment efficiency?. *Journal of Accounting and Economics, 48*(2–3), 112–131.

Black, F. (1976). The pricing of commodity contracts. *Journal of Financial Economics, 3*(1), 167–179.

Breiman, L. (1996). Bagging predictors. *Machine Learning, 24*(2), 123–140.

Carr, P., & Wu, L. (2009). Variance risk premiums. *The Review of Financial Studies, 22*, 1311–1341.

Chen, C., Fengler, M. R., Hárdle, W. K., & Liu, Y. (2018). Textual sentiment, option characteristics, and stock return predictability. *Economics Working Paper Series, 1808*, University of St. Gallen, School of Economics and Political Science.

Chin, C. W., Harris, R. D. F., Stoja, E., & Chin, M. (2018). Financial market volatility, macroeconomic fundamentals and investor sentiment. *Journal of Banking & Finance, 92*, 130–145.

Feldman, R., & Sanger, J. (2007). *The text mining handbook: Advanced approaches in analyzing unstructured data*. Cambridge: Cambridge University Press.

Glorot, X., & Bengio, Y. (2010). Understanding the difficulty of training deep feedforward neural networks. In *Proceedings of the 13th International Conference on Artificial Intelligence and Statistics*, Sardinia, 249–256.

Groth, S. S., & Muntermann, J. (2011). An intraday market risk management approach based on textual analysis. *Decision Support Systems, 50*(4), 680–691.

Hajek, P. (2018). Combining bag-of-words and sentiment features of annual reports to predict abnormal stock returns. *Neural Computing and Applications, 29*(7), 343–358.

Hajek, P., & Henriques, R. (2017). Mining corporate annual reports for intelligent detection of financial statement fraud - A comparative study of machine learning methods. *Knowledge-Based Systems, 128*, 139–152.

Hajek, P., Olej, V., & Myskova, R. (2014). Forecasting corporate financial performance using sentiment in annual reports for stakeholders' decision-making. *Technological and Economic Development of Economy, 20*(4), 721–738.

Hart, R. P. (2001). Redeveloping DICTION: Theoretical considerations. *Progress in Communication Sciences, 16*, 43–60.

Kaeck, A. (2018). Variance-of-variance risk premium. *Review of Finance, 22*, 1549–1579.

Kaeck, A., & Alexander, C. (2013). Continuous-time VIX dynamics: On the role of stochastic volatility of volatility. *International Review of Financial Analysis, 28*, 46–56.

Keerthi, S. S., Shevade, S. K., Bhattacharyya, C., & Murthy, K. R. K. (2001). Improvements to Platt's SMO algorithm for SVM classifier design. *Neural Computation, 13*(3), 637–649.

Kim, S. H., & Kim, D. (2014). Investor sentiment from Internet message postings and the predictability of stock returns. *Journal of Economic Behavior & Organization, 107*, 708–729.

Kira, K., & Rendell, L. A. (1992). A practical approach to feature selection. In *Proceedings of the 9th International Workshop on Machine Learning*, Aberdeen, 249–256.

Knittel, Ch. R., & Pindyck, R. S. (2016). The simple economics of commodity price speculation. *American Economic Journal: Macroeconomics*, American Economic Association, *8*(2), 85–110.

Kothari, S. P., Xu, L., & Short, J. E. (2009). The effect of disclosures by management, analysts, and business press on cost of capital, return volatility, and analyst forecasts: A study using content analysis. *The Accounting Review, 84*(5), 1639–1670.

Kumar, B. S., & Vadlamani, R. (2016). A survey of the applications of text mining in financial domain. *Knowledge-Based Systems, 114*, 128–147.

Liaw, A., & Wiener, M. (2002). Classification and regression by RandomForest. *R News, 2*(3), 18–22.

Loughran, T., & McDonald, B. (2011). When is a liability not a liability? Textual analysis, dictionaries, and 10âĂŘKs. *The Journal of Finance, 66*(1), 35–65.

Manning, C. (1999). *Foundations of statistical natural language processing*. Cambridge: MIT Press.

Myskova, R., Hajek, P., & Olej, V. (2018). Predicting abnormal stock return volatility using textual analysis of news - A meta-learning approach. *Amfiteatru Economic, 20*(47), 185–201.

Oliveira, N., Cortez, P., & Areal, N. (2017). The impact of microblogging data for stock market prediction: Using Twitter to predict returns, volatility, trading volume and survey sentiment indices. *Expert Systems with Applications, 73*, 125–144.

Quinlan, J. R. (1999). Simplifying decision trees. *International Journal of Human-Computer Studies*, *51*(2), 497–510.

See-To, E. W., & Yang, Y. (2017). Market sentiment dispersion and its effects on stock return and volatility. *Electronic Markets*, *27*(3), 283–296.

Seng, J., & Yang, H. (2017), The association between stock price volatility and financial news – A sentiment analysis approach. *Kybernetes*, *46*(8), 1341–1365.

Shi, Y., Ho, K. Y., & Liu, W. M. (2016). Public information arrival and stock return volatility: Evidence from news sentiment and Markov regime-switching approach. *International Review of Economics & Finance*, *42*, 291–312.

Staritz, C. (2012). *Financial markets and the commodity price boom: Causes and implications for developing countries*. Working Paper, Austrian Foundation for Development Research (ÄÜFSE).

Tetlock, P. C. (2007). Giving content to investor sentiment: The role of media in the stock market. *The Journal of Finance*, *62*(3), 1139–1168.

Xing, F. Z., Cambria, E., & Zhang, Y. (2019). Sentiment-aware volatility forecasting. *Knowledge-Based Systems*, *176*, 68–76.

Zhao, L. T., Liu, L. N., Wang, Z. J., & He, L. Y. (2019). Forecasting oil price volatility in the era of big data: A text mining for VaR approach. *Sustainability*, *11*(14), 3892.

Chapter 6

Random projection methods in economics and finance*

Roberto Casarin and Veronica Veggente

6.1 Introduction

Nowadays, very huge datasets are available in each field of science due to the possibility of recording and storing every relevant and apparently irrelevant information. Not only structured data but also unstructured ones are available in different forms such as images, histograms and text documents. All of them can be used as inputs in algorithms in order to improve the efficiency of decision processes, and to discover new relationships in nature, financial markets and society. The power of these data is potentially infinite and in recent years an active area of research emerged in economics and finance, which aims at handling inference on high-dimensional and complex data by combining machine learning methods with econometric models. Chinese Restaurant Processes and Bayesian nonparametric inference have been considered in Bassetti et al. (2018b), Billio et al. (2019), Bassetti et al. (2018a) and Bassetti et al. (2014); graphical models for time series analysis are developed in Bianchi et al. (2019), Ahelegbey et al. (2016a) and Ahelegbey et al. (2016b); random forest and nonparametric inference have been studied in Athey et al. (2019) and Wager and Athey (2018).

Nevertheless, it should not be forgotten that an algorithm or inference procedure might not work properly if all input data are not carefully refined. For this purpose, *data preprocessing techniques* are exploited to ensure that the input dataset is suitable for a data analysis process so that its efficiency is increased (see García et al. (2015) for further details). Data preprocessing is organized into two main steps: *data preparation* and *data reduction*. Data preparation consists

*This research used the SCSCF multiprocessor cluster system and is part of the project Venice Center for Risk Analytics (VERA) at Ca' Foscari University of Venice.

in *data cleaning*, which includes correction of bad data, filtering of incorrect data and reduction of unnecessary details, and *data transformation*, which includes data conversion, missing values imputation and data normalization. *Data reduction* techniques, which are the main focus of this chapter, allow for reducing sample size, and cardinality and dimensionality of the original data.

Sample size reduction ensures a data reduction through the estimation of parametric or nonparametric models which preserve some data properties. *Cardinality reduction* includes for example binning processes which divide data into intervals (bins) and identify a representative feature value for each bin. *Dimensionality reduction techniques* allow for reducing the number of variables and divide into three types of approaches. The first is *feature selection* which identifies the best subset of variables to represent the original data. The second is *feature construction* which compounds new features through the application to the original data of constructive operators such as logical conjunction, string concatenation and numerical average (Sondhi, 2009). The third is *feature extraction* which defines new features through a mapping of the original variables into a lower dimensional space. Within this approach, we will review *Principal Component Analysis*, *Factor Analysis* and *Projection Pursuit* (Section 6.2) and focus on random projection methods (Section 6.3) which have recently been applied to statistics and machine learning (Breger et al., 2019; Fard et al., 2012; Guhaniyogi and Dunson, 2015; Kabán, 2014; Li et al., 2019; Maillard and Munos, 2009; Thanei et al., 2017) and econometrics (Koop et al., 2019). Also, see Boot and Nibbering (2019) for a review of sub-space projection methods in macro-econometrics.

Data reduction is a necessary preprocessing step for high-dimensional data since they come with a lot of unwanted modeling, inference and prediction issues. In statistical models, the number of parameters increases exponentially with the number of variables (*over-parametrization*) implying good in-sample prediction and poor out-of-sample prediction performances (*overfitting*). Also, the number of observations needed to achieve an effective model fitting is large and is not reached in many practical situations (*inefficiency* issues). Similar issues arise in machine learning. The most relevant feature of a learning algorithm is that it should be trained on a large dataset in order to achieve good fitting or forecasting performances. When the number of covariates (features) increases, the algorithm needs a very large training set and can be subject to overfitting the training data if the number of observations is not large enough. All the issues mentioned above originate from the curse of dimensionality (Bellman, 1961) and *multicollinearity* problems in high-dimensional spaces (Vershynin, 2019; Wang, 2012).

An intuitive explanation of the *curse of dimensionality* is that in high-dimensional spaces there is exponentially more room than in low-dimensional spaces. For example, a cube with side 2 in R^3 has an area 2^3 times larger than the one of the unit cube. The same 2-side cube in $\mathbb{R}^d$ has an area 2^d times larger than the unit cube lying in the same d-dimensional space. The larger volume available in high-dimensional spaces makes more difficult that random observations fall in the "center" of the distribution: the tails in high-dimensional probability distributions are much more important than the center.

Two similar situations are as follows: a hypersphere inscribed in a cube and two embedded hyperspheres. It can be shown that when the dimension increases, if data points are drawn randomly in the hypercube, it is more likely that they fall in the complement of the hypersphere inscribed in the hypercube; similarly, if data are drawn randomly in the larger hypersphere there is a higher probability that they fall in the complement of the smaller hypersphere. In high-dimensional spaces, data concentrates in unexpected parts of those spaces. This mathematical fact is referred in the literature as *empty space phenomenon* and is illustrated in Figure 6.1. Given

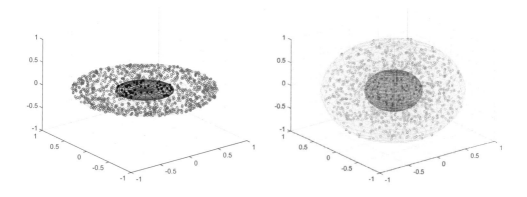

Figure 6.1   When the dimension of the space (*d*-sphere) increases from *d* = 2 (2-sphere on the left) to *d* = 3 (3-sphere on the right), the proportion of random points (black dots) falling into the internal sphere (red area) of radius $1 - \varepsilon$, with $\varepsilon = 0.6$, decreases, whereas the proportion of points (empty circles) in the complement of the internal sphere (gray area) increases.

1,000 points randomly generated in a unit *d*-sphere, the percentage of random points (black dots) in the inscribed *d*-sphere of radius $1 - \varepsilon$ (red area), with $\varepsilon \in (0, 1)$, decreases when *d* increases from 2 (left plot) to 3 (right plot).

As in the examples of the hypercube and hyperspheres, the graph of a multidimensional Gaussian distribution can be considered. In dimension $d = 1$ the volume of this distribution contained in a 1-sphere (or interval) of radius 1.65 is 0.9; it can be proved that if the dimension of the space increases, the volume contained in that sphere decreases and it becomes almost 0 in dimension 10. This shows that as *d* goes to infinity, the tails of a distribution become much more important than its center. For a wide and comprehensive discussion of this topic, the reader can refer to Verleysen and François (2005).

This result permits to argue a new concept: since data concentrate in extreme areas of the distribution in high-dimensional spaces, as *d* increases the distance between data and the center becomes higher; consequently, all points have similar distance from the center. Hence, substituting the Euclidean norm $||\mathbf{x}|| = \sqrt{x_1^2 + \ldots + x_d^2}$ of each point $\mathbf{x} = (x_1, \ldots, x_d) \in \mathbb{R}^d$ with the mean of the norms $\mu_{||x||}$ computed over a subset of points $\mathbf{x}_1, \ldots, \mathbf{x}_k \in \mathbb{R}^d$ leads to a negligible error in computing relative distances from the center of the distribution (Verleysen and François, 2005). This fact opens the way to the application of dimensionality reduction techniques when learning or making inference on high-dimensional distributions.

Another issue in modeling high-dimensional data is *collinearity*, also called *multicollinearity* in the multivariate case. It is a phenomenon that arises when one or more variables in a regression model can be nearly perfectly predicted by a linear combination of the other covariates (near-collinearity). As a result, this phenomenon creates a substantial variability in the coefficient estimate for each variable. Nevertheless, the predictive effectiveness of a model as a whole is not affected, what becomes senseless is the value of each regression coefficient that cannot be interpreted in the usual way. In practice, this means that the effect of a unit change in a variable controlling for the others cannot be well estimated. In addition, standard errors of these estimates become larger and a small change in the input data can make them vary substantially.

In the case of perfect collinearity, that is much more unusual than near-collinearity, a variable is the exact linear combination of another. In this case, the input matrix has not full rank and the model is not well specified (Stock and Watson, 2015). As the space dimension increases, the possibility that some variables are linearly correlated with the others increases substantially and the model is more likely to suffer of the multicollinearity issues described above. Nevertheless, it is possible to exploit multicollinearity to reduce the dimensionality of an input dataset. In the following, we will call *extrinsic dimension* the dimension of the original dataset and *intrinsic dimension* the number of independent variables in the reduced dataset.

The remainder of this chapter is organized as follows. In Section 6.2, dimensionality reduction techniques are presented as a way to overcome the issues discussed in the introduction. Section 6.3 introduces random projection and Section 6.4 provides some illustrations on simulated time series data and three original applications to tracking and forecasting a financial index and to predicting electricity trading volumes.

6.2 Dimensionality reduction

There are many different techniques available to reduce the dimension of a dataset from the extrinsic dimension to the intrinsic one. The way the intrinsic dimension is computed is one of the main differences among reduction methods. The aim of this section is to provide an overview and to get the reader introduced to random projection (RP in what follows) techniques which is the main focus of this chapter. In the following, we review linear techniques and refer the reader to Schölkopf et al. (1998) for an introduction to *Kernel PCA* and to Roweis and Saul (2000) for *Local Linear Embedding*, which are widely used non-linear techniques.

In all reduction techniques, a given sample of d covariates (or features) $(x_{i,1}, x_{i,2}, \ldots, x_{i,d})$, $i \in 1, 2, \ldots, n$, is represented as a data matrix:

$$X = \begin{bmatrix} x_{1,1} & x_{1,2} & \cdots & x_{1,d} \\ x_{2,1} & x_{2,2} & \cdots & x_{2,d} \\ \vdots & \vdots & \ddots & \vdots \\ x_{n,1} & x_{n,2} & \cdots & x_{n,d} \end{bmatrix} \tag{6.1}$$

where d is the extrinsic dimension and a *variance-covariance matrix*

$$\Sigma = \begin{bmatrix} \sigma_{1,1} & \sigma_{1,2} & \cdots & \sigma_{1,d} \\ \sigma_{2,1} & \sigma_{2,2} & \cdots & \sigma_{2,d} \\ \vdots & \vdots & \ddots & \vdots \\ \sigma_{d,1} & \sigma_{d,2} & \cdots & \sigma_{d,d} \end{bmatrix}$$

is assumed to exist for the model which is generating the data. In linear techniques, a representation of the data on a low-dimensional space is generated by extracting k variables that are linear transformations of the d covariates (where $k < d$).

6.2.1 Principal component analysis (PCA)

Principal component analysis is the most used dimensionality reduction technique. See Dunteman (1989) for an introduction, Jolliffe and Cadima (2016) for a review with recent developments, Ruppert (2011) for applications to economic time series and Fu et al. (2020) for an application to finance.

This procedure identifies k variables that explain a certain percentage of the total variability in the original d variables. More formally, PCA is a statistical procedure that applies an *orthogonal transformation* to the $n \times d$ data matrix in order to produce a set of k linearly independent variables, which are called *principal components*.

Let $\mathbf{u}_j$, $j = 1, \ldots, d$, be the *eigenvectors* of symmetric matrix A. According to the *spectral decomposition theorem*, A can be decomposed as

$$A = U \Lambda U'$$

where U is the orthogonal matrix with the eigenvectors of A in its columns, i.e. $U = (\mathbf{u}_1, \mathbf{u}_2, \ldots, \mathbf{u}_d)$, U' its transposed, and $\Lambda = \mathrm{diag}(\lambda_1, \lambda_2, \ldots, \lambda_d)$ is a diagonal matrix composed of all the *eigenvalues* corresponding to the eigenvectors of A, disposed in the same order. Consider a *normed linear combination* of the components $\mathbf{x}_i \in \mathbb{R}^n$:

$$C = \sum_{i=1}^{d} \alpha_i \mathbf{x}_i$$

where $||\alpha|| = 1$.

The combination C with the maximum variance will be the first principal component, the component with the second highest variance and orthogonal to the first will be the second principal component and so on. Formally, this is an optimization problem of the type

$$\alpha = \arg \max_{||\alpha||=1} Var(X'\alpha)$$

It can be shown that the vector α which maximizes the variance of the normed linear combination is $\mathbf{u}_1$, that is the eigenvector corresponding to the largest eigenvalue (λ_1). This vector is called the first principal axis and the projection of $\mathbf{u}_1'X$ on this axis is called the first principal component.

The following principal components are found adopting the same procedure repetitively. Relevantly, each principal component explains a percentage of the total variance of the model and the variance due to the ith principal component is equal to

$$\frac{\lambda_i}{(\lambda_1 + \lambda_2 + \cdots + \lambda_d)}$$

This quantity decreases for each principal component, the variance due to the first principal component being the largest.

The main drawbacks of the PCA are presented in the following.

■ Even if the principal components are all linear combinations of the original variables, sometimes it is difficult to interpret them in the sense of the initial problem.

- There is not a unique rule to decide the number k of components to include in the reduced matrix that is the dimension of the projection sub-space. Generally, a rule of thumb is used; components are added until a satisfactory percentage of the original variance is explained.
- It can be not effective when original data lie on non-linear manifolds,[1] because PCA is only able to project onto a linear sub-space.[2]

6.2.2 Factor analysis

Factor analysis is a linear method where all variables are represented as linear functions of some *common factors* which are not observable. See Bartholomew (1984) and Fodor (2002) for an introduction, Stock and Watson (2002b) for an application to macroeconomics and Stock and Watson (2002a) for a forecasting application with large datasets.

Consider the matrix X in 6.1, the columns represent the variables and the rows are the responses of each statistical unit to each variable. Let X' be the transpose of X and $\mathbf{x}_j \in \mathbb{R}^d$ the jth column of X', with $j \in 1, \ldots, n$. The factor model is

$$X' = \Upsilon F + E \tag{6.2}$$

where Υ is a $d \times k$ matrix of constants, F is a $k \times n$ matrix with unit-specific k-dimensional vectors of random factors $\mathbf{f}_j$ in the columns and E is a $d \times n$ matrix with unit-specific d-dimensional vectors of idiosyncratic errors $\mathbf{e}_j$ in the columns. The assumptions for the factor models are presented in the following:

1. all factors are standardized; that is, their expected value is null (i.e. $E(\mathbf{f}_j) = 0$) and their variance-covariance matrix is equal to the identity (i.e. $E(\mathbf{f}_j \mathbf{f}_j') = I$);
2. all specific factors have null expected value (i.e. $E(\mathbf{e}_i) = 0$);
3. idiosyncratic terms are mutually independent (i.e. $Cov(\mathbf{e}_i, \mathbf{e}_j) = \mathbf{0}, i \neq j$);
4. idiosyncratic terms and random factors are mutually independent (i.e. $Cov(\mathbf{f}_i, \mathbf{e}_j) = \mathbf{0}$).

Since all columns of F and E are independent, the variance $Var(X')$ is equal to $Var(\Upsilon F + E) = Var(\Upsilon F) + Var(E)$ and according to the *fundamental theorem of factor analysis* (Bartholomew, 1984) the variance-covariance matrix can be decomposed as

$$\Sigma = \Upsilon \Upsilon^T + \Psi$$

where Ψ is the variance-covariance matrix of the idiosyncratic term (E). From the specification of the factor model in Equation 6.2, each $x_{i,j}$, $i = 1, \ldots, j = 1, \ldots, d$, satisfies

$$x_{j,i} = \sum_{l=1}^{k} \upsilon_{j,l} f_{l,i} + e_{j,i}$$

As a consequence, its variance can be decomposed as

$$\sigma_{i,i} = \sum_{j=1}^{k} \upsilon_{i,j}^2 + \psi_{i,i} \tag{6.3}$$

The first term in Equation 6.3, $h_i^2 = \sum_{j=1}^{k} \upsilon_{i,j}^2$, is called the *communality* and is common to all variables while the second term $\Psi_{i,i}$ is called the *specific* or the *unique* variance, and it is the part of variability due to the idiosyncratic term $\mathbf{e}_i$. If many $\mathbf{x}_i$s have high coefficients ($\upsilon_{i,j}$) for the same factor $\mathbf{f}$, they highly depend on this same unknown factor, so they are probably redundant. Exploiting this feature of the data, dimensionality of a dataset can be consistently reduced, including in the analysis only non-redundant factors.

6.2.3 Projection pursuit

Projection pursuit is a dimensionality reduction technique which determines an *interesting* low-dimensional linear orthogonal projection of a higher dimensional dataset by maximizing a *projection index*. See Huber (1985) and Carreira-Perpinán (1997) for an introduction, Serneels (2019) for an application in finance and Chen and Tuo (2020) for an application to statistical models. PCA is a special case of projection pursuit, where the projection index is the maximum variance.

Projection pursuit is an unsupervised technique, and its aim is to find the low-dimensional projection (linear or non-linear) that provides most information about the structure of the original high-dimensional data (that is called interesting projection). With this aim, a $k \times d$ matrix of directions $(A)^3$ is found such that $Q(A)$ is maximized, where Q is a real-valued functional in $\mathbb{R}^k$ representing the projection index that defines the interestingness of a direction.

The main intuition behind this method is that the components of A should be determined in a way that the projection (through A) leads to the most interesting representation of the data into a lower dimensional space. Each column (a_i) is a projection direction and the most interesting projection is found according to the selected projection index $Q(A)$.

Dimensionality reduction techniques have also been extended to the non-linear case. A full discussion of this topic is beyond the scope of this chapter; for a wide explanation, the reader can refer to Lee and Verleysen (2007).

6.3 Random projection

Random projection techniques compress randomly a large-dimensional data matrix into a smaller matrix in such a way that the information content of the initial dataset is not lost. We need to introduce some new concepts in order to make the notion of *information preservation* more precise from a mathematical point of view.

Intuitively, for the techniques presented in the previous section, the determination of the dimension reduction heavily depends on the structure of the data, which implies high computational costs. The main feature of random projection technique is that projection matrices are not constructed with regard to the data.[4]

Random projection can be applied to perform both a *row-wise* (Woodruff, 2014) and a *column-wise* compression. In the former case, the number of observations (n) is reduced while in the latter a reduction of the number of covariates in the dataset (d) is obtained. In this chapter, we focus on column-wise dimensionality reduction.

In Section 6.3.1, random projection is described, starting from its mathematical foundations. Johnson-Lindenstrauss lemma (Johnson and Lindenstrauss, 1984) and norm preservation theorem are discussed as the fundamental presupposition for its validity and reliability. In Section 6.3.2, a review of different types of projection matrices is provided.

6.3.1 Johnson-Lindenstrauss lemma

We illustrate the Johnson-Lindenstrauss lemma (JL lemma in what follows) from a probabilistic perspective. The norm preservation theorem will be presented when the function f is a *Gaussian random projection function*.

The JL lemma is a fundamental result concerning the distortion implied by projecting data from a high-dimensional space to a sub-space of very low dimension. This lemma shows that it is possible to embed high-dimensional space into a sub-space in such a way that distances between points are nearly preserved.

The mapping used must be at least *Lipschitz*. A function is said to be Lipschitz when it presents a strong form of uniform continuity. For the purpose of this work, it is sufficient to know that a Lipschitz continuous function is limited in how fast it can change.[5]

Lemma 6.3.1 (Johnson-Lindenstrauss). *Let $Q \subset \mathbb{R}^d$ be a set of n points, $k = 20 \log(n)\epsilon^{-2}$ the dimension of the representation space, sub-space of $\mathbb{R}^d$, and $\epsilon \in (0, 1/2)$ the largest error allowed in the dimensionality reduction. Hence, a Lipschitz mapping $f : \mathbb{R}^d \longrightarrow \mathbb{R}^k$ does exist such that $\forall\, \mathbf{u}, \mathbf{v} \in Q$:*

$$(1 - \epsilon)\|\mathbf{u} - \mathbf{v}\|^2 \leq \|f(\mathbf{u}) - f(\mathbf{v})\| \leq (1 + \epsilon)\|\mathbf{u} - \mathbf{v}\|^2$$

where $\| \cdot \|$ is the Euclidean norm.

Lemma 6.3.1 states that the distance between two transformed points $f(\mathbf{u})$ and $f(\mathbf{v})$ is bounded by below (above) by the distance between the original points $\mathbf{u},\mathbf{v}$ decreased (increased) by a percentage ϵ. Otherwise said a function f exists such that the distance between the points of the transformed space $f(Q)$ is close to the distance between the points in original space Q. This distance can be viewed as the information content cited before.

The norm preservation theorem is stated in the following not only because it is of great importance in the proof of the JL lemma, but also because it provides a useful bound to the approximation error due the random projection. Although a Gaussian projection matrix is assumed, the result has been confirmed to be valid also under different distributional assumptions for the projection matrix.

Theorem 6.3.2 (Norm Preservation). *Let $\mathbf{x} \in \mathbb{R}^d$ and A a $k \times d$ matrix with entries $a_{i,j}$ sampled independently from a standard normal distribution $\mathcal{N}(0, 1)$; hence*

$$P\left((1 - \epsilon)\|\mathbf{x}\|^2 \leq \left\|\frac{1}{\sqrt{k}}A\mathbf{x}\right\|^2 \leq (1 + \epsilon)\|\mathbf{x}\|^2 \right) \geq 1 - 2e^{-(\epsilon^2 - \epsilon^3)\frac{k}{4}} \qquad (6.4)$$

Given that the norm preservation theorem has been proved using the Gaussian random projection function (Dasgupta and Gupta, 1999), a last issue must be solved: the existence of some couples $\mathbf{u}, \mathbf{v} \in Q$ such that the JL lemma holds using the Gaussian random projection.

Set f in Equation 6.4 equal to the Gaussian random projection function so that the norm preservation theorem holds

$$f(\mathbf{x}) = \frac{1}{\sqrt{k}}A\mathbf{x} \qquad (6.5)$$

with $k = 20 \log(n)/\epsilon^{-2}$, and assume $\mathbf{u}, \mathbf{v} \in Q \subset \mathbb{R}^d$ are both $O(n^2)$. Using probabilistic arguments it can be shown that the probability that a couple of vectors $\mathbf{u}$ and $\mathbf{v}$ exists such that JL lemma does not hold is lower than one. Equivalently, under proper assumptions, the probability to have **u** and **v** such that the lemma holds true is greater than zero. This ensures us that the JL lemma is valid from a probabilistic point of view.

6.3.2 Projection matrices' specification

In the previous section, a Gaussian random matrix A was chosen to perform random projection and to present the JL lemma. The main advantage of random projection above other dimensionality reduction techniques is the fact that the matrix used for the projection is built regardless of the original dataset. This ensures the researcher a substantial saving of time and the possibility to apply the same technique to solve many different problems. In random projection literature, other suitable forms for the matrix A have been proposed after the Gaussian random matrix. In this section, a review of this matrices is proposed.

JL lemma has been proved using different types of random matrices; in the previous section, we provided a statement considering a Gaussian projection matrix. Other proposals have been made for the projection matrix and the most relevant contribution (Achlioptas, 2003) introduced two new types of random projection A, the first with entries

$$a_{i,j} = \begin{cases} +\sqrt{3} & p = \frac{1}{6} \\ 0 & p = \frac{2}{3} \\ -\sqrt{3} & p = \frac{1}{6} \end{cases} \tag{6.6}$$

and the second with entries

$$a_{i,j} = \begin{cases} +1 & p = \frac{1}{2} \\ -1 & p = \frac{1}{2} \end{cases}$$

The first type allows for a higher degree of sparsity in the projection matrix. This characteristic has two main advantages: first, it strongly reduces the computational costs as two-thirds of the entries are zeros; moreover, this feature reflects the fact that economic and financial data are sparse. Take as an example financial returns; following the literature, they are generally well described by distributions with null mean and fat tails.

In the Bayesian literature, random projection was implemented to cope with problems of *large-scale regressions* (Guhaniyogi and Dunson, 2015) and *large-scale vector autoregressions* (Koop et al., 2019). In both these works, the authors used a projection matrix A with entries

$$\Phi_{i,j} = \begin{cases} +\frac{1}{\sqrt{\phi}} & p = \phi^2 \\ 0 & p = 2(1-\phi)\phi \\ -\frac{1}{\sqrt{\phi}} & p = (1-\phi)^2 \end{cases}$$

with $\phi \sim \mathcal{U}(0.1, 0.9)$.

6.4 Applications of random projection

In this section, we provide four applications of random projection. The first one is a linear regression problem on simulated data with large number of covariates; the second is a financial portfolio replication problem; the last two applications are forecasting exercises for the S&P500 index returns and the trading volumes in the Australian electricity market, respectively. These four original applications allow us to illustrate how to combine dimensionality reduction with standard econometric models and to discuss the main features, advantages and limitations of random projection.

6.4.1 A compressed linear regression model

Since RP has been used mainly in image and text data processing, its strength has been exploited to manage massive datasets. The goal of our numerical experiments is to show that random projection can be effective also when a moderate number of covariates is considered, producing a significant efficiency gain.

Data are generated as follows:

$$Y_j = \beta_0 + \mathbf{x}_j'\beta + \eta_j, \quad \eta_j \overset{iid}{\sim} \mathcal{N}\left(0, \sigma_\eta^2\right)$$

$j = 1, \ldots, n$, where $x_j = (x_{j,1}, \ldots, x_{j,d})'$ is a d-dimensional column vector of covariates, and $\beta = (\beta_1, \ldots, \beta_d)'$ a d-dimensional column vector of coefficients. The covariates are generated as follows:

$$x_{j,i} = \frac{i}{d+1} x_{j-1,i} + \varepsilon_i, \quad \varepsilon_i \overset{iid}{\sim} \mathcal{N}(0, \sigma_\varepsilon^2)$$

and their coefficients are drawn randomly

$$\beta_i = \left(\gamma \frac{i}{d+1} + \zeta_i\right) s_i, \quad \zeta_i \overset{iid}{\sim} \mathcal{N}(0, \sigma_\zeta^2), \quad s_i \overset{iid}{\sim} \mathcal{B}ern(p)$$

with $i = 1, \ldots, d$. The Bernoulli random variable s_i allows for setting the coefficient β_i at zero randomly with probability $1 - p$, thus excluding some covariates from the model which is generating the data. We apply a random projection approach to reduce the dimensionality of a linear regression model. The dimension of the projection sub-space is given by the error bound estimates of the JL lemma $k = 20 \log(n)/\epsilon^{-2}$.

The numerical illustration in Figure 6.2 shows that in our experiment settings with $n = 2{,}000$ and $n = 1{,}100$ observations, the optimal sub-space dimensions are $k = 634$ and $k = 588$, respectively. We fit the following random projection (RP) regression model:

$$Y_j = \beta_0 + \mathbf{w}_j(A)'\beta + \eta_j, \quad \eta_j \overset{iid}{\sim} \mathcal{N}\left(0, \sigma_\eta^2\right)$$

for $j = 1, \ldots, n$, where $\beta = (\beta_1, \ldots, \beta_k)'$ is a k-dimensional column vector of coefficients and

$$\mathbf{w}_j(A) = \frac{1}{\sqrt{k}} A\mathbf{x}_j, \quad j = 1, \ldots, n$$

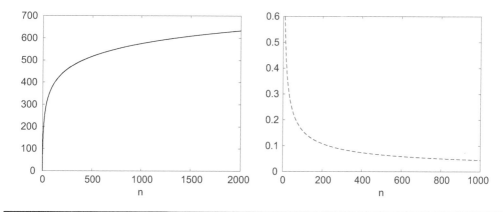

Figure 6.2 Dimension *k* of the projection sub-space given by the JL lemma (vertical axis, left) and the upper bound in the norm preservation theorem (vertical axis, right) as a function of the number of observations *n* (horizontal axes).

the k-dimensional column vector of projected covariates, A is a $(k \times d)$-dimensional random projection matrix.

In the different experimental settings of Table 6.1, we evaluate the *mean square error (MSE)* on a validation set of 1,000 samples generated from the true model. The results are given in Table 6.2. Since the random projection strategy is over-performing OLS for n close to the number of covariates d and for a low probability of inclusion of the covariates in the data generating process, we focus our attention on the parameter p. Within setting 1 (see Table 6.1), we estimate the mean square error with p varying in the interval $(0, 1)$. As is visible in the results reported in Table 6.2 (boldface figures), random projection seems to outperform the OLS estimation when a subsample of 1,100 observations is used. Moreover, it works better both with $n = 2,000$ and $n = 1,100$ in experiment 4, when the probability to include the covariates into the data generating

Table 6.1 Experimental settings. Each experiment includes the number of observations, the intercept β_0, the regression variance σ_η^2, the parameters of the covariate generating process $\gamma, \sigma_\epsilon^2, \sigma_\zeta^2$ and the probability p of inclusion of a covariate in the true model

	Model parameters					
Experiment	n	β_0	σ_η^2	γ	σ_ϵ^2	σ_ζ^2	p
1	2,000	0.1	3^2	0.9	1	0.01^2	0.2
2	2,000	0.1	1	0.9	1	0.01^2	0.2
3	2,000	0.1	3^2	0.9	1	0.01^2	0.8
4	2,000	0.1	3^2	0.9	1	0.01^2	0.01
5	2,000	0.1	3^2	0.9	1	0.01^2	0.05

Table 6.2 Mean square error for the different estimation strategies (columns) and experimental settings (rows) given in Table 6.1

Experiment	Sample size			
	OLS *n* = 2,000	OLS *n* = 1,100	RP OLS *n* = 2,000	RP OLS *n* = 1,100
1	27.98	221.04	115.53	213.17
2	3.38	44.95	117.17	167.40
3	29.95	209.51	468.81	943.79
4	36.24	326.48	**22.95**	**41.42**
5	24.97	304.51	39.59	**76.09**

process is lower (see Figure 6.3). This is to say that when data are sparser, the gain in effectiveness using random projection instead of OLS is substantial.

6.4.2 Tracking the S&P500 index

In order to test the efficiency of random projection, a problem of financial index tracking was set up. Index replication strategies require to build a portfolio of financial assets whose behavior mimics that of a given financial index (e.g., see Corielli and Marcellino (2006), Kim and Kim (2020)). Typically, much fewer stocks should appear in the replica than in the index. The objective of our experiments is to replicate the S&P500 index by investing in a specific subset of its components.

We assume one is interested in replicating the index fluctuations by trading stocks of the healthcare sector. With this goal, we retrieved data from 1st August 2019 to 31st December 2019 for S&P500 index and for all components of the S&PHealthcare index. The dataset includes $n = 104$ time observations of the log-returns of 59 stocks and of 1 index (see Figure 6.4).

Initially, it is argued that it is possible to replicate an index using just a subset of its components; analytically, it means that the log-return of S&P500 can be expressed as a linear combination of the log-returns of the stocks belonging to the healthcare sector plus an error term. In formulas

$$R_{SP,t} = R'_{HC,t} \beta + \varepsilon_t, \quad t = 1, \ldots, n$$

where $R_{SP,t}$ is the S&P500 log-return at time t, $R_{HC,t}$ is a $d \times 1$ vector of log-returns for all $d = 59$ stocks belonging to the healthcare sector, β is a $d \times 1$ vector of coefficients and ε_t is the idiosyncratic error term. According to this representation, β is the vector of weights to be attributed to each stock to replicate the log-return of the S&P500. In this application, we exploit the compressed regression

$$R_{SP,t} = R'_{HC,t} \frac{1}{\sqrt{k}} A \beta^c + \varepsilon_t, \quad t = 1, \ldots, n$$

where the matrix A is Gaussian random projection matrix to efficiently determine an optimal investment strategy.

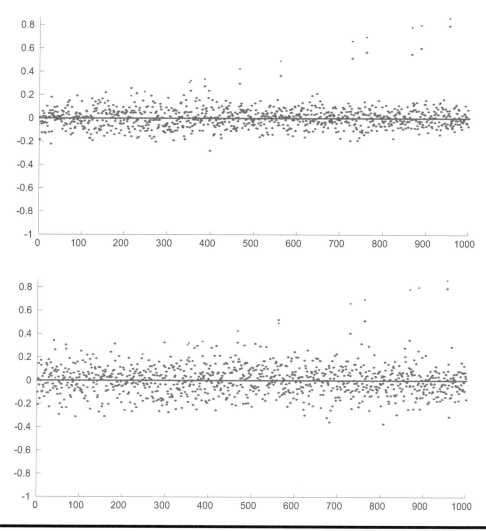

Figure 6.3 Results of experiment 4, where the probability of inclusion of a covariate in the data generating process is small, that is $p = 0.01$. In each plot: true parameter values (blue dots) and estimated parameter values (red dots) for a random projection OLS on the entire samples of 2,000 observations (top) and on a subsample of 1,100 observations (bottom).

In all analyses, the number of observations is $n = 104$ and the projection sub-space has dimension $k = 15$. We followed the suggestion in Guhaniyogi and Dunson (2015) and choose the new dimension in the interval $[2 \log(d), \min(n, d)]$. Random projection is performed 1,000 times generating A_i, $i = 1, \ldots, 1{,}000$, independent projection matrices. The elements of the projection $R'_{HC,t} A_i$ can be interpreted as random portfolios and the optimal coefficients β^c_i are portfolio weights conditionally to the projections A_i. To recover the regression coefficients in the original dimension d, we perform a reverse random projection of each $\hat\beta^c_i$ vector as follows:

$$\hat\beta_i = A_i \hat\beta^c_i$$

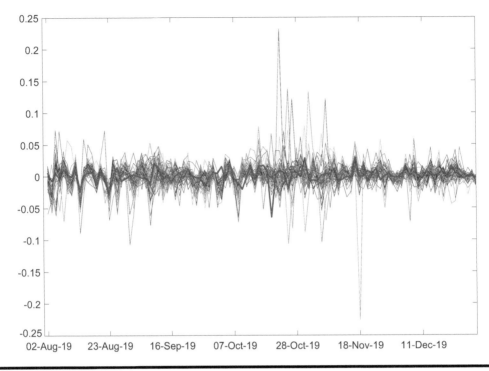

Figure 6.4 **Log-returns of the S&P500 index (red line) from 1st August 2019 to 31st December 2019 and log-returns of all S&PHealthcare components (colored lines).**

Finally, we apply Bayesian model averaging (Hoeting et al., 1999) and obtain a d-dimensional vector of portfolio weights:

$$\bar{\beta}^* = \frac{1}{1000} \sum_{i=1}^{1000} \hat{\beta}_i^* \qquad (6.7)$$

The results in this section are averages over the 1,000 independent random projections.

Different portfolio strategies were set up according to different weight calculation methods and different training sample sizes. Weight calculation is based alternatively on the coefficients produced by the simple OLS regression (OLS method in Table 6.3), or on the Gaussian random projection coefficients of Equation 6.7 (GRP method in Table 6.3).

Three different sizes of the training sample are considered: 80.77%, 67.31% and 57.69% of the original sample size, which corresponds to the first 84, 70 and 60 observations of the original sample, respectively. In the experiments with 57.69% of the original sample, the number of observations available equals the number of coefficients to estimate plus one, which makes the OLS estimates highly inefficient. These experiments mimic scenarios where there is a large number of replicating assets and a few temporal observations available to determine the optimal weights. We expect random projection techniques help to deal with this inefficiency issue.

Figure 6.6 presents the log-returns of the S&P500 index and of the replicating strategies. The corresponding average tracking errors are given in Table 6.3. Results in Table 6.3 and Figure 6.5 show that random projection outperforms OLS in all of our experiments. Random projection

Table 6.3 *Mean Absolute Error (MAE), Tracking Error (TE) and Tracking Error with normalized weights (TE-n) for different strategies. A strategy is given by a combination of estimation method (OLS without Random Projection (OLS) and OLS with Gaussian Random Projection (RP)) and training sample size (percentage of the original samples (P) equal to $n_{sub}/104$)*

	Strategy		Tracking performances		
	Method	P (%)	MAE (%)	TE (%)	TE-n (%)
1	OLS	80.77	0.0097	1.20	1.20
2	RP	80.77	0.0054	0.59	0.71
3	OLS	67.31	0.0167	2.17	1.72
4	RP	67.31	0.0055	0.56	0.87
5	OLS	57.69	0.5074	60.5	58.13
6	RP	57.69	0.0059	0.53	1.03

displays a smaller mean absolute error and is more accurate in backtesting. When the subsample is chosen really small, and the number of observations is close to the number of regressors, OLS-based portfolios have a large variability (bottom plot of Figure 6.5) and random projection OLS strongly outperforms the simple OLS method in terms *mean absolute error* (MAE) computed as

$$MAE = \frac{1}{n} \sum_{t=1}^{n} \left| \hat{R}_{SP,t} - R_{SP,t} \right|$$

where $\hat{R}_{SP,t} = R'_{HC,t} \bar{\beta}^*$. We evaluate the performances of the investment strategies by computing the Tracking Error (TE) that is a measure of the deviation of a tracking portfolio from the target index:

$$TE = \sqrt{\frac{1}{n-1} \sum_{t=1}^{n} ((\hat{R}_{SP,t} - \bar{\hat{R}}_{SP}) - (R_{SP,t} - \bar{R}_{SP}))^2}$$

where $\bar{\hat{R}}_{SP}$ and $\bar{R}_{SP}$ are the average returns of the replication and target portfolio, respectively (Basak et al., 2009). The TE is computed as the standard deviation of the difference of the index and portfolio returns. The TE values confirm that random projection has a better performance in terms of portfolio replication. The results are confirmed when the regression coefficients are normalized to obtain a replicating portfolio with self-financing constraint and initial capital equal to 1 (last column of Table 6.3).

6.4.3 Forecasting S&P500 returns

Using the same methodology applied in the previous section for the index tracking problem, we forecast the S&P500 considering the components of the S&PHealthcare as regressors. Although the procedure is the same, the model fitted is slightly different

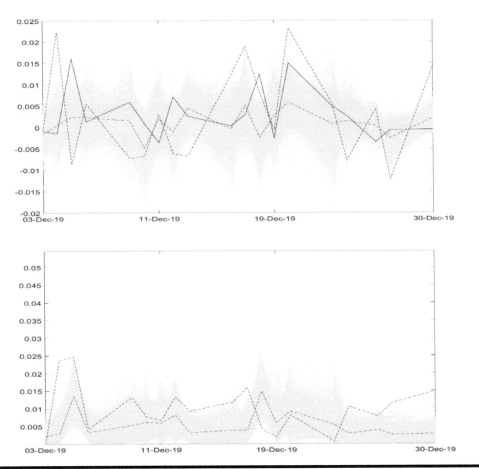

Figure 6.5 Results for Gaussian random projection model estimated on whole sample. Top: true values (black), and OLS (blue dashed) and random projection OLS (red dashed) fitted values. Bottom: mean absolute error for OLS (blue dashed) and random projection OLS (red dashed). Gray lines represent the results of each one of the 1,000 random projection estimates.

$$R_{SP,t+1} = R'_{HC,t}\beta + \varepsilon_t$$

meaning that lagged variables are considered to produce a forecasting estimate.

The dataset used for this application is the same employed in the previous one; the only difference is that data are taken with a lag, so observations are 103 instead of 104. The experimental settings are quite similar to the ones presented in the previous section. Time series of 103 observations were retrieved for S&P500 index and for all the 59 components of the S&PHealthcare index. In this application, model is fitted using a training set of 52 observations and a test set of 51 observations. Also, the new dimension for random projection k is set equal to 15 following the same arguments exposed in Section 6.4.2.

Similarly to what done in the previous application, the training sample (52 observations) is used ten times to fit a multiple regression preprocessing data through a Gaussian random projection. The ten random projection matrices and the corresponding vectors of coefficients produced

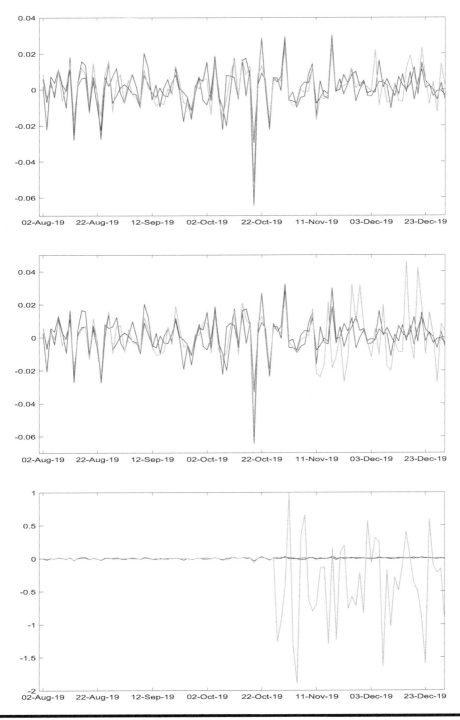

Figure 6.6 Performance of S&P500 index (blue), OLS-based portfolio (yellow) and (RP+OLS)-based portfolio (red). Weights computed using the whole sample (top), a subsample of 70 observations (middle) and a subsample of 60 observations (bottom).

by the compressed regressions are stored. The aim of this application is to forecast the values of the test set (51 observations) through a multiple regression performing a weighted model averaging of these ten different trials. Particularly, mean absolute error is computed for each of these models applied to the training set in order to derive a vector of weights to perform model averaging. To compute it, a vector of absolute errors is produced for each Monte Carlo simulation:

$$AE_i = \left| R_{SP} - \hat{R}_{SP,i} \right| \tag{6.8}$$

where AE_i is a 52×1 vector of absolute errors for the ith fitted model and $i = 1, \ldots, 10$. Averaging all the values in each vector, a measure for the error committed by each regression is produced (MAE_i). Then, its reciprocal is used to calculate weights

$$P_i = \frac{MAE_i^{-1}}{\sum_{j=1}^{10} MAE_j^{-1}} \tag{6.9}$$

where P_i is the weight attached to the ith model and $i = 1, \ldots, 10$.

In the forecasting procedure of the test set, model averaging is performed according to these weights, applying the previously stored projection matrices to compress the test set and then the stored vectors of coefficients to produce outputs. In the end, a weighted average of these predicted values is computed for each observation in the test set according to the weights in Equation 6.9.

The graphical results in Figure 6.7 shows the higher predictive performance of the compressed regression model (top chart) with respect to the standard linear regression (bottom chart). To compare the two models, we consider the *Mean Absolute Percentage Error* (MAPE) computed as

$$MAPE = \frac{1}{n} \sum_{t=1}^{n} \frac{\left| \hat{R}_{SP,t} - R_{SP,t} \right|}{R_{SP,t}}$$

For OLS estimate it is equal to 658.93 while preprocessing data using random projection allows for an appreciable reduction of MAPE to a value of 3.67.

6.4.4 Forecasting energy trading volumes

In the last decades, following the liberalization of the electricity market, there has been an increasing attention to predicting electricity prices and volumes to support optimal resources allocation (Raviv et al., 2015; Weron, 2014). We propose to apply random projection to predict electricity trading volumes in the Australian market. Wholesale trading in Australia is conducted by the *Australian Energy Market Operator* (AEMO) which generates electricity based on the requests presented with a five minutes frequency. Accordingly, spot prices are determined in each region (New South Wales, the Australian Capital Territory, Queensland, South Australia, Victoria and Tasmania) and then averaged over the six regions to obtain the average half hour trading price in the *NEM (National Energy Market)*. The spot price is the basis for the settlement of the transactions in the market.

The original dataset includes time series data for volumes and spot prices for electricity traded in the NEM for all regions from 7th December 1998 to 4th April 2010. Data have been transformed from 30 minutes frequency to daily frequency applying simple average. Figure 6.8 shows

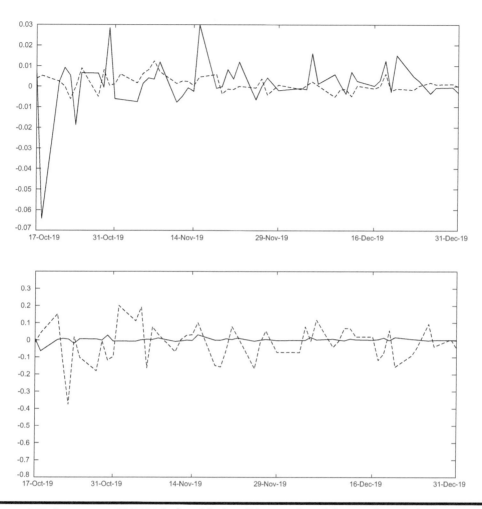

Figure 6.7 **Returns on S&P500 index (black solid), OLS-based forecasting (dashed, top) and (OLS+RP)-based forecasting (dashed, bottom).**

the electricity volumes traded during a period of 21 days. Every Sunday there is a decrease in the trading volumes, and every Tuesday and Wednesday there are peaks. These seasonal patterns in the data call for the use of forecasting models with periodic components such as seasonal step-wise dummies, and sine and cosine functions (Pedregal et al., 2007). In this application, we consider a Fourier regression model with the aim of forecasting trading volumes in the Queensland at a daily frequency.

We propose an augmented Fourier regression model

$$Y_t = \phi_t + \mu_t + \xi_t + \varepsilon_t \tag{6.10}$$

with ε_t being the idiosyncratic component, ϕ_t the Fourier period component

$$\phi_t = \sum_{j=1}^{F} \alpha_j \cos(2\pi f_j t) + \sum_{j=1}^{F} \beta_j \sin(2\pi f_j t)$$

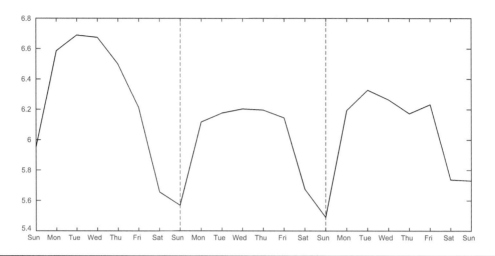

Figure 6.8 Daily trading volumes of electricity in thousands of Megawatt (MW) (black) from 7th March 2010 to 28th March 2010. The vertical dashed line indicates the end of the week.

where $f_j = j/n$ and $j = 1, \ldots, n/2$ are the Fourier frequencies and α_j and β_j the Fourier coefficients. The augmentation terms are the quadratic time trend component

$$\mu_t = \alpha + \beta t + \gamma t^2$$

for the long-term dynamics in the trading volumes, with coefficients α, β and γ, and the seasonal component

$$\xi_t = \sum_{j=1}^{6} \gamma_j D_{j,t}^{W}$$

for the day-of-the-week seasonality, where $D_{j,t}^{W}$ takes value 1 when t is the jth day of the week and 0 otherwise and γ_j are the coefficients representing the increase or decrease in the trading volumes with respect to the baseline day, which corresponds in our application to the seventh day of the week (Sunday).

In order to apply random projection, we write Equation 6.10 in a more compact form

$$\mathbf{y} = X_1 \beta_1 + X_2 \beta_2 + \varepsilon$$

where the vector $\mathbf{y} = (y_1, \ldots, y_n)'$ contains the observations for the response variable, the matrix

$$X_1 = \begin{bmatrix} 1 & 1 & 1^2 & D_{1,1}^{W} & D_{2,1}^{W} & \cdots & D_{6,1}^{W} \\ 1 & 2 & 2^2 & D_{1,2}^{W} & D_{2,2}^{W} & \cdots & D_{6,2}^{W} \\ \vdots & \vdots & \vdots & \vdots & & \ddots & \vdots \\ 1 & n & n^2 & D_{1,n}^{W} & D_{2,n}^{W} & \cdots & D_{6,n}^{W} \end{bmatrix}$$

has in its columns the intercept, the linear and quadratic components of the deterministic trend and the dummy variables, the regression matrix

$$X_2 = \begin{bmatrix} \sin(1 \cdot 2\pi f_1) & \cos(1 \cdot 2\pi f_1) & \dots & \sin(1 \cdot 2\pi f_F) & \cos(1 \cdot 2\pi f_F) \\ \sin(2 \cdot 2\pi f_1) & \cos(2 \cdot 2\pi f_1) & \dots & \sin(2 \cdot 2\pi f_F) & \cos(2 \cdot 2\pi f_F) \\ \vdots & \vdots & \ddots & \vdots & \vdots \\ \sin(2 \cdot n\pi f_1) & \cos(2 \cdot n\pi f_1) & \dots & \sin(2 \cdot n\pi f_F) & \cos(2 \cdot n\pi f_F) \end{bmatrix}$$

has the periodic components at different frequencies in the different columns and the vector ε contains the error terms. The dimension of the original dataset is n = 4,132 temporal observations, $d = 1 + 2 + 6 + 2F$ covariates which is equal to 4,141 when all Fourier frequencies are considered, i.e. F = 2,066. We apply data preprocessing to a subset of covariates. The column vectors in the regression matrix X_1 are not compressed, whereas we apply the $(d - 9) \times k$ random projection matrix A of the type exposed in Equation 6.6 to the columns of X_2. The resulting partially compressed regression model is

$$\mathbf{y} = X_1\beta_1 + X_2A\beta^c + \varepsilon$$

where β^c is a k-dimensional vector of coefficients, referred to the compressed regression matrix X_2A, and ε is an $n \times 1$ vector of idiosyncratic errors.

The model in Equation 6.10 is fitted 100 times to the training set using different random draws of the projection matrix. For each draw, the mean absolute error MAE_i is computed and the coefficients are used to predict the observations in the second part of the sample (validation set) conditioning on the random projection matrix. The unconditional out-of-sample predictions are obtained by averaging the conditional predictions over all draws of the random projection matrix. The combination weights of the Bayesian model averaging are proportional to MAE_i^{-1}, that is the inverse of the mean absolute error computed at each simulation step. In Figure 6.9 results

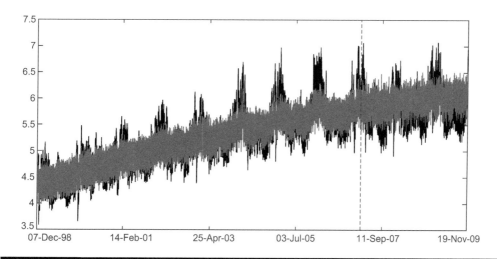

Figure 6.9 **Electricity trading volumes in thousands of Megawatt (MW) (black) for Queensland and RP combined with OLS forecasting (red) in sample (from 7th December 1998 to 22nd February 2007) and out of sample (from 23rd February 2007 to 31st March 2010). The vertical dashed line indicates the end of the in-sample analysis.**

of the forecasting performance are shown for the RP combined with OLS. Since the number of covariates is very large and very close to the sample size, the OLS without data preprocessing is not efficient. In our application, the standard deviation of coefficients estimated with OLS method takes values in the range [0, 22.19] with an average value of 0.062, whereas preprocessing data allows for reducing the coefficient standard deviation to the range [0, 0.019] and to an average value of 0.0003.

6.5 Appendix: Matlab code

Use the following code to generate a synthetic dataset. Replace this block of code to upload the dataset of your application.

```
1   n=2000;                              % Number of observations
2   nsub=1100;                           % Inference with smaller sample
        size
3   ntest=10000;                         % Number of observations in test
        set
4   d=1000;                              % Number of covariates
5   fs=14;                               % Font size graphical part
6
7   % Experiment Number 4
8   p=0.01;
9   sigmaeta=3;
10  sigmaeps=1;
11  sigmaz=0.01;
12
13  % Data generation
14  eps=randn(n+ntest,d);
15  eta=randn(n+ntest,1);
16  u=zeros(n+ntest,d);
17  y=zeros(n+ntest,1);
18
19  sl=rand(d,1)<p;                      % Selecting covariates to include
20  nsl=sum(sl);
21  bet=((1:d)'/(d+1)*0.9+randn(d,1)*sigmaz).*sl;
22  for i=2:n+ntest
23      u(i,:)=(1:d)/(d+1).*u(i-1,:)+sigmaeps*eps(i,:);
24      y(i,1)=0.1+bet'*u(i,:)'+sigmaeta*eta(i,1);
25  end
26
27  Xtest=[ones(ntest,1),u(n+1:n+ntest,:)];
28  ytest=y(n+1:n+ntest,:);
```

Use the following code to find the JL's bound following the number of observations n and the number of covariate d in the dataset.

```
29  epsi=49/100;                         % Error JL lemma
30  k=20*log((1:n))/(epsi^2);            % New dimension
31  % Left plot in Figure 2 of the Chapter
32  figure(1)
33  plot((1:n),k,'k-');
```

```
34   legend('k','location','northwest');
35   xlabel('n');
36
37   % Right plot in Figure 2 of the Chapter
38   figure(2)
39   u=2*exp((-epsi^2+epsi^3)*k/4).*((1:n).^2);
40   plot((1:n),u,'r--');
41   legend('upper bound','location','northwest');
42   xlabel('n');
```

Use the following code to perform Ordinary Least Square (OLS) and OLS with random projection (RP). The analyses are performed on the while sample and a smaller subsample.

```
43   % Whole Sample OLS  Analysis
44   X1=[ones(n,1),u(1:n,:)];
45   bethat1=inv(X1(1:n,:)'*X1(1:n,:))*(X1(1:n,:)'*y(1:n));
46   yhat1=Xtest*bethat1;                  % Test set prediction
47   mse1=mean((ytest-yhat1).^2);
48
49   % Sub Sample OLS  Analysis
50   Xsub=[ones(nsub,1),u(1:nsub,:)];
51   ysub=y(1:nsub);
52   bethat2=inv(Xsub'*Xsub)*(Xsub'*ysub);
53   yhat2=Xtest*bethat2;                  % Test set prediction
54   mse2=mean((ytest-yhat2).^2);
55
56   % Whole Sample OLS + RP Analysis
57   ka=floor(20*log(n)/(epsi^2))+1;
58   A=randn(d,ka)/sqrt(ka);               % Generating Projection
         Matrix
59   Xran=[ones(n,1),u(1:n,:)*A];          % Projecting Covariates
60   yran=y(1:n);
61   bethat3=inv(Xran'*Xran)*(Xran'*yran);
62   yhat3=[ones(ntest,1),(u(n+1:n+ntest,:)*A)]*bethat3; % Test set
         prediction
63   mse3=mean((ytest-yhat3).^2);
64
65   % Sub Sample OLS + RP Analysis
66   kasub=floor(20*log(nsub)/(epsi^2))+1;
67   Asub=randn(d,kasub)/sqrt(kasub);             % Generating
         Projection Matrix
68   Xransub=[ones(nsub,1),u(1:nsub,:)*Asub];     % Projecting
         Covariates
69   yransub=y(1:nsub);
70   bethat4=inv(Xransub'*Xransub)*(Xransub'*yransub);
71   yhat4=[ones(ntest,1),(u(n+1:n+ntest,:)*Asub)]*bethat4; % Test set
          prediction
72   mse4=mean((ytest-yhat4).^2);
73
74   % Left plot in figure 3 of the chapter
75   figure(3)
76   sz=10;
```

```
77  sz0=5;
78  scatter((1:d)',bet,sz0,'MarkerEdgeColor','none','MarkerFaceColor'
        ,[0 0 1]);
79  hold on;
80  scatter((1:d)',A*bethat3(2:end),sz,'MarkerEdgeColor','none','
        MarkerFaceColor',[1 0 0]);
81  hold off;
82  legend('true',['Estim. RP','(k=',num2str(ka),', n=',num2str(n),')
        '],'location','northwest');
83  ylim([-1+min(bet),max(bet)]);
84
85  % Left plot in figure 3 of the chapter
86  figure(4)
87  sz=10;
88  sz0=5;
89  scatter((1:d)',bet,sz0,'MarkerEdgeColor','none','MarkerFaceColor'
        ,[0 0 1]);
90  hold on;
91  scatter((1:d)',Asub*bethat4(2:end),sz,'MarkerEdgeColor','none','
        MarkerFaceColor',[1 0 0]);
92  hold off;
93  legend('true',['Estim. RP','(k=',num2str(kasub),', n=',num2str(
        nsub),')'],'location','northwest');
94  ylim([-1+min(bet),max(bet)]);
```

Notes

1 A *manifold* is a topological space that locally resembles a *Euclidean space* near each point. This means that each point of an n-dimensional manifold has a neighborhood that is homoeomorphic.
2 Anyway, when data lie on a non-linear manifold, it is possible to apply PCA locally (Kambhatla and Leen, 1997).
3 A is composed of orthonormal column vectors $\mathbf{a}_i$, subject to $Cov(\mathbf{a}_i, \mathbf{a}_j) = 0 \ \forall i \neq j$.
4 Nevertheless, Zhao and Mao (2015) propose to build projection matrices after a preliminary analysis of the features of the original dataset.
5 For example, if a bound exists for the first derivative of a function f, it is said to be Lipschitz.

References

Achlioptas, D. (2003). Database-friendly random projections: Johnson-Lindenstrauss with binary coins. *Journal of Computer and System Sciences*, 66(4):671–687.

Ahelegbey, D. F., Billio, M., and Casarin, R. (2016a). Bayesian graphical models for structural vector autoregressive processes. *Journal of Applied Econometrics*, 31(2):357–386.

Ahelegbey, D. F., Billio, M., and Casarin, R. (2016b). Sparse graphical multivariate autoregression: A Bayesian approach. *Annals of Economics and Statistics*, 123/124:1–30.

Athey, S., Tibshirani, J., Wager, S., et al. (2019). Generalized random forests. *The Annals of Statistics*, 47(2):1148–1178.

Bartholomew, D. J. (1984). The foundations of factor analysis. *Biometrika*, 71(2):221–232.

Basak, G. K., Jagannathan, R., and Ma, T. (2009). Jackknife estimator for tracking error variance of optimal portfolios. *Management Science*, 55(6):990–1002.

Bassetti, F., Casarin, R., and Leisen, F. (2014). Beta-product dependent Pitman–Yor processes for Bayesian inference. *Journal of Econometrics*, 180(1):49–72.

Bassetti, F., Casarin, R., and Ravazzolo, F. (2018). Bayesian nonparametric calibration and combination of predictive distributions. *Journal of the American Statistical Association*, 113(522): 675–685.

Bassetti, F., Casarin, R., Rossini, L., et al. (2020). Hierarchical species sampling models. *Bayesian Analysis*, 15(3), 809–838.

Bellman, R. (1961). *Adaptive Control Processes: A Guided Tour.* Chapter 5, pages 94–95. Princeton.

Bianchi, D., Billio, M., Casarin, R., and Guidolin, M. (2019). Modeling systemic risk with Markov switching graphical sur models. *Journal of Econometrics*, 210(1):58–74.

Billio, M., Casarin, R., and Rossini, L. (2019). Bayesian nonparametric sparse var models. *Journal of Econometrics*, 212(1):97–115.

Boot, T. and Nibbering, D. (2019). Forecasting using random subspace methods. *Journal of Econometrics*, 209(2):391–406.

Breger, A., Orlando, J., Harar, P., Dörfler, M., Klimscha, S., Grechenig, C., Gerendas, B., Schmidt-Erfurth, U., and Ehler, M. (2019). On orthogonal projections for dimension reduction and applications in augmented target loss functions for learning problems. *Journal of Mathematical Imaging and Vision*, 62:376–394.

Carreira-Perpinán, M. A. (1997). A review of dimension reduction techniques. *Department of Computer Science. University of Sheffield. Tech. Rep. CS-96-09*, 9:1–69.

Chen, G. and Tuo, R. (2020). Projection pursuit Gaussian process regression. *arXiv preprint arXiv:2004.00667.*

Corielli, F. and Marcellino, M. (2006). Factor based index tracking. *Journal of Banking & Finance*, 30(8):2215–2233.

Dasgupta, S. and Gupta, A. (1999). An elementary proof of the Johnson-Lindenstrauss lemma. *International Computer Science Institute, Technical Report*, 22(1):1–5.

Dunteman, G. H. (1989). *Principal components analysis.* Number 69. Sage.

Fard, M. M., Grinberg, Y., Pineau, J., and Precup, D. (2012). Compressed least-squares regression on sparse spaces. In *AAAI'12: Proceedings of the Twenty-Sixth AAAI Conference on Artificial Intelligence. Toronto, Ontario, Canada.*

Fodor, I. K. (2002). *A survey of dimension reduction techniques.* Technical report, Lawrence Livermore National Lab., CA (US).

Fu, J., Zhou, Q., Liu, Y., and Wu, X. (2020). Predicting stock market crises using daily stock market valuation and investor sentiment indicators. *The North American Journal of Economics and Finance*, 51:100905.

García, S., Luengo, J., and Herrera, F. (2015). *Data preprocessing in data mining.* Springer.

Guhaniyogi, R. and Dunson, D. B. (2015). Bayesian compressed regression. *Journal of the American Statistical Association*, 110(512):1500–1514.

Hoeting, J. A., Madigan, D., Raftery, A. E., and Volinsky, C. T. (1999). Bayesian model averaging: A tutorial. *Statistical Science*, 14(4):382–401.

Huber, P. J. (1985). Projection pursuit. *The Annals of Statistics*, 13(2):435–475.

Johnson, W. B. and Lindenstrauss, J. (1984). Extensions of Lipschitz mappings into a Hilbert space. *Contemporary Mathematics*, 26:189–206.

Jolliffe, I. T. and Cadima, J. (2016). Principal component analysis: A review and recent developments. *Philosophical Transactions of the Royal Society A: Mathematical, Physical and Engineering Sciences*, 374(2065):20150202.

Kabán, A. (2014). New bounds on compressive linear least squares regression. *Artificial Intelligence and Statistics*, 33:448–456.

Kambhatla, N. and Leen, T. K. (1997). Dimension reduction by local principal component analysis. *Neural Computation*, 9(7):1493–1516.

Kim, S. and Kim, S. (2020). Index tracking through deep latent representation learning. *Quantitative Finance*, 20(4):639–652.

Koop, G., Korobilis, D., and Pettenuzzo, D. (2019). Bayesian compressed vector autoregressions. *Journal of Econometrics*, 210(1):135–154.

Lee, J. A. and Verleysen, M. (2007). *Nonlinear dimensionality reduction*. Springer Science & Business Media.

Li, L., Vidyashankar, A. N., Diao, G., and Ahmed, E. (2019). Robust inference after random projections via Hellinger distance for location-scale family. *Entropy*, 21(4):348.

Maillard, O. and Munos, R. (2009). Compressed least-squares regression. *Advances in neural information processing systems*, volume 22, pages 1213–1221.

Pedregal, D. J. and Trapero, J. R. (1999). Electricity prices forecasting by automatic dynamic harmonic regression models. *Energy Conversion and Management*, 48(5):1710–1719.

Raviv, E., Bouwman, K. E., and Van Dijk, D. (2015). Forecasting day-ahead electricity prices: Utilizing hourly prices. *Energy Economics*, 50:227–239. Elsevier.

Roweis, S. T. and Saul, L. K. (2000). Nonlinear dimensionality reduction by locally linear embedding. *Science*, 290(5500):2323–2326.

Ruppert, D. (2011). *Statistics and data analysis for financial engineering*, volume 13, chapter 18, pages 517–527. Springer.

Schölkopf, B., Smola, A., and Müller, K. R. (1998). Nonlinear component analysis as a kernel eigenvalue problem. *Neural Computation*, 10(5):1299–1319.

Serneels, S. (2019). Projection pursuit based generalized betas accounting for higher order co-moment effects in financial market analysis. *arXiv preprint arXiv:1908.00141*.

Sondhi, P. (2009). Feature construction methods: A survey. *sifaka.cs.uiuc.edu*, 69:70–71.

Stock, J. H. and Watson, M. W. (2002a). Forecasting using principal components from a large number of predictors. *Journal of the American Statistical Association*, 97(460):1167–1179.

Stock, J. H. and Watson, M. W. (2002b). Macroeconomic forecasting using diffusion indexes. *Journal of Business & Economic Statistics*, 20(2):147–162.

Stock, J. H. and Watson, M. W. (2015). *Introduction to econometrics*. Pearson.

Thanei, G. A., Heinze, C., and Meinshausen, N. (2017). Random projections for large-scale regression. In Ahmed, S. Ejaz (ed.), *Big and complex data analysis*, pages 51–68. Springer.

Verleysen, M. and François, D. (2005). The curse of dimensionality in data mining and time series prediction. In *International Work-Conference on Artificial Neural Networks*, pages 758–770. Springer.

Vershynin, R. (2019). *High-dimensional probability*, chapter 3, pages 42–43. Cambridge University Press.

Wager, S. and Athey, S. (2018). Estimation and inference of heterogeneous treatment effects using random forests. *Journal of the American Statistical Association*, 113(523):1228–1242.

Wang, J. (2012). *Geometric structure of high-dimensional data and dimensionality reduction*. Springer.

Weron, R. (2014). Electricity price forecasting: A review of the state-of-the-art with a look into the future. *International Journal of Forecasting*, 30(4):1030–1081.

Woodruff, D. P. (2014). Sketching as a tool for numerical linear algebra. *arXiv preprint arXiv:1411.4357*.

Zhao, R. and Mao, K. (2015). Semi-random projection for dimensionality reduction and extreme learning machine in high-dimensional space. *IEEE Computational Intelligence Magazine*, 10(3):30–41.

Chapter 7

The future of cloud computing in financial services
A machine learning and artificial intelligence perspective

Richard L. Harmon and Andrew Psaltis

7.1 Introduction

The age of cloud computing is upon us. In the Financial Services Industry, we will see a significant acceleration in the migration of core banking applications and related workloads to public and private clouds over the next three years. This will help drive innovation, agility and digital transformations but it will also contribute to enhanced complexity and potential operational risk concerns if institutions build out a siloed cloud environment.

This chapter will focus on the future of cloud computing in financial services and highlight a few examples where machine learning (ML) and artificial intelligence (AI) are transforming how the financial services industry is driving innovation by leveraging data to improve products and services, and reduce risk. We also highlight the foundational role cloud computing provides by enabling institutions to have an enterprise-grade hybrid and multi-cloud architecture that provides full portability of data and applications while having a single data management, data governance and data security capability across all environments. This allows for the full life cycle industrialisation of ML and AI that provides capabilities to support real-time data ingestion, data analysis, model development, validation and deployment with ongoing model management and monitoring.

We showcase two examples where ML and AI provide innovative capabilities to address critical business problems. We then briefly touch on regulatory concerns around cloud computing at a firm and industry level and explain how the next generation of cloud computing platforms when used in conjunction with a modern data management, ML and AI platform addresses many of these firm-specific risk concerns but not the industry-level financial stability concerns which require regulatory involvement.

7.2 The role of machine learning and artificial intelligence in financial services

There are many well-documented business benefits for the adoption of ML and AI across the Financial Services Industry. These include the ability for institutions to automate and optimise a wide range of operational processes, to leverage a comprehensive single view of customers that takes into account many different data sources to identify key behavioural characteristics for improved personalisation and customer interaction. ML and AI can improve and automate fraud and Anti-Money Laundering (AML) detection capabilities using a more holistic "Know Your Customer" (KYC) view of customers, transactions and relationships coupled with a massive reduction of false positives that drive up the cost of investigations and reporting. ML and AI enable near real-time automated credit risk decisions and risk management alerts that reduce risk while expanding revenue opportunities.

As an illustration, imagine the success a business can achieve in revenue growth and market share in a corporate banking environment if the Chief Marketing Officer (CMO) is able to double the number of new corporate prospects that come with automatically pre-qualified lines of credit or business approvals. This is starting to become a possibility when combining global lists of businesses, directors, investors and shareholders, along with an institution's current customer data. From this data, ML and AI systems can more accurately identify what the best customers look like, scour these global lists of prospects, find similar businesses, rate them based on a wide range of factors, present a qualified targeted list of the best prospects to the CMO and even identify which of the institution's existing customers could make a warm introduction. This is just one example of the potential for ML and AI to drive automation, innovation and operational efficiencies across many lines of business.

While there are many well-known benefits of the use of ML and AI, it also comes with a range of risks, especially with respect to concerns about how these models are utilised. Beyond concerns about the lack of explainability of many advanced ML and AI algorithms, there are direct challenges to address the potential for models to replicate embedded societal biases. There are also concerns about the ethical application of models even including how autonomous pricing algorithms can collude with other algorithms to set non-competitive prices.

A recent study by the Financial Stability Board (FSB) has highlighted an interesting aspect of a potential risk-related side effect of the continued advancement and widespread use of ML and AI:[1]

Applications of AI and machine learning may enhance the interconnections between financial markets and institutions in unexpected ways. Institutions' ability to make use of big data from new sources may lead to greater dependencies on previously unrelated macroeconomic variables and financial market prices, including from various nonfinancial corporate sectors (e-commerce, sharing economy, etc.). As institutions find algorithms that generate uncorrelated profits or returns, there is a risk these will be exploited on a sufficiently wide scale that correlations actually increase.[2]

A related aspect of these concerns about ML and AI for the Financial Services industry is a requirement for Model Risk Management (MRM). This is a regulatory requirement as well as a core aspect of a bank's operational risk management framework. A recent McKinsey paper[3] highlights how the Coronavirus pandemic has identified shortcomings of existing MRM capabilities:

> ... the real failure is not that banks used models which failed in this crisis but rather that they did not have fallback plans to manage when the crisis did come.

It highlights several reasons for models that have failed during the COVID-19 crisis:

1. Model assumptions and boundaries defined at the design stage were developed in a pre-COVID-19 world.
2. Most models draw on historical data without the access to high-frequency data that would enable recalibration.
3. While access to the needed alternative data is theoretically possible, models would not be able to integrate the new information in an agile manner, because the systems and infrastructure on which they are built lack the necessary flexibility.

The last point, regarding the lack of ML and AI system's flexibility, is critical to the global efforts of many firms and analytic vendors to develop what is widely called the industrialisation of ML and AI. At Cloudera we have been working for years to enable the modern machine learning life cycle for large teams across massive data and heterogeneous compute environments with an open platform built for enterprise scale that runs anywhere. We call this Cloudera Machine Learning (CML). CML provides the following key features and benefits:[4]

- **ML workspaces without waiting**: Cloudera Machine Learning lets administrators deploy new machine learning workspaces for teams in a few clicks, giving data science teams access to the project environments and resources they need for end-to-end ML without waiting.
- **Democratised access to governed data**: With Cloudera Machine Learning, administrators can easily replicate governed data sets across hybrid and multi-cloud environments to give data science teams self-service access to the business data they need while maintaining enterprise data security and governance controls.
- **Data science teams' preferred, open tools**: Beyond Python, R and Scala, modern data science teams need the latest open source tools and libraries for innovation and to collaborate while working in their preferred IDE. Cloudera Machine Learning gives practitioners the freedom to use their favourite tools while preserving security, efficiency and scalability without administrative overhead.

■ **Elastic, auto-suspending resources including GPUs**: Innovation can be unpredictable but should be unstoppable. Cloudera Machine Learning gives data science teams access to the scale-out, heterogeneous computing resources they need to get work done fast while maintaining adjustable guardrails that help IT easily manage and optimise infrastructure resources and costs.

■ **Comprehensive, cohesive user experience**: Machine learning can't begin until data is ready, and it doesn't end when a model is trained. ML for business requires data engineering, model training and experiment tracking, and deploying and managing models in production. Cloudera Machine Learning gives teams the tools for it all in one cohesive environment without switching or stitching workflows together multiple tools.

■ **Portable and consistent**: In a hybrid or even multi-cloud world, shouldn't your ML platform be portable? Cloudera Machine Learning lets the business move data and infrastructure anywhere without creating disconnected silos and without changing the consistent user experience that data science teams rely on for building robust workflows and processes for end-to-end ML.

■ **Model catalogue and lineage**: Unique model cataloguing and lineage capabilities allow visibility into the entire ML life cycle to eliminate silos and blind spots for full life cycle transparency, explainability and accountability.

■ **Model monitoring**: A first-class model monitoring service is designed to track and monitor both technical aspects and accuracy of predictions in a repeatable, secure and scalable way.

While the McKinsey paper provides a clear outline of the shortcomings of existing Model Risk Management (MRM) capabilities, we think a more critical element is missing in their analysis. This would be the lack of alternative or challenger approaches to the historical data-dependent algorithms that are foundational to most ML and AI approaches. What is required within this context is a more out-of-the-box approach that incorporates simulation-based frameworks, such as Agent-Based Models (ABMs), that fall within the wider AI group of capabilities. We will illustrate below (Section 7.4) how ABMs can play a critical supportive role in modelling situations where traditional ML algorithms fail.

7.3 The enterprise data cloud

The demands of additional data management, use cases, technology infrastructure, user experiences, privacy, governance and security have increased exponentially over the past decade. Where prior software needs were planned for deployment across months and quarters (sometimes years!), expectations and needs have shifted to requiring services to be spun up in minutes. Those desires have been partially driven by four major technological shifts that have been underway in the computing industry.

■ **Cloud experience**: easy to use, self-service, on-demand, elastic, consumption-based.
■ **Compute and storage**: the separation of computing and storage as commonly seen in public and private clouds for increased performance.
■ **Kubernetes and containers**: adoption as a standard operating environment for flexibility and agility.
■ **Streaming and ML/AI**: multi-function real-time analytics for the data-driven enterprise.

The manifestation of these shifts has resulted in what Gartner[5] has termed the "Cloud Data Ecosystem" where data management in the cloud has shifted from a developer-oriented "some assembly required" focus to an enterprise-oriented, solution-based focus where enterprises may run workloads across multiple Cloud Service Providers (CSPs), on-premise or in a hybrid model utilising on-premise resources and cloud computing. Coupling the industry shifts with the Gartner research one arrives at the following core principles a modern data architecture must fulfil:

- Data must reside where it is best suited – on-premises or in the cloud workloads must be processed in the most efficient compute pools.
- There must be the ability to move workloads and data between compute environments – CSPs and on-prem.
- Management, security and governance for the entire multi-cloud ecosystem must be delivered through one management console.

Cloudera has continued to evolve its data management platform with these technological changes, customer demands, and emerging "new" realities of increased data and workloads across on-prem, hybrid and cloud in mind. The culmination of which has resulted in the creation of the Enterprise Data Cloud industry segment.[6]

The Cloudera Data Platform (CDP) is an integrated platform allowing businesses of all sizes to realise the benefits of an Enterprise Data Cloud. By simplifying operations, CDP reduces the time to onboard new use cases across the organisation. It uses machine learning to intelligently autoscale workloads up and down for a more cost-effective use of cloud infrastructure. CDP manages data in any environment, including multiple public clouds, bare metal, private cloud and hybrid cloud. With Cloudera's Shared Data Experience (SDX), the security and governance capabilities in CDP are ensured, IT can confidently deliver secure analytics, and ML and AI are running against data anywhere. CDP is a new approach to enterprise data, anywhere from the Edge to AI. The high-level architecture is depicted in Figure 7.1.[7]

This entire platform is delivered as a service, often referred to as a Platform as a Service (PaaS). Our focus throughout this chapter will be on ML and AI and where appropriate we will identify aspects of CDP supporting the discussed use cases.

7.4 Data contextuality: machine learning-based entity analytics across the enterprise

ML and AI can generate significant insight into an institution's customers, suppliers and business relationships from huge volumes of seemingly disparate sources of data. This underpins the ability to make automated unique decisions as per individual or organisation on a whole range of topics. It can also identify hidden trends and patterns of behaviour.

Digital transformation, credit and market risk, anti-money laundering (AML), fraud, customer retention, customer cross-sell, customer acquisition and many other key business tasks all benefit from the ability to more fully understand data by building the context of relationships between people, organisations and accounts.

An innovative Cloudera partner, called Quantexa, specialises in building out this data contextuality through the use of advanced ML and AI but also leveraging capabilities to help ensure that

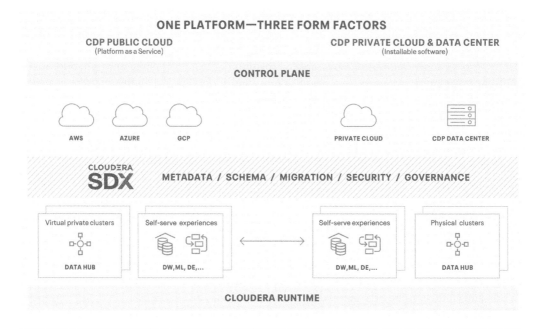

Figure 7.1 High-level architecture of Cloudera data platform.

the data is correct. Bringing together entities from multiple internal and external data sources in real time or batch allows Quantexa to create a single entity view across an enterprise.

Quantexa is able to do this by using dynamic entity resolution. Dynamic entity resolution relies on the ability to look at all of the data possible in a single relationship view. This involves aggregating potentially billions of data points to assemble an investigative, predictive, preventative and analytical single view. Quantexa does this in real time, making it accessible and applicable for any use case.[8]

Figure 7.2 provides an example of how Quantexa is able to empirically identify entity-based relationships. In this case, the single view of the customer is built with all the relevant and important data parts that lead to a complete contextual understanding. This provides the ability to see opportunities, threats and risks that each party presents to an institution in a quick and clear manner. Being able to do this at scale requires that one architect the business to be running at a microservices level enabling data and analytics to be rapidly deployed to address an institution's most immediate or evolving needs.[9]

As described in Section 2, the agility and scalability of the Big Data platform (CDP) provides this capability to make dynamic entity resolution at scale a reality. This is done by first having all of the data accessible within a single source and then being able to leverage the scalable computational capabilities of CDP to support the analytics. Figure 7.3 provides a high-level architecture overview of the Quantexa application running on the Cloudera platform.

Let's take a moment to discuss the key aspects of the high-level architecture in Figure 7.3.[10] Starting at the bottom we have the data layer where we leverage the Hadoop Distributed Files System (HDFS) to store the massive amounts of data required to have a complete understanding of entity relationships, this may be a mix of structured and unstructured data. At this layer you

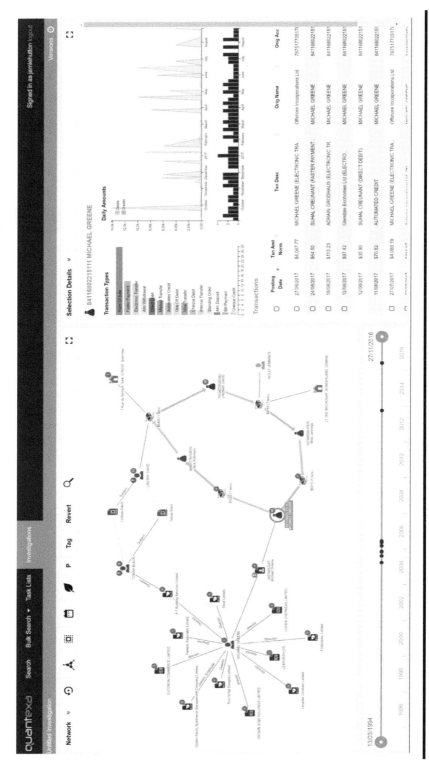

Figure 7.2 Quantexa's visualisation of entity-based resolutions.

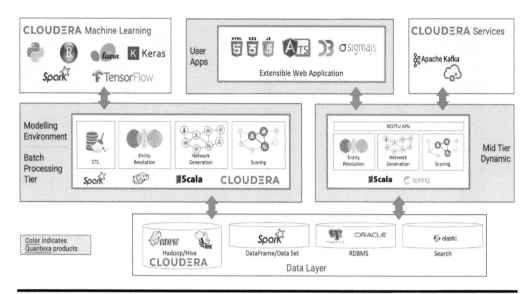

Figure 7.3 Quantexa architecture.

also see a variety of tools used to allow ad hoc discovery and investigation of the raw and processed data. Hive (a data warehousing tool), Spark for data engineering and Oracle for traditional SQL-like queries and transformations along with elastic search for a Google-like search experience over the unstructured data.

Moving up the diagram, in the middle we see the Batch Processing and Mid Dynamic Tiers and above them what is commonly referred to as the Access Layer. The Batch Processing and Mid Dynamic Tiers are both representations of the types of technologies that are indirectly in use to help satisfy the use cases of the Access Layer. For example, on the top left is Cloudera Machine Learning, which is part of CDP. This provides a data scientist with an enterprise-grade advanced machine learning and artificial intelligence environment utilising the latest technologies. On the opposite side, the top-right corner, we see Cloudera Services with Apache Kafka; this is also part of the CDP and is the de facto tool of choice across all industries for exposing data and/or ingesting data in a stream.

Today, many financial institutions find that their traditional anti-money laundering (AML) transaction monitoring systems are insufficient when relied on to detect risk in financial markets. In short, they fail to enrich, connect or operationalise the various forms of data associated with such markets, often causing investigators to miss suspicious patterns of behaviour that may exist within this data. Similarly, these legacy approaches overburden investigators with exceptionally high volumes of false-positive alerts, making the process of detecting risks related to financial crime to be both inefficient and ineffective.[11]

The Quantexa solution outlined above offers an innovative ML- and AI-driven approach that allows financial institutions to resolve related entities into a single view and make connections between distinct entities through interactions and relationships to derive context, and this context gives investigators a far more unified and accurate picture of where true risk lies. Furthermore, advanced analytics at the transaction, entity and network level can support the generation of risk-scored alerts, allowing analysts to prioritise and focus their efforts.

7.5 Identifying Central Counterparty (CCP) risk using ABM simulations

The complex and emergent behaviour of financial markets, especially under stress, has proven difficult to model with traditional mathematical approaches. A simulation-based approach that comes out of the complexity science literature is starting to gain traction in Financial Services. This approach is referred to as Agent-Based Modelling (ABM). ABM is a bottom-up approach to the modelling of complex and adaptive systems with heterogeneous agents.

A key factor that is not addressed by traditional machine learning-based approaches is that the sequencing of events within a period of time can be vitally important for capturing interconnecting effects that develop into trigger points for wider contagion effects. This allows ABMs to explain how the behaviour of individual institutions or agents can affect outcomes in complex systems and offers the opportunity to understand potential vulnerabilities and paths through which risks can propagate across the financial system. Additionally, such models offer the ability to depict the heterogeneity of agents, as well as idiosyncratic rules for how financial institutions operate, which are important for replicating real market conditions.[12]

An ABM simulation framework allows regulators and financial services institutions to develop dynamic simulation environments that can evaluate thousands of stress test scenarios at the system-wide level. This can be an indispensable tool to identify and quantify emerging financial stability risks around third-party cloud outsourcing and cloud concentration.

One clear example where this can be applied is on the financial stability risks that potentially exist within the global Central Counterparty (CCP) system. A recent consultative document by the Financial Stability Board (FSB)[13] highlights regulatory concerns about Central Counterparty (CCP) for being a source of system risks:

> Central clearing of standardised over-the-counter (OTC) derivatives is a key pillar of the G20 Leaders' commitment to reform OTC derivatives markets in response to the global financial crisis. Central counterparties' (CCPs) criticality to the overall safety and soundness of the financial system means that authorities must take steps to ensure that CCPs do not themselves become a source of systemic risk and that any CCP can be successfully resolved without exposing taxpayers to loss.

They propose that regulators and the resolution authority follow a five-step process for assessing the adequacy of financial resources and tools available to authorities to support the resolution of a CCP:[14]

- Step 1: Identifying hypothetical default and non-default loss scenarios (and a combination of them) that may lead to resolution;
- Step 2: Conducting a qualitative and quantitative evaluation of existing resources and tools available in resolution;
- Step 3: Assessing potential resolution costs;
- Step 4: Comparing existing resources and tools to resolution costs and identifying any gaps;
- Step 5: Evaluating the availability, costs and benefits of potential means of addressing any identified gaps.

These five steps are to be utilised to outline the minimum requirements that a CCP must address as part of a regular supervisory review process.

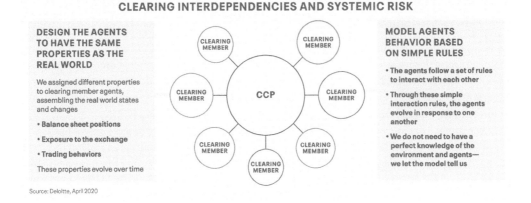

Figure 7.4 The Deloitte-Simudyne Agent-Based Model (ABM) for CCPs.

Two Cloudera partners, Deloitte and Simudyne, have developed a cloud-enabled ABM simulation model of CCPs on the CDP.[15] As illustrated in Figure 7.4, CCPs have clearing members which not only transact but are responsible for replenishing a default fund in the case of clearing member defaults.

This model is able to capture many of the risk exposures of CCPs (e.g., concentration risk, liquidity risk and wrong-way risk) which can have wide financial stability implications. This model will also be able to directly support the FSB's five-step risk and resiliency evaluation requirements.

The Deloitte-Simudyne ABM-based CCP model records all state changes for each agent and the environment at every time step, as well as associated behaviour and interaction changes for visualisation, analysis and quantification. This model captures three key components relevant to the CCP structure.

1. **Financial market simulator**: It simulates a market environment for different types of clearing members and end users, with evolving states in response to participants' idiosyncratic behaviours and interactions over time.
2. **Margin call framework**: It calculates initial margin and variation margin requirements for clearing members portfolios and makes associated margin calls.
3. **Default management framework**: It simulates the default management protocols triggered by a clearing member as default.

Within this ABM structure, the market simulator, the margin call and default management processes will synchronously lead to changes in the states of the Clearing Members (CMs) and the environment. By simulating the path of these agents over time, the model captures emergent behaviour and the impact of adaptive agents responding to different financial market environments. From hundreds of thousands of simulation runs, institutions can analyse the effects of any potential changes in regulatory policy, CCP risk management practices, CCP default fund changes, stressed market conditions or other circumstances on the CCP, the CMs, other CCPs as well as the wider financial system.[16]

The model is built on the Simudyne platform and runs on Cloudera's CDP. The Simudyne platform provides an easy-to-use, highly customisable SDK, together with libraries of support functions specifically optimised for ABMs. Architecturally, the Simudyne SDK uses Apache Spark to distribute ABM simulations by performing calculations in parallel across a large number of processor nodes that are managed by CDP. It also has a user-friendly front-end console built into the SDK, which greatly simplifies data and process visualisation. This is illustrated in Figure 7.5.

The Cloudera platform provides a fast, easy and secure data platform that supports the models to be run in a hybrid or multi-cloud environment. CDP is a key enabler for storing the massive amount of data generated by the simulations. Taken together, the combined technologies of Simudyne and Cloudera provide a highly scalable simulation environment, enabling seamless scaling to millions of simulations, as well as storage of all information required for making decisions based on deeper insights into the dynamics of the underlying behavioural relationships.

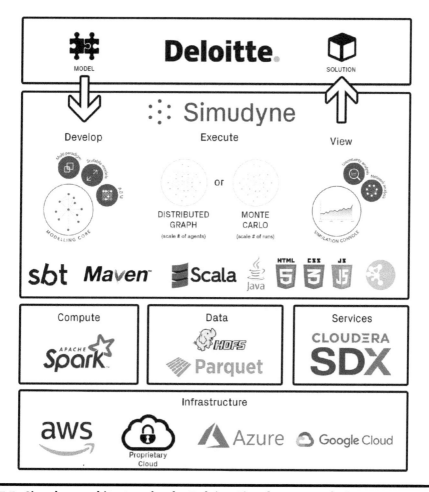

Figure 7.5 Simudyne architecture for the Deloitte-Simudyne CCP solution.

The Deloitte-Simudyne ABM CCP cloud-based solution is a notable example for regulators and financial institutions to consider the use of ABMs as a complementary approach to traditional approaches for quantifying potential future systemic risk events.

7.6 Systemic risk and cloud concentration risk exposures

The growth in cloud adoption across the Financial Services Industry and the associated increasing reliance on third-party infrastructure providers have gained the attention of regulators at global, regional and national levels.[17]

At a high level, a core regulatory concern is the operational resiliency in the "shared responsibility model" that exists between a Cloud customer and the CSP. Within the context of the Infrastructure as a Service (IAAS) offering, while the CSPs retain responsibility over the lower level layers of infrastructure, the financial institution is responsible for the data stored and processed, the overall security of the solutions developed on the Cloud and the ability to assess the CSP's compliance with required resiliency requirements.[18]

At the global level, the Financial Stability Board (FSB) and the Bank of International Settlements (BIS) have recently issued a few publications focused on the operational and supervisory risks of third-party cloud service providers. The most recent FSB study[19] identified an emerging risk concern:

> Potential concentration in third-party provision could result in systemic effects in the case of a large-scale operational failure or insolvency.

Similarly, the Basel Committee for Banking Supervision, part of the Bank of International Settlements, noted the impact that Cloud computing is having on the progress of a key regulatory mandate (BCBS-239)[20] outlining the "Principles for effective risk data aggregation and risk reporting"

> In recent years, changes in business and technology have intensified, including developments such as fintech and cloud technologies, compelling banks to upgrade their IT capabilities. … Some banks have faced challenges in ensuring data accuracy, timeliness and completeness for outsourced data-related processes against the backdrop of growing use of third-party support for data-related processes.

Globally, regulators have taken a variety of approaches to address third-party cloud service providers though they have not yet addressed in sufficient detail specific concerns about potential systemic risk impacts. This is especially true of the risks associated with Cloud Concentration Risk.[21]

Currently, detailed Cloud IAAS market share estimates of the major CSPs for the Financial Services Industry are not publicly disclosed by the CSPs. Fortunately, in January 2020, the Bank of England published some high-level results of an annual survey of the 30 largest banks and 27 largest insurers that it supervises to understand how these institutions utilise the cloud. This includes a good selection of some of the largest global banks since many have significant operations in London.[22] This is presented in Figure 7.6.

It should be noted that in this publication the Bank of England stated:

> Our survey indicates that for banks and insurers, the provision of IT infrastructure in the cloud is already highly concentrated.

Furthermore, they mentioned that

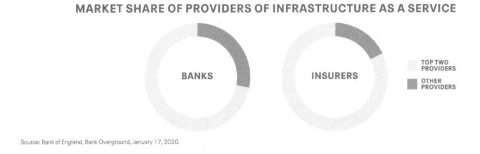

Figure 7.6 **Bank of England's IAAS cloud market share survey (January 2020).**

We will use the results of the survey to inform and adjust our supervisory approach to cloud oversight.

While a diverse list of operational resiliency concerns has been identified across many regulator publications, we perceive the following six items reflect the most critical factors in evaluating future systemic risk exposures.

1. **Lack of unified data security and governance**: Each cloud native product re-creates its own silo of metadata making data management, security and governance much more complex. Without a unified security and governance framework, institutions will be challenged to identify, monitor and address crucial issues in data management that are critical for the proper measurement of risk exposures across different platforms. This is especially true for hybrid or multi-cloud environments.

2. **Cyber attack resiliency**: The consolidation of multiple organisations within one CSP presents a more attractive target for cyber criminals than a single organisation.[23] A further complication is that Cloud security is a shared responsibility between the CSP and the institution.

3. **Vendor lock-in**: The market share concentration of a small group of CSPs can result in significant lock-in effects, whereby an institution is unable to easily change its cloud provider either due to the terms of a contract, a lack of feasible alternatives, proprietary technical features or high switching costs.

4. **Operational resiliency**: Much of the operational resiliency concerns by regulators is the "shared responsibility" model inherent in the relationship between a Cloud customer and the CSP. Regulators have consistently made it clear that institutions at all times remain fully responsible for all the operational functions they outsource to third-party providers. This addresses the liability aspect but does not address the fundamental risk exposure that still exists.

5. **Lack of transparency**: A CSP is unlikely to share detailed information about its processes, operations and controls. This restricts not only an individual institution but also the regulator from being able to fully ensure sufficient oversight. From a reporting perspective, the UK and Luxembourg regulators require institutions to periodically report all functions outsourced to the Cloud, alongside requiring pre-authorisation for migration of critical applications.

6. **Cloud concentration risk**: Regulators are concerned about institutions' over reliance on one service provider to support their banking services. This not only presents cloud operational risks for individual institutions but creates financial stability risks for the financial system within a single country as well as globally. Concentration risks also arise if a significant number of institutions have a key operational or market infrastructure capability (e.g., payment, settlement and clearing systems) in a single CSP. For instance, there is abundant research on the potential systemic risk exposures from CCPs and their default fund structures but little discussion among regulators on Cloud Concentration Risk in these risk assessments.

Specifically, with regard to the issue of Cloud Concentration Risk, we can segment this into two distinct categories: Firm-Specific and Systemic Concentration Risk.[24]

- **Firm-specific concentration risks:** These consist of risks due to cloud lock-in, a lack of unified data security and governance across CSPs, third-party operational resiliency concerns such as auditability, multi-cloud controls and cyber security exposures.
- **Systemic concentration risks:** These consist of risks that affect the stability of the financial system. This includes a lack of transparency on what critical applications currently have or will be migrated to a specific CSP. Regulators are also concerned about the systemic risk of having a concentration of many large financial service firms' critical application(s) all residing on the same CSP. These include applications such as payment, settlement and clearing systems.

This bifurcation of oversight complexities of Cloud Concentration Risk highlights the need for the Financial Services Industry, the CSPs and Regulators to collaboratively work towards resolving these issues. Fortunately, as illustrated in Section II, recent innovations in developing a comprehensive hybrid, multi-cloud architecture directly eliminate many of the regulatory concerns around Vendor Lock-in dangers as well as the lack of a unified multi-cloud data security and governance capability that help to address firm-specific Cloud Concentration Risks.

In addressing regulators' overall concerns around operational resilience, institutions must first specify the most important business functions that can impact financial stability risks. This requires a careful mapping of the systems, facilities, people, processes and third parties that support those business services. From this, institutions need to identify how the failure of an individual system or process running in the cloud environment could impact the operations of a specific business function and assess to what extent these systems or processes are capable of being substituted during disruption so that business services can continue to be delivered. Only when this thorough mapping has been completed can the institution begin to assess the vulnerabilities and concentration risk exposures that might result.

But this only addresses the operational risks that are specific to each institution. With the current high level of CSP vendor concentration, any disruption of a key CSP has the potential under certain circumstances to trigger wider systemic impacts. For instance, the European Systemic Risk Board's (ESRB) systemic cyber risk study[25] highlights a prominent type of incident effect whereby a "systemic cyber incident" could threaten financial stability. The key tipping point in these circumstances would occur when confidence in the financial system was so severely weakened that important financial institutions would cease all lending activity because they were no longer willing to lend, as opposed to being (technically) unable to lend. This is reflective of the Lehman Brother collapse on September 15, 2008 and the resulting impact across the wider financial system.

7.7 How should regulators address these challenges?

The obvious first step in addressing Cloud Concentration Risks is the need for transparency in identifying the types of applications each institution currently has running as well as future applications planned for each CSP. Ideally, this would incorporate a standardised classification system for key financial infrastructure capabilities.

This is critical for addressing systemic cloud concentration risks. As previously mentioned, systemic cloud concentration risk that can result from a significant number of institutions having a key application or market infrastructure capability (e.g., payment, settlement and clearing systems) concentrated in a single CSP.

Collecting this data permits regulators and industry participants to better identify potential contagion scenarios and trigger points that require regulatory oversight and possibly intervention. This is an area that will see significant regulatory and academic research.

In conclusion, the future of cloud computing in financial services is very bright with machine learning and artificial intelligence helping to drive innovation and automation across all lines of business. This will support the development of new products and services to help all customers benefit from the agility and speed that cloud computing provides. The role of technology is the foundation for this to be successful as well as helping to address many of the near-term regulatory risk concerns in migrating to the Cloud. We are confident that cloud computing will enable firms to be able to more effectively protect their customers and their business from many new challenges the future will bring.

Notes

1 See, for example, Calvanoz et al. (2019).
2 Financial Stability Board (2017).
3 Laurent et al. (2020).
4 Cloudera (2020a).
5 Gartner (2020).
6 Cloudera (2020b).
7 Cloudera (2020b).
8 Quantexa(2020).
9 Quantexa(2020).
10 Quantexa(2020).
11 Quantexa(2020).
12 There are many examples of ABM simulation models developed for systemic risk and policy evaluations. One example that would be similar in design is a paper by Bookstaber et al. (2018).
13 Financial Stability Board (2020).
14 Financial Stability Board (2018).
15 Westin and Zhang (2020).
16 Westin and Zhang (2020).
17 See Harmon (2020).
18 Strachan (2019).
19 Financial Stability Board (2019).
20 BCBS (2020).
21 Harmon (2020).

22 Bank of England (2020).
23 In 2017, the ESRB established the European Systemic Cyber Group (ESCG) to investigate systemic cyber risk and examine whether and how a cyber incident could cause a systemic crisis. The analysis conducted shows that a cyber incident could indeed evolve into a systemic cyber crisis that threatens financial stability with the potential to have serious negative consequences for the real economy. See ESRB (2020).
24 Harmon (2020).
25 ESRB (2020).

References

Bank of England (2020, January). How reliant are banks and insurers on cloud outsourcing? *Bank Overground*, January 17, 2020.

Basel Committee on Banking Supervision (2020, April). Progress in adopting the principles for effective risk data aggregation and risk reporting. *Bank for International Settlements*.

Bookstaber, R., Paddrik, M. & Tivanax, B. (2018). An agent-based model for financial vulnerability. *Journal of Economic Interaction and Coordination*, vol. 13, issue 2, 433–466.

Calvanoz, E., Calzolari, G., Denicolox, V. & Pastorello, S. (2019, December). Artificial intelligence, algorithmic pricing and collusion. *SSRN Working Paper*.

Cloudera (2020a). Cloudera machine learning. *Cloudera Product Assets*.

Cloudera (2020b). Cloudera data platform. *Cloudera Product Assets*.

European Systemic Risk Board (2020, February). Systemic cyber risk. *ESRB*.

Financial Stability Board (2017, November). Artificial intelligence and machine learning in financial services: Market developments and financial stability implications. *Financial Stability Board*.

Financial Stability Board (2018, November). FSB 2018 resolution report: "Keeping the pressure up". *Financial Stability Board*.

Financial Stability Board (2020, May). Guidance on financial resources to support CCP resolution and on the treatment of CCP equity in resolution. *Financial Stability Board Consultative Paper*.

Gartner (2020, January). Cloud data ecosystems emerge as the new data and analytics battleground. *Gartner*.

Harmon, R. (2018, May). Cloud concentration risk: Will this be our next systemic risk event? *Cloudera White Paper*.

Harmon, R. (2020, June). Cloud concentration risk II: What has changed in the past 2 years? *Cloudera White Paper*.

Hoque, I. (2019, November). The AI revolution is now: Why you should embrace AI decisioning. *Quantexa Blog*.

InsideBigData (2019, August). What good is data without context? *InsideBigData.Com*.

Laurent, M., Plantefeve, O., Tejada, M. & Weyenbergh, F. (2020, May). Banking models after COVID-19: Taking model-risk management to the next level. *McKinsey Paper*.

Psaltis, A. (2017). Streaming data understanding the real-time pipeline. *Manning Publications*.

Quantexa (2020, April). Situational awareness: Creating a contextual view to understand your commercial customers in a changing world. *Quantexa White Paper*.

Strachan, D. (2019, September). Financial services on the cloud: The regulatory approach. *Deloitte Blog*.

Westin, S. & Zhang, T. (2020, April). Agent-based modelling for central counterparty clearing risk: CCP Resilience - from one crisis to the next. *Deloitte*.

Chapter 8

Prospects and challenges of using artificial intelligence in the audit process

Emon Kalyan Chowdhury

8.1 Introduction

In the field of business, accounting is the area where the Information and Communication Technology (ICT) tools and latest technologies were used for the first time (Kwilinski, 2019). In accounting, the ICT tools and techniques were used to transform the manual accounting process to automation. Later on, the analysis and interpretation parts were also included (Carr, 1985). At the initial stage, the adoption rate of ICT in accounting was very slow due to the conservative attitude of accounting practitioners (Barras and Swann, 1984). In the early 1990s, as the competition was skyrocketing, organizations were trying to improve operational efficiency and to reduce expenses by replacing manual book-keeping and accounting process with automation (Manson, 2001). In our daily life, seldom we find any such area where the ICT is not used. Organizations use ICT tools for easy tasks like arithmetic calculations and for complex tasks like programming, logit modeling and Enterprise Resource Planning (ERP). Deloitte uses ICT tools for Visual Assurance while PricewaterhouseCooper (PwC) uses it for Risk Control Workbench. Most of the large-scale audit firms use computer technology in their audit process such as image processing, Electronic Fund Transfer (ETF) and Electronic Data Interchange (EDI) to ensure accuracy of their data assessment and improve the quality of audit report, audit judgment and overall audit services (Bell et al., 1998).

8.1.1 Background and relevant aspect of auditing

The term "audit" refers to a systematic process of objectively obtaining and evaluating evidence regarding assertions about economic actions and events ascertaining the degree of correspondence between the assertions and established criteria, and communicating the results to interested users (Hayes et al., 2014). Here, the systematic process refers to a structured, documented audit plan using different generally accepted techniques. Objectively it means an auditor is independent and works with certain objectives and gives expert opinion after examining and evaluating necessary documents. Assertions mean the assurance of management regarding the existence of economic actions that are reported in financial statements. Ascertaining the degree of correspondence indicates that the auditor verifies whether the presentation and disclosure of different accounts have been done in compliance with applicable financial reporting framework, such as International Financial Reporting Standards (IFRS), local law, regulations and standards. The objective of an audit is to issue a report containing the opinion of an auditor about the reliability of information, which may be used by a third party. Audits are classified into three types: audits of financial statements, operational audits and compliance audits.

1. Audit of financial statements: auditors examine financial statements to verify the true and fair view of financial position, results and cash flows.
2. Operational audits: auditors measure the performance of a unit or department of an organization.
3. Compliance audits: auditors assure whether an organization is complying the specific rules, regulations and procedures set by concerned higher authority.

The success of an audit depends on the appropriate planning, participation of concerned parties and smooth communication between client and the auditor. The audit process begins with the acceptance of an organization's offer by an auditor to audit their firm. The offer is made either to acquire a new client or to continue with an existing client. During the second stage, an auditor determines the volume of evidence and review required to assure that the financial statements of the clients are free from material misstatement. During the third stage, an auditor tests necessary supporting documents to support internal control and the fairness of the financial statements. Finally, the auditor issues an opinion on the financial position through completion of rigorous audit procedure. The manual audit process is very lengthy, time consuming, boring and costly; moreover, there is a possibility of committing human errors. Due to lack of security, data may be copied, stolen and destroyed.

In an organization, decisions are taken using pieces of information which are processed through ICT-based tools. Nowadays, business organizations generate information using Artificial Intelligence where no human intervention is required. An AI is a computer software that can behave like a human being and has the capacity to plan, learn and solve problems (Bakarich and O'Brien, 2020). In our daily life, we interact with AI in some form or another. Due to thriving inner capacity of AI, most of the businesses adopt it to stay competitive in today's challenging world. Audit being an indispensable part of a business, the application of AI in the audit process has become an important research topic. This study extensively covers different aspects of AI in the audit process such as the importance of using AI in the audit process; steps to convert manual to AI-based audit process; and impact of AI-based audit process on audit firms, business, customers, users of financial reports and other relevant stakeholders. Till date, no study was found converging the full-fledged implications of AI in the audit process on different parties. This study will impeccably bridge the gap and advance the existing literature by outspreading the scope to broader areas with relevant examples. Furthermore, the empirical interview-based study on current inadequacies and future prospects of applying AI in the audit process in Bangladesh will create another dimension of imminent research.

The chapter continues as follows. Section 2 focuses on literature review. Section 3 overviews the application of AI in auditing. Section 4 presents the required framework to implement AI in the audit process. Section 5 illustrates the digitalization process of audit activities and its impact on audit quality and audit firms. Section 6 cites few real examples of AI applications in the audit process. Section 7 shows the current scenario of application of AI in Bangladesh and Section 8 concludes the chapter.

8.2 Literature review

There have been dramatic changes in the accounting profession due to the advancement of latest technologies (Zhang et al., 2020). The objective of using AI in auditing is to reduce clerical work load (Ferreira and Morais, 2020). There are many repetitive and structured tasks in the audit process. AI can easily handle these complex and sensitive tasks with the highest accuracy and quickly (Agnew, 2016). Abdolmohammadi (1999) identified six audit stages and 50 sub-stages where AI can be applied by collecting data from 49 audit officers and thoroughly evaluating 332 audit tasks. Out of the total 332 tasks, 131 are structured, 135 are semi-structured and 66 are unstructured. Sixty-seven percent of the total tasks are substantive audit related where auditors need to take judgmental decisions on various grounds. He also revealed that automation can play a vital role in vouching, footing, verification and re-computation. Few structured works include checking the correctness of all paper documents, footing of cash payment and receipts journals, reconciliation of cash ledger posting and bank statement, re-computation of taxes, amortization and depreciations, verification of voucher register, cross-checking of supervisory review and inspection of subsidiary ledgers. Srinivasan (2016) developed a model for external audit activities and showed that human auditors will not be required at all if processes are automatized. However, he clearly did not mention exactly what activities will be taken over by the AI. There are few firms which use AI technology to analyze performance review, risk assessments, materiality assessment and going concern judgment, and to evaluate internal control systems (Baldwin et al., 2006). Issa et al. (2016) identified seven different audit stages from pre-planning to preparation of audit report where AI can be used to convert tasks in a sequential manner. Brennan et al. (2017) observed that AI is frequently used in data acquisition, data extraction, data comparison and data validation. AI helps to extract information from the data in such way which can be used to take major decision. Brennan et al. (2017) recommended to use AI in time-consuming processes such as transactions analysis, verification of receipts and payments, and generation of supporting data. Agnew (2016) mentioned that AI tools have the capacity to search complicated documents like image, contracts, vouchers, notes and other relevant accounting-related information. Rapoport (2016) found that AI can trace unusual transactions, data anomalies and abnormal equipment lease term.

Public accounting firms use AI technology to address auditing and assurance problems (Gillett, 1993). It can successfully detect fraudulent insurance claims (Viaene et al., 2002). Arthur Andersen uses WinProcess, Deloitte uses Touche, PwC uses Planet and KPMG uses KRisk to plan audit process and to manage risk assessment (Bell et al., 2002; Brown, 1991; Zhang and Zhou, 2004). Auditors have become more concerned about audit quality and the acceptability of their audit reports. Due to numerous accounting scandals in the last few decades, audit firms are now in serious image crisis and it is expected that the application of blockchain and AI may be a way out to restore their lost confidence and reliability. This chapter will focus on how to apply AI in the audit process to ensure more transparency and count each document to avoid unexpected errors.

8.3 Artificial intelligence in auditing

8.3.1 Artificial intelligence

The concept of AI is very extensive and diverse. It refers to the use of technology which can imitate human behavior like decision-making, visual perception, language translation and speech recognition. Machine learning (ML) is one of the dimensions of AI. ML can perform complex, lengthy and boring statistical and mathematical calculations very quickly without any error. ML-based models are capable to categorize and foresee new data point (Kazim and Koshiyama, 2020).

Auditors utilize machine-learning–based models to detect frauds, and analyze unstructured data such as posts in social media, audio clips and emails through deep learning. It also helps auditors to interact with key parties of an organization like Chief Financial Officer (CFO), board members and the audit committee members. AI analyzes various types of contracts at least time and cost with greater accuracy and quality. The ongoing pressure on auditors to deliver authentic information on the true and fair view of the organizations is increasing the importance of using AI in the audit process. Along with ML, AI also covers Expert Systems (ESs) and Neural Networks (NNs). Few practical examples of AI are stated below.

Profiling: Using personal data such as phone call lists, food habits, records of credit card usage and details of foreign trips, AI figures out the nature of personality, likes-dislikes and interests of a person, and predicts the future moves. Kreditech, a German online lending company, provides data points up to 20,000 to the loan applicant based on their performance on social media, nature of social media friends and e-commerce transactions records (Fowler, 2013).

Autonomous machines: These are smart machines which can perform tasks themselves. Using natural language processing system, a machine can communicate with human beings. Different drones, house-cleaning robots, Google translate and self-driven cars made by Tesla are few examples of autonomous machine.

Decision-making capacity: Based on factual and digitally created data, machine can take decisions without any human intervention. In the banking sector, AI can decide whether to sanction a loan or not to a party by verifying the relevant data. In the case of human resource management, AI is used to select the desired candidates based on their performances in the online aptitude test.

Natural language processing: It is a computer program that has the ability to interact with human being through speech generation and recognition. Few popular examples include Apple's Siri, Google's Assistant, Amazon's Alexa and Microsoft's Cortana.

Facial recognition: Trained algorithms are used to capture the past records of a person using his/her photo. In China, police department uses smart glasses through facial recognition technology in different railway stations to spot criminals. The system has the capacity to detect 10,000 faces from a data bank within 100 milliseconds (Chan, 2018).

Image recognition: It is such a system which can recognize age, and mental and physical condition of a person. In the healthcare industry, using computer vision and image recognition technology, robots record informative timeline of patients to analyze their emotional state while they get admitted, stay and get discharged from the hospitals. Google uses this technology to search the records of a person through the image search option (Choudhury, 2019).

8.3.2 Use of expert systems in auditing

ESs are software-based systems that assemble the excellence of few experts to detect probable troubles which deter the delivery of quality service. It helps to make better decisions (Arnold et al., 2016). ES includes both system and process to replicate the decision-making capacity of experts (Baldwin-Morgan and Stone, 1995). They proposed a two-dimensional framework to solve multiple effects of ES on accounting firms. The first dimension is levels of impact such as task, individual, organization and industry and the second dimension is the categories of effect such as environment, education, expertise, effectiveness and efficiency. If both the dimensions are taken into consideration, it helps to reduce potential mistakes and take effective accounting decisions. Dillard and Yuthas (2001) showed that ES can also be used in the audit process adhering to the ethical issues. They used the theory of "the responsible self" to define the limit of ethical areas and a mechanism for detecting important actions to have a regular communication among the concerned parties who are supposed to be influenced by the implementation of ES.

8.3.3 Use of neural network in auditing

A neural network (NN) is a sequence of algorithms that attempts to identify interrelations among the set of data in such a way that replicates the way a human brain works. An NN is used to predict future trend by analyzing large past database. As audit decisions are based on proofs generated from the historical accounting data, the importance of using NN in the audit process is increasing gradually. Applying evaluation of analytical procedure expectations on financial data, Green and Choi (1997) developed an NN fraud classification model. This model helps auditors to conduct a substantive test when a financial statement is classified as deceitful. Bell and Carcello (2000) developed a fraud detection tool called the "logistic regression model" which can successfully predict the possibility of fraudulent financial reporting of the clients based on few specific risk components, namely, fast company growth, internal control environment, management's deceitful information to the auditors and varying relative profitability. They applied the model in 77 cases and observed that this gives better result than the practicing auditors in estimating risks.

8.4 Framework for including AI in auditing

The role of internal audit in AI is to provide necessary guideline on how an organization can evaluate, understand and communicate the extent to which AI can influence the organization's ability to add values in different time periods like short, medium and long term.

Internal auditors can apply the auditing framework prescribed by the Institute of Internal Auditors (IIA)[26] in designing AI-based services for the organization. Figure 8.1 depicts the

Figure 8.1 AI-based auditing framework.

Source: The Institute of Internal Auditors (IIA).

AI-based framework having three major components – namely, AI strategy, governance and human factor – and seven elements – namely, cyber resilience, AI competencies, measuring performance, data quality, data architecture and infrastructure, ethics and the black box. The following section contains a brief introduction on the AI-based audit framework.

8.4.1 Components

8.4.1.1 AI strategy

An organization designs its own AI strategy according to its own requirements to exploit the best benefits that AI can offer. Every organization has its own digital data strategy, and the AI strategy will be an important addition to it. Organizations can perform much better if they tie the AI strategy with their existing digital capability (Chui, 2017). An organization must fulfill the following criteria to enable a successful AI strategy:

1. Clear goal on AI-related affairs
2. Sufficient budget for AI-based research and development
3. Preparation to extract the benefits and to combat the threats related to AI
4. Internal audit should make the top management and board members understand about the importance of having AI strategy to stay ahead of its competitors

8.4.1.2 Governance

AI governance includes procedures, structures and processes to manage, direct and monitor organization's AI-related activities which play a vital role in achieving the desired goals. The structure and scope of governance depends on the nature and type of the organization. AI governance should be result-oriented which will comply the ethical, legal and social issues. An organization should have a sufficient number of skilled and experienced people to oversee the AI-based day-to-day activities.

8.4.1.3 Human factor

Due to human errors in the manual system, the world is now flipping to automation. Behind every human-based algorithm there is a human factor; therefore, human errors and prejudices influence the performance of these algorithms. To reduce the risk of human error, the following issues need to address:

1. The algorithms should be aligned with organization's main goal
2. AI results should be used for ethical, legal and responsible purposes
3. AI should be free from human biases and errors

8.4.2 Elements

8.4.2.1 Cyber resilience

It refers to the capacity of an organization to stay prepared, respond and recover from any unexpected cyber-attacks. It is a continuous process and helps the organization to keep the risk of losses due to cyber-attack as low as possible. Cyber resilience broadly covers the following issues (EY, 2017):

1. Identify, construct and protect organization's systems
2. Detect, respond and communicate system-related issues
3. Run testing systems and keep recovery plans

8.4.2.2 AI competencies

AI competency means ability of an organization to adopt AI-based operations. It includes software, hardware, skilled people, budget, necessary supports from peer and approving authority.

8.4.2.3 Data quality

It emphasizes on the reliability, accuracy and completeness of well-defined data on which AI algorithms are built. Data should be highly customizable and perfectly communicated among the connected systems.

8.4.2.4 Data architecture and infrastructure

It includes detailed guidelines on how the organization's data will be managed and used. It also focuses on the privacy issue, roles and responsibilities of data, and collection, usage, storage and destruction of data.

8.4.2.5 Measuring performance

An organization measures the performance of activities on the basis of achievement of goals. In an AI-based organization, the activities should be AI driven so that they can play a role in achieving the goals; thus, the measurement of performance becomes easier. Top management needs to monitor the AI-based activities on a regular basis.

8.4.2.6 Ethics

Designing AI for an organization should adhere to few ethical issues. The people who are behind the designing, development, decision process and outcomes of AI should remain accountable. The values and norms of the user group should be given due importance. The AI process should be easily understandable and free from any sort of biasness.

8.4.2.7 Black box

According to the *Cambridge Dictionary*, black box refers to an electronic device that keeps the records of a driver's driving information. The internal mechanism of this device is unknown to the user. In auditing, an auditor can verify the input data and the output data but he/she totally remains in dark about the data process. This sophisticated algorithm is known as black box. An auditor takes physical printouts of input and output documents and conducts testing of such documents.

Carlson (1978) stated that a basic decision process has three important parts such as intelligence, design and choice. Intelligence includes collection of data, specification of goals, analysis of problems, authentication of data and rationalization of problems. During the design stage, processed data is assembled, objectives are quantified and alternatives are created by assigning relevant weight to each alternative. Third is choice where the desired alternative(s) is(are) selected after conducting through analysis of each alternative. Therefore, AI is an important part of a decision process that is used in both managerial and technical operations in modern business world.

8.5 Transformation of the audit process

Traditional auditing plays three important roles, namely, monitoring, information and insurance as a part of governance (Wallace, 2004).

1. In the monitoring role, managers who are known as agents reduce agency costs by improving the quality of accounting information through control and, hence, limit their discretionary powers.

2. Shareholders and other stakeholders take important decisions based on the information generated by the managers. Auditors ensure reliability and fairness of these information by discharging their information role.

3. In the insurance role, auditors ensure that the information which is transferred to other organization truly expresses the financial position of the company and there is nothing to hide. However, it cannot solve the problem of information asymmetry between shareholders and managers.

Under this circumstance, the principal role of an auditor is to assure the investors that there exists no risk in relying on the information of organization. Technology can help auditors to make this job easier by accelerating data processing rate and reducing human errors. Comprehensive and integrated Accounting Information System reduces information asymmetry between managers and stakeholders and the risk associated with the transfer of information. Therefore, the roles of auditors will be occupied by technological developments. Jeacle (2017) and Andon et al. (2014) assess that a new audit role will emerge which will be expanded to other areas of assurance such as e-commerce, social and environmental responsibilities, reliability of information systems, cyber security and performance measurements, although it depends on the legitimacy and ability of audit firms to adopt these new changes.

8.5.1 *Impact of digitalization on audit quality*

Governance mechanism has its own limits. The notorious financial scams of Enron in 2001, WorldCom and Tyco in 2002, Healthsouth and Freddie Mac in 2003, American International Group in 2005, Lehman Brothers in 2008 and Satyam in 2009 proved that existing governance mechanism can be manipulated by managers in their own way. These loop holes necessitate introducing a new auditing system. Quality of audit lies with detecting the inconsistencies in the financial statements and reveals them to relevant parties. The higher the quality of audit, the better the control of managers and it will be more helpful for decision makers to take investment decisions. But the quality of audit requires efficient auditors' efforts and investment, which has a negative relation with the earnings of an organization (Chen et al., 2019). Many organizations in the world are now digitalizing their process to exploit the benefits of big data and ultra-modern digital tools to provide quality services to their valuable parties with more relevance. The application of big data eases the analysis of each and every data, leaving the outdated sampling method far behind. This helps auditors to eliminate the risk of audit by avoiding sampling method in which a few vital and sensitive data may be ignored. It also helps to improve the risk assessment process and judgment capacity by detecting all the irregularities.

Big data also aids to use current data along with historical data which helps to foresee future sales and expenses and of course with a clear vision of sustainability. Since the extra burden is taken away by the technology, managers can focus on more important issues and thus can enhance the quality of corporate governance.

8.5.2 *Impact of digitalization on audit firms*

The main reason behind digitalizing the audit firms is to respond to the market demand. The intense competition and expectations of clients for better services compel audit firms to convert their process (Porter and Heppelmann, 2014). Audit firms have no other options but to stay innovative and to embrace technological advancements to win over the tough competitors in this challenging world (Van den Broek and van Veenstra, 2018). The research of Macaulay (2016) indicated that 58% of the audit process would be influenced by new technologies. Leading audit firms such as PwC, Deloitte and KPMG would massively invest in artificial intelligence tools (Kokina and Davenport, 2017). Montes and Goertzel (2019) observed that audit firms prioritize adopting artificial intelligence and big data among other digital tools to convert their audit process. Researchers are continuously trying to ensure the best use of big data in conducting audit. For example, Kim et al. (2017) instrumented how to use the big data to identify, classify and eliminate redundant data in a protected way. Zhang et al. (2015) found that big data helps auditors to mitigate data gap like identification of gap in data structure, finding incomplete data, data contradictions, aggregation and confidentiality. Since data collection and processing will be taken care by technology, auditors can spend their valuable time to analyze data (Krahel and Titera, 2015). Big data automatically rectifies data (Kogan, 2014) and influences auditors toward their judgment and decision-making process. Big data can be used as a proxy for the so-called audit evidence (Yoon et al., 2015), to detect frauds (Nigrini, 2019) and to measure the level of risk for clients (Brown et al., 2015). However, by digitalizing audit operations, audit firms can provide quality services to the clients. It helps to predict the possibility of bankruptcy and detect any such alarming issues of clients (Cao et al., 2015). Although there are many benefits of using artificial intelligence or big data in an audit firm, safety and privacy should be given due importance to mitigate the risks related to cyber security.

8.5.3 Steps to transform manual audit operations to AI-based

Figure 8.2 illustrates the step-by-step transformation process of manual to AI-based audit operations.

Step 1: Purpose and Structure of Algorithm

The key objectives of applying the algorithm need to specify. In this case, other established algorithms for similar objectives may be studied. The important factors to generate desired results need to incorporate. Necessary regulatory compliances must follow for setting objectives with the application of artificial intelligence.

Step 2: Issues on the Sources of Data

The data need to be collected from the original sources. If the source is not original, it should be reliable. The data collection method, changes of pattern, frequency, entry method and characteristics of data need to address to ensure the quality of data. If there are other sources of data for which the model or machine is not trained, then we need to keep a provision for that.

Step 3: Pre-processing Data

There should have been necessary clarifications and options to solve for any such missing and incomplete data. Selection methods and standardization for training and testing datasets need to elaborate.

Step 4: Constructing Model

In constructing model, detailed information on the AI techniques need to be provided. Reasons for selecting a particular technique or rejecting other techniques need to be explained. If the algorithms are required to modify, the criteria need to be specify. There should have been necessary information on the sources, pattern, criteria and computer programming packages of codes of algorithms.

Step 5: Testing

The metrics for testing the accuracy of model need to be mentioned. Information regarding sensitivity of algorithms toward minor changes in model need to postulate.

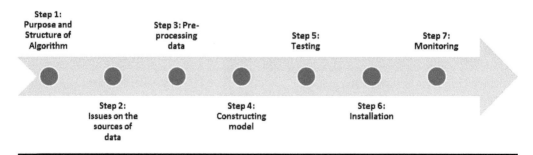

Figure 8.2 Conversion process of manual to AI-based audit operations.

Step 6: Installation

The implementation process of the AI model in practice should be mentioned. Necessary guidelines regarding involvement of different parties should be framed. The model should rigorously be reviewed by qualified third party before final installation. The final results and the objectives need to reconcile very carefully.

Step 7: Monitoring

Monitoring measures the capacity of the organization to implement, maintain and supervise the AI model. It also compels concerned parties to discharge their respective responsibilities and to maintain regulatory compliances in achieving organization's goals in a social and ethical way.

8.6 Applications of artificial intelligence in auditing – few examples

The real application of AI in accounting and audit process is possible if practitioners have the positive attitude. Very handful firms use AI in the audit process fully, many firms apply partially and most of the firms are still at the development stage. They apply AI for predictive and analysis purposes by examining the total population rather than using samples.

8.6.1 KPMG

KPMG uses AI in their audit process for its reasoning competences. It executed a contact with IBM's Watson in March 2016 to provide this service. The technology uses Application Program Interfaces (APIs) for a wide range of purposes such as extractions of document entity to facial recognitions (Lee, 2016). It applies advanced forecasting ability of AI in auto racing firms like McLaren Applied Technologies (Sinclair, 2015).

8.6.2 Deloitte

Deloitte uses AI to enhance its cognitive capabilities in the audit process and create a base to receive services from different vendors. According to the Chief Innovation Officer, Deloitte applies AI for document review, inventory counts, confirmations, predictive risk analytics, disclosure research and preparation of client request lists (Kokina and Davenport, 2017). Deloitte partnered with Kira Systems to review complicated documents such as leases, contracts, employment agreements, invoices and other legal documents. The system can interact with human beings and enhance capacity in extracting more relevant information over time (Whitehouse, 2015).

8.6.3 PwC

PwC uses "Halo" to analyze accounting journals. Although few are passed using human-support–based business intelligence, rest are done using automated algorithms (PricewaterhouseCoopers, 2016).

8.6.4 Ernst and Young (EY)

EY uses big data analytics in audits to process clients' large datasets. It engages its clients in this process to ease the total audit process and to make the clients comfortable with the AI process.

8.6.5 K.Coe Isom

This is a consulting and accounting firm specialized for food- and agriculture-based business. It applies AI to diagnose complete financial conditions and produce exclusive reports for clients. During the initial stage, it used AI to analyze the extent of materiality and used low-, medium- and high-risk items for the test purpose. During the risk assessment test period, AI detected two such transactions which would literally be impossible in a traditional process. The customized AI of K.Coe Isom allows reassessment of audit planning and testing procedure.

8.6.6 Doeren Mayhew

In a traditional audit process, audit firms need to wait for long time to get reply on any such query and require further investigation for justifications. Doeren Mayhew solved this slow process of mutual communication by applying AI. Both the parties share real-time data and thus can complete the audit process efficiently and quickly.

8.6.7 CohnReznick

CohnRezick is an advisory, assurance and tax consultancy firm currently enjoying competitive advantage by adopting AI technology to provide security of public funds for local agency, state and federal. It also assists government agencies to enhance their operating efficiency, enhance service quality and ensure job satisfaction of employees. By applying AI both CohnRezick and government are improving the public trust and ensuring transparency of responsibilities at different managerial and operational levels taking every data into consideration.

8.6.8 The Association of Certified Fraud Examiners (ACFE)

The ACFE is a professional body to examine frauds. It mainly conducts research on tools used to detect frauds, provide training on frauds and produce information related to frauds. It also offers professional degree on frauds called "Certified Fraud Examiner". According to ACFE's reports, two out of three fraud cases are related to misrepresentation of financial statement and misappropriation of asset. Both types of frauds are done by manipulating or tempering records. It uses AI to detect these types of frauds as AI can easily detect any sort of manipulation of records with 100% accuracy rate.

8.7 Prospects of an AI-based audit process in Bangladesh

In Bangladesh, automation is used partially to reduce the burden of complex and tedious operating process. The use of AI is seen in some specific areas such as ride-sharing, flight and hotel booking, natural language processing for Bangla and real-time mapping (Samarajiva, 2020).

The Bangladesh government is moving ahead with the mission "Digital Bangladesh" to ensure transparency, justice, accountability, human rights, democracy and delivery of government services to the people of Bangladesh by utilizing the modern technology to improve the day-to-day life-style. In line with this mission, different organizations are now adopting and implementing AI in their operations gradually. There are more than 160 million population in Bangladesh, of which 34% are young and extremely technology freak (Deowan, 2020). Bangladesh is thriving to accustom itself with the wave of technological development in different industrial sectors. The recent concepts – namely Big Data, Artificial Intelligence, Internet of Things and Blockchain – are attaining huge attentions and being popular among Bangladeshi people; therefore, AI has an incredible future in Bangladesh.

To know the current scenario and future prospects of applications of AI in the audit process in Bangladesh, ten renowned accounting professionals and ten key officials from reputed organizations were interviewed. The summary of the interviews is presented below in three parts. The first part characterizes issues of both audit firms and business organizations. The second part deals with issues related to audit firms and the third part focuses on business organizations.

8.7.1 General aspects

The application of AI requires compliances of certain issues such as cyber security, rules and regulations, different acts, ethics and privacy of data. These compliance issues should be addressed first to extract the best outcome from the AI-based society. The scope of AI application in the audit process needs to define clearly. A central national body is required to form consisting of experts from different areas to create, develop and monitor framework and compliance-related issues. A comprehensive data bank of different sectors at least for several decades is required to help long-term data comparison, and for analysis of financial and other performances. To reduce the cost of data collection, storage and distribution, a culture of data sharing and dependency network system needs to develop, which will also confirm checks and balances among the available AI-based systems. AI-based audit should be made compulsory for all the organizations irrespective of sectors, nature and size. There should have been a dedicated AI department or extension of IT department like other functional departments in all the organizations to ensure smooth functioning and unremitting services.

8.7.2 Audit firm specific aspects

Assuring audit quality is the main concern of every audit firm. To ensure desired audit quality, firms are continuously trying to embrace the technological changes to cope up with the market demand. In Bangladesh, advanced audit firms commonly follow Computer-Assisted Auditing Tools and Techniques (CAATTs). It helps to analyze massive volumes of data. Auditors use this technology to measure specific risk like in the case of insurance claim; this technology automatically closes the process after termination of policy and in the case of warranty, any claim is rejected after the expiration of warranty period. However, the use of automation is not the application of AI in the audit process. Financially capable audit firms still cannot use AI in the audit process for absence of few necessary groundworks as mentioned in the above section and lack of clients' preparations.

8.7.3 Business organization aspects

In Bangladesh, most of the companies use specially designed software for recording the transactions, inventory management, preparation of financial statements and analysis of the results. Few firms use customized audit management software in consultation with audit firms to complete the audit tasks within short time with more accuracy and efficiency. As a result, auditors do not need to visit firms physically to collect and verify documents as data are stored in the cloud server and are reachable from any place through smart devices. Software service providers customize their software according to the requirements of the clients. Standardized software helps to compare the performance of the departments across the company over the period of time. Based on the nature and financial capacity of the firms, the software comes in different categories. Latest audit software can perform different types of audits, namely, financial audit, process audit, manufacturing audit, safety audit, product audit, compliance audit, internal and external audit. Although initial installation costs are very high, it helps to reduce the operating and office expenses in the long run by smart sizing human resources, using limited space, saving additional document generation costs, etc. Due to initial high installation costs, insufficient supply of expert people and most importantly lack of top management's support and interest, many firms use the manual audit process. The manual audit process requires huge time and the possibility of human error is very high. Auditors need to use sampling technique which sometimes gives misleading results and thus reduces the quality of reports. Last but not the least, many companies in Bangladesh are not psychologically ready to nurture the culture of automation for many reasons like hiding revenues, showing fabricated expenses, making illegal profits and avoiding taxes, duties and excises.

8.8 Conclusion

Artificial intelligence is now being extensively used in different areas of accounting and finance. Astoundingly, the implementation rate of this technology is very sluggish in the field of auditing. Big data technology has tremendous potentiality to change the way now auditors work. It can bring turnaround change in the mindset of users of financial statements by ensuring reliability, confidence, stability and fairness. The slow adoption rate of big data technology in auditing may put this sector under serious challenge. To make different parties familiar with the concept of using big data in auditing, massive training program is required to launch and curricula of different courses and programs should be updated. Accounting and auditing standards should also be revised with necessary guidelines on how to adopt and use technology in the process of auditing. Inclusion of big data technology with traditional audit techniques and expert judgment ensures rigorous analytical procedures and helps to prepare quality report. Despite having many benefits, lack of objectivity, insufficient studies on the existing system and human biasness may create obstacle in achieving the desired goals. There should have been sufficient transparency in developing an AI-based system as "black box" processing remains behind the scene to auditors, regulatory authority, government and even the person who inputs the data in the system. A transparent process is a pre-requisite for taking sensitive decisions and giving judgments on different audit affairs. This chapter comprehensively focused on the technical aspects of AI, benefits and challenges of using AI in the audit process, conversion of manual to AI-based audit process in a few simple steps and the impact of digitalization of audit process on different concerned parties citing few real examples. This chapter delineated the prospects and challenges of applying AI in a developing market economy with reference to Bangladesh. As per opinion of expert professionals and successful businessmen, due to the absence of sufficient groundworks and orthodox mindset of top management of business organizations, the use of AI in the audit process is stuck and may take several years to come. This study used interview method to collect data for nationwide lockdown due to COVID-19 pandemic crisis. In future, researchers may apply other methods of data collection and can examine the cost-benefit of implementing AI in the audit process for both audit firms and business organizations.

Bibliography

Abdolmohammadi, M. J. (1999). A comprehensive taxonomy of audit task structure, professional rank and decision aids for behavioral research. *Behavioral Research in Accounting, 11*, 51.

Agnew, H. (2016). Auditing: Pitch battle. *Financial Times.* Retrieved from https://www.ft.com/content/268637f6-15c8-11e6-9d9800386a18e39d

Andon, P., Free, C., & Sivabalan, P. (2014). The legitimacy of new assurance providers: Making the cap fit. *Accounting, Organizations and Society, 39*(2), 75–96.

Arnold, V., Collier, P. A., Leech, S. A., & Sutton, S. G. (2004). Impact of intelligent decision aids on expert and novice decision-makers' judgements. *Accounting and Finance, 44*, 1–26.

Bakarich, K. M., & O'Brien, P. (2020). The robots are coming… But aren't here yet: The use of artificial intelligence technologies in the public accounting profession. *Journal of Emerging Technologies in Accounting.* doi:10.2308/JETA-19-11-20-47

Baldwin, A. A., Brown, C. E., & Trinkle, B. S. (2006). Opportunities for artificial intelligence development in the accounting domain: The case for auditing. *Intelligent Systems in Accounting, Finance & Management: International Journal, 14*(3), 77–86. doi:10.1002/isaf.277

Baldwin-Morgan, A. A., & Stone, M. F. (1995). A matrix model of expert systems impacts. *Expert Systems with Applications, 9*(4), 599–608.

Barras, R., & Swann, J. (1984). *The adoption and impact of information technology in the UK accountancy profession.* Technical Change Centre.

Bell, T. B., Bedard, J. C., Johnstone, K. M., & Smith, E. F. (2002). KRiskSM: A computerized decision aid for client acceptance and continuance risk assessments. *Auditing: A Journal of Practice & Theory, 21*(2), 97–113.

Bell, T. B., & Carcello, J. V. (2000). A decision aid for assessing the likelihood of fraudulent financial reporting. *Auditing: A Journal of Practice and Theory, 19*(1), 169–182.

Bell, T. B., Knechel, W. R., Payne, J. L., & Willingham, J. J. (1998). An empirical investigation of the relationship between the computerisation of accounting system and the incidence and size of audit differences. *Auditing: A Journal of Practice and Theory, 17*(1), 13–26.

Brennan, B., Baccala, M., & Flynn, M. (2017). *Artificial intelligence comes to financial statement audits.* CFO. com (February 2). Retrieved from http://ww2.cfo.com/auditing/2017/02/artiïñÁcial-intelligence-audits

Brown, C. E. (1991). Expert systems in public accounting: Current practice and future directions. *Expert Systems with Applications, 3*(1), 3–18.

Brown-Liburd, H., Issa, H., & Lombardi, D. (2015). Behavioral implications of Big Data's impact on audit judgment and decision making and future research directions. *Accounting Horizons, 29*(2), 451–468.

Cao, M., Chychyla, R., & Stewart, T. (2015). Big Data analytics in financial statement audits. *Accounting Horizons, 29*(2), 423–429.

Carlson, E. D. (1978). An approach for designing decision support systems. *ACM SIGMIS Database: The DATABASE for Advances in Information Systems, 10*(3), 3–15. doi:10.1145/1040730.1040731

Carr, J. G. (1985). *Summary and conclusions. IT and the accountant.* Aldershort: Gower Publishing Company Ltd/ACCA.

Chan, T, R. (2018). Chinese police are using facial-recognition glasses to scan travelers. *Independent.* Retrieved from https://www.independent.co.uk/news/world/asia/china-police-facial-recognition-sunglasses-security-smart-tech-travellers-criminals-a8206491.html

Chen, Q., Jiang, X., & Zhang, Y. (2019). The effects of audit quality disclosure on audit effort and investment efficiency. *The Accounting Review, 94*(4), 189–214.

Choudhury, A. (2019), 8 uses cases of image recognition that we see in our daily lives. *Analytics India Magazine.* Retrieved from https://analyticsindiamag.com/8-uses-cases-of-image-recognition-that-we-see-in-our-daily-lives/

Chui, M. (2017). Artificial intelligence the next digital frontier?. *McKinsey and Company Global Institute, 47*, 3–6.

Deowan, S. A. (2020). *Artificial intelligence: Bangladesh perspective, The Business Standard.* Retrieved from https://tbsnews.net/tech/artificial-intelligence-bangladesh-perspective-44017

Dillard, J. F., & Yuthas, K. (2001). A responsibility ethic for audit expert systems. *Journal of Business Ethics, 30*(4), 337.

EY. (2017). Cyber resiliency: Evidencing a well-thought-out strategy. *EYGM Limited.* Retrieved from https://www.ey.com/Publication/vwLUAssets/EY-cyber-resiliency-evidencing-a-well-thought-out-strategy/$FILE/EY-cyber-resiliency-evidencing-a-well-thought-out-strategy.pdf

Ferreira, C., & Morais, A. I. (2020). Analysis of the relationship between company characteristics and key audit matters disclosed. *Revista Contabilidade & FinanÃ§as, 31*(83), 262–274.

Fowler, N. (2013) *Samwer brothers' Global Founders Capital co-invests millions in Wonga rival Kreditech.* Retrieved from https://web.archive.org/web/20130423160012/http://venturevillage.eu/oliver-samwers-global-founders-capital-kreditech

Gillett P. R. (1993). Automated dynamic audit programme tailoring: An expert system approach. *Auditing: A Journal of Practice and Theory, 12*(2), 173âŞ-189.

Green, B. P., & Choi, J. H. (1997). Assessing the risk of management fraud through neural network technology. *uditing: A Journal of Practice and Theory, 16*(1), 14âŞ-28.

Hayes, R., Wallage, P., & Gortemaker, H. (2014). *Principles of auditing: An introduction to international standards on auditing.* Pearson Higher Ed.

Issa, H., Sun, T., & Vasarhelyi, M. A. (2016). Research ideas for artificial intelligence in auditing: The formalization of audit and workforce supplementation. *Journal of Emerging Technologies in Accounting, 13*(2), 1–20. doi:10.2308/jeta-10511

Jeacle, I. (2017). Constructing audit society in the virtual world: The case of the online reviewer. *Accounting, Auditing & Accountability Journal, 30*(1), 18–37.

Kazim, E., & Koshiyama, A. (2020). *A Review of the ICO's Draft Guidance on the AI Auditing Framework.* Available at SSRN: https://ssrn.com/abstract=3599226

Kim, D., Song, S., & Choi, B. Y. (2017). *Data deduplication for data optimization for storage and network systems.* Springer International Publishing.

Kogan, A., Alles, M. G., Vasarhelyi, M. A., & Wu, J. (2014). Design and evaluation of a continuous data level auditing system. *Auditing: A Journal of Practice & Theory, 33*(4), 221–245.

Kokina, J., & Davenport, T. H. (2017). The emergence of artificial intelligence: How automation is changing auditing. *Journal of Emerging Technologies in Accounting, 14*(1), 115–122.

Krahel, J. P., & Titera, W. R. (2015). Consequences of Big Data and formalization on accounting and auditing standards. *Accounting Horizons, 29*(2), 409–422.

Kwilinski, A. (2019). Implementation of blockchain technology in accounting sphere. *Academy of Accounting and Financial Studies Journal, 23*, 1–6.

Lee, D. (2016). KPMG recruits IBM Watson for cognitive tech audits, insights. *Accounting Today* (March 8). Retrieved from http://www. accountingtoday.com/news/kpmg-recruits-ibm-watson-for-cognitive-tech-audits-insights

Macaulay, M. T. (2016). Financial Executive, How cognitive tech is revolutionizing the audit. *Business Source Premier, 32*, 18–24.

Manson, S., McCartney, S., & Sherer, M. (2001). Audit automation as control within audit firms. *Accounting, Auditing and Accountability Journal, 14*(1), 109–130.

Montes, G. A., & Goertzel, B. (2019). Distributed, decentralized, and democratized artificial intelligence. *Technological Forecasting and Social Change, 141*, 354–358.

Nigrini, M. (2019). The patterns of the numbers used in occupational fraud schemes. *Managerial Auditing Journal, 34*(5), 606–626. doi:10.1108/MAJ-11-2017-1717

Porter, M. E., & Heppelmann, J. E. (2014). How smart, connected products are transforming competition. *arvard Business Review, 92*(11), 64–88.

PricewaterhouseCoopers. (2016). *Halo for Journals.* Retrieved from http://halo.pwc.com/

Rapoport, M. (2016). Auditing firms count on technology for backup. *Wall Street Journal.*

Samarajiva, R. (2020). Is it time for a policy on artificial intelligence? *The Daily Star.* Retrieved from https://www.thedailystar.net/opinion/perspective/news/it-time-policy-artificial-intelligence-1733191

Sinclair, N. (2015). How KPMG is using Formula 1 to transform audit. *CA Today* (October 27). Available at: https://www.icas.com/catoday-news/kpmg-and-formula-one-big-data

Srinivasan, V. (2016). Will financial auditors become extinct?. In Venkat Srinivasan (ed.), *The Intelligent Enterprise in the Era of Big Data*, 171–183. New York: Wiley. doi:10.1002/9781118834725.ch7

Van den Broek, T., & van Veenstra, A. F. (2018). Governance of big data collaborations: How to balance regulatory compliance and disruptive innovation. *Technological Forecasting and Social Change, 129*, 330–338.

Viaene, S., Derrig, R. A., Baesens, B., & Dedene, G. (2002). A comparison of stateâĂŘofâĂŘtheâĂŘart classification techniques for expert automobile insurance claim fraud detection. *Journal of Risk and Insurance, 69*(3), 373–421.

Wallace, W. A. (2004). The economic role of the audit in free and regulated markets: A look back and a look forward. *Research in Accounting Regulation, 17*, 267–298.

Whitehouse, T. (2015). The technology transforming your annual audit. *Compliance Week* (December 1). Retrieved from https://www. complianceweek.com/news/news-article/the-technology-transforming-your-annual-audit#.WGQkebYrLPA

Yoon, K., Hoogduin, L., & Zhang, L. (2015). Big Data as complementary audit evidence. *Accounting Horizons, 29*(2), 431–438.

Zhang, J., Yang, X., & Appelbaum, D. (2015). Toward effective Big Data analysis in continuous auditing. *Accounting Horizons, 29*(2), 469–476.

Zhang, Y., Xiong, F., Xie, Y., Fan, X., & Gu, H. (2020). The impact of artificial intelligence and blockchain on the accounting profession. *IEEE Access, 8*, 110461–110477.

Zhao, N., Yen, D. C., & Chang, I. C. (2004). Auditing in the eâĂŘcommerce era. *Information Management & Computer Security, 12*(5), 389–400

Chapter 9

Web usage analysis
Pillar 3 information assessment in turbulent times

Anna Pilkova, Michal Munk, Petra Blazekova and Lubomir Benko

9.1 Introduction

The stability of the financial system is a long-term challenge for governments, regulators and academics. The 2007–2009 financial crisis proved stability's importance and highlighted the weaknesses of the financial regulatory system around the world which was not able to avoid the failures and losses generated by the turbulence in the banking industry. Regulators, policy makers and academics learnt many lessons from this period and have attempted to fix the identified weaknesses. One of these areas is market discipline. There are different definitions of this term and one of them is a mechanism to use by market participants to discipline risk-taking by financial institutions. Basel supervisors stressed this mechanism's importance in the Basel II architecture (BCBS, 2006) by the introduction of Pillar 3 components that complemented the other two pillars: Pillar 1 – minimum risk-based capital requirements and other quantitative requirements; Pillar 2 – supervisory review processes. At that time, it aimed to provide meaningful regulatory information to market participants on a consistent basis and to be able to assess a bank's risk. However, the 2007–2009 financial crisis additionally exposed some weaknesses in Basel II and also with Pillar 3. In Basel III (a revision of Basel II after the financial crisis), Pillar 3 started to become more detailed, structured and with information more frequently disclosed. Lengthy discussion among regulators and stakeholders on the new content, structure and frequency of information disclosure just confirmed some authors' opinions that it would have been more accurate to label Pillar 3 "information disclosure" rather than "market discipline" (Flannery & Bliss, 2019). Above all, in Europe the ideas on global financial stability and cross-border banking have to be achieved through centralization in the European Central Bank (Miklaszewska & Pawłowska, 2014). All in all, the current version of Pillar 3 is highly standardized with limited room for banks regarding flexibility of the content, structure and frequency of reporting. Due to high standardization and low differentiation disclosure reporting, according to Pillar 3, for some banks it can be a very costly process which does not incentivize their stakeholders to behave in such a manner that would discipline banks. It is the case with banks when insured deposits are major items in their liabilities. According to research findings (Flannery & Bliss, 2019), insured depositors have no incentive to spend resources on monitoring. In addition to that, they are probably not sophisticated enough to interpret bank results correctly. Other specific cases are also banks with majority ownership (many times more than 90%) by single foreign bank/financial group and when key stakeholders are uninsured depositors. These stakeholders have an interest in information about banks to be able to monitor the bank's risk. To cover their requirements, it is important to establish which information they are particularly interested in and furthermore to design the most effective structure regarding both content and time points of disclosed information. This study analyses the interest in information disclosures aimed at a specific type of stakeholders (depositors) in foreign-owned commercial banks, not traded on the capital market. These types of banks can represent a "model" in CEE countries where many commercial banks have similar ownership and liability structures. Stakeholders' behaviour related to Pillar 3 disclosed information can be expected to be similar in these countries.

The main goal is as follows: first, to assess interests of depositors in the disclosed two groups of information (Pillar 3 disclosure requirements, Pillar 3 related information during the period 2009–2012, year of crisis and subsequent years); second, to conduct robustness checks by verifying results by applying two approaches based on different time variables (week, quarter during 2009–2012).

The study has the following structure: the first section contains market discipline status of the research; methodology of the research is introduced in the second section; results are dealt with in the third section where the outcomes are compared based on different time frameworks; subsequently, discussion and conclusion are dealt with in the last section.

9.2 Related work

Market discipline mechanisms work via the prospect of failure and financial losses to minimize risk-taking, by which market participants discipline banks for their risk-taking behaviour. The market disciplining effect has been broadly identified by many studies and also by substantial evidence concerning market participants' reactions (Distinguin, 2008; Evanoff & Wall, 2000; Hadad, Agusman, Monroe, Gasbarro & Zumwalt, 2011; Jagtiani, Kaufman & Lemieux, 1999; Jordan, Peek & Rosengren, 2000; Sironi, 2003). Market discipline as a concept is evaluated empirically and factors which influence its enhancement have also been analysed. This concept has been analysed from different perspectives, which also point out its weak points. It is important to note that these frailties are important generally, but their impact on financial markets can be increased in turbulent times. Consequently, market discipline can be weakened by implicit government guarantees such as insured deposits (Distinguin, Rous & Tarazi, 2006), and by negative aspects of financial regulation highlighted by the crisis (Calomiris, 2009). Substantially, this involves disclosure standards, which reinforce an accurate reaction to turbulent times in the financial markets. However, Cubillas et al. (2012) conclude that while market discipline is weakened by banking crises and policy implications, regulations and interventions strengthen market discipline. At this point, these outcomes of disclosures as a market disciplining tool can differ; they are important in the functioning of market discipline mechanisms and as a background for market discipline enhancement. Furthermore, recapitalization and forbearance have negative effects on market discipline, but less supervisory power and more private ownership and supervision of banks have opposite effects. Generally, market discipline's efficiency is important, and mainly during crises, due to stronger risk-taking incentives which can be eliminated by market discipline (Nier & Baumann, 2006).

Market discipline framework is important in the concept of market discipline. This framework may represent a functional system and is a key component in modern banking regulation (Bartlett, 2012). However, this is true only in the case when the following four blocks are in perfect coherence (Stephanou, 2010): information disclosure, market participants, discipline mechanism and internal governance. Moreover, the interaction of these four blocks influences the market discipline effectiveness, which depends on the enhancement of accurate and timely financial disclosures (Jagtiani & Lemieux, 2001) and market disclosure of private information that penetrates the market (Berger & Davies, 1998).

There is no doubt that disclosures are one of the most effective tools for the enhancement of market discipline (Fonseca & González, 2010) and serve as a macro-prudential tool in reducing uncertainty in the capital markets during a financial crisis (Ellahie, 2012; Peristiani, Morgan & Savino, 2010). Moreover, Sowerbutts et al. (2013) conclude that disclosures' mechanism failure contributed to the last financial crisis, because of inadequate public disclosure that was followed by the inability of investors to judge risk and the withdrawal of lending in times of systemic stress. Therefore, a few studies have been reviewed in which the authors concentrate on the factors of disclosures, which contribute to the market discipline efficiency. Most of the authors concentrate on the impact of the increase of information disclosures on commercial banks. According to Bouaiss et al. (2017), the increase in disclosure levels enhances transparency and efficient market discipline and supervises excessive risk-taking. It positively influences investor's attitude to banks' risk profiles and actively increases banks' value (Zer, 2015). Furthermore, it increases the ability to attract interbank funding (Guillemin & Semenova, 2018), boosts depositors' sensitivity to equity levels (Kozłowski, 2016), improves sensitivity to risk-taking (Goldstein & Sapra, 2014) and prevents market breakdown. Additionally, an increase in disclosures is connected with a reduction of risk-taking by commercial banks (Naz & Ayub, 2017) and with a lower probability of default (Li, Li & Gao, 2020). However, it also implies the potential threat of disclosing too much information, which destroys risk-sharing opportunities (Goldstein & Leitner, 2015).

The nature of the disclosure content as a base for adequate, accurate and timely disclosures depends on the level of transparency, which is connected to the enhancement of market discipline. Accordingly, the bank stability and the probability of falling into crisis are influenced by transparency that increases accountability and leads to greater market efficiency (Gandrud & Hallerberg, 2014; Nier, 2005) and enables banks to raise cheaper capital (Frolov, 2007). However, Moreno and Takalo (2016) conclude that only an intermediate level of transparency is socially optimal and effective (Bouvard, Chaigneau & Motta, 2015). Key explanation of this finding is the statement that more transparency can decrease efficient liquidity and increase rollover risk. This development has a negative impact on the share prices of banks and the cost of trading corporate bonds can decrease (Parwada, Lau & Ruenzi, 2015). This is in conjunction with Iren et al. (2014)

that concludes that transparency can have a positive impact on bank performance only up to some level.

After the last financial crisis market discipline has become a background for stable financial markets and its implementation by regulatory requirements was preceded by a complex discussion process, which has led to significant changes and improvement of Pillar 3. The Pillar 3 disclosure requirements enhance the efficiency of market discipline in order to achieve a resilient banking system. Numerous studies evaluate Pillar 3 disclosures as a market disciplining tool and the majority of authors concentrate on the benefits of Pillar 3 disclosures as an effective market disciplining tool. First, Pillar 3 improves the safety of the banking system (Vauhkonen, 2012) and decreases information asymmetry (Niessen-Ruenzi, Parwada & Ruenzi, 2015), and its quarterly reporting is useful to investors (Parwada, Ruenzi & Sahgal, 2013). Second, banks' adequate disclosures (Pillar 3 and annual reports) have a significant effect on market risk-taking behaviour and can minimize risks (Sarker & Sharif, 2020). Third, the similarity of Pillar 3 regulation and COREP (Common Reporting Standards (COREP) used in Europe) reports leads to a positive relationship between these regulations and market discipline effectiveness (Yang & Koshiyama, 2019). However, a few authors concentrate on Pillar 3 weaknesses. Concretely, an implementation of additional regulations is effective in the area of financial reporting quality, but there arise differences for smaller banks, which face disproportionately higher increases in the costs of compliance but big banks can be engaged in higher risk acceptance (Poshakwale, Aghanya & Agarwal, 2020). Correspondingly, Freixas and Laux (2011) in their study put doubt about the transparency of Pillar 3 reports, mainly thanks to stories that occurred during the financial crisis. Moreover, Pillar 3 has excessive superstructure and monitoring costs (Benli, 2015), which can bring a range of issues.

The content of Pillar 3 disclosures is also an important factor in any assessment of the efficiency of Pillar 3 as a market disciplining tool. According to Giner et al. (2020), the most relevant categories of Pillar 3 disclosures are credit risk, liquidity risk and market risk category (Scannella, 2018). This is in conjunction with Bischof et al. (2016), who conclude that the improved content of Pillar 3 disclosures translates into higher market liquidity. Scannella and Polizzi (2019) concentrated on improvement in the disclosure of derivatives and hedging strategies, which is important for the enhancement of interest of the market participants. Additionally, IT risk popped up as one of the key risk categories that are positively correlated with a firm's future stock price decrease (Song, Cavusoglu, Lee & Ma, 2020).

However, the related work review suggests a lack of studies assessing the interest of stakeholders to the content of Pillar 3 formation disclosures in commercial banks, which is crucial in order to implement effective supervisory market discipline.

First, the sensitivity of stakeholders to negative content in disclosures is validated by a few authors. It can trigger inefficient bank runs (Faria-e-Castro, Martinez & Philippon, 2017) and qualitative information disclosed in a negative way that contributes to explain the bank risk insolvency and increase probability of default (Del Gaudio, Megaravalli, Sampagnaro & Verdoliva, 2020). Second, Araujo and Leyshon (2016) revealed a window in the content relevancy of disclosures in relation to banks' risk profile, because stakeholders are most responsive to information related to the value of the bank's assets, off-balance sheet and ratings. These authors also highlight important factors, influencing Pillar 3 content efficiency, such as the overall quality of risk disclosures and the valuation of quantitative information more than qualitative information.

Research in the CEE region focused on the analysis of disclosures is rare. A few authors concentrate on their weaknesses (Bartulovic & Pervan, 2012). According to Arsov and Bucenska (2017), disclosures in CEE countries lack transparency and independent verification of the data in the presented reports (Habek, 2017). Moreover, for some financial institutions in Poland, there is a lack of resources strongly related to disclosures (Fijalkowska, Zyznarska-Dworczak & Garsztka, 2017). But it is clear that research in the field of Pillar 3 disclosures in CEE countries is even more rare. Despite Matuszaka and Rozanska's interesting study (Matuszak & Rozanska, 2017), which points out the Pillar 3 benefits but the research which would evaluate the performance of commercial banks in Poland (positive relationship between Pillar 3 disclosure and banks' profitability measured by ROA and ROE of commercial banks), research which would evaluate its content relevancy is insufficient.

As has been already stated in the introduction, depository markets are important in CEE countries. Research studies identify a few challenges these markets cope with. According to Distinguin et al. (2012), it is a high correlation between the level of interbank deposits and the risk of the bank. Higher proportion of interbank deposits in the bank's balance sheet means lower levels of risk in this region. They also conclude that explicit deposit insurance (implemented in the 1990s) contributed to effective market discipline in CEE. Moreover, Karas et al. (2013) discovered that in Russia the introduction of deposit insurance for households caused lower sensitivity for insured deposits flows than for uninsured ones. According to researchers, the uninsured depositors have stronger market discipline than insured ones. However, Lapteacru (2019) suggests that external support has no impact on non-deposit funding at any type of banks according to ownership. Hasan et al. (2013) present a relevant finding for banks owned by foreign investors (which is the case in many CEE banks): a more positive correlation in interest to negative rumours on the banks' parent companies than to banks' disclosures. This is in conjunction with Accornero and Moscatelli (2018), who concluded that depositors of threatened banks used to be more sensitive than other depositors to negative rumours. Substantially, it can be agreed with Berger and Bouwman (2013) that particularly depository discipline research in Europe is not sufficient and according to the findings even more rare in CEE countries. At this point, it can be agreed also with authors (Miklaszewska & Pawłowska, 2014) who questioned post-crisis regulatory architecture, especially for CEE banks in the competitive and unstable environment, which may produce negative effects on relatively stable CEE banks. Based on these findings, this study aims to cover the gap in the field of adequate and relevant Pillar 3 disclosures, which would also contribute to higher interests of stakeholders to enhance the efficiency of market discipline.

9.3 Research methodology

The methods described in this chapter were created to analyse the behaviour of the visitors to a web portal – a bank web portal. The source data comes from webservers that are set as load balancers and are saved in an extended log file format. It contains only useful information for the analysis of user behaviour. In the log file (Munk, Pilková, Drlik, Kapusta & Švec, 2012) are identified user sessions to distinct visits of stakeholders. The log file contains variables connected to the Basel II, Pillar 3 regulations. Pillar 3 are exact regulatory disclosures requirements set out in the Basel II framework and incorporated into EU law and the subsequent laws of the EU states. Those regulations order the bank to publish various information and stakeholders can better understand the risk. The log file consists of around two million logged accesses that were obtained after data preparation. The data preparation is very important as was proved in previous experiments (Drlik & Munk, 2019; Munk, Benko, Gangur & Turčáni, 2015; Munk, Drlik & Vrabelova, 2011; Munk, Kapusta & Švec, 2010; Munk, Kapusta, Švec & Turčáni, 2010) where bad data preparation can lead to different results from the analysis.

The chapter deals with a comparison of two different approaches to model the behaviour of web users. Both approaches deal with the time variable as an indicator of the analysis. The first approach deals with the analysis of weekly accesses to web categories of banking portal. The multinomial logit model is used to analyse the data. The second approach deals with the evaluation of frequent itemsets based on quantity. The itemsets were evaluated based on quarters. Both approaches deal with the period 2009–2012. The year 2009 represents the year of the financial crisis. Contrary, the years 2010–2012 represent the years after the financial crisis. The investigated categorical dependent variable is a variable category that represents a group of web parts that deal with a similar issue. The variable contains these categories of the web content: *Business Conditions, Pricing List, Pillar3 related, Reputation, Pillar3 disclosure requirements* and *We support*. In this experiment, the focus will be on two of these categories that are related to the topic of Pillar3: *Pillar3 related* and *Pillar3 disclosure requirements*. The *Pillar3 related* category consists of parts: Rating, Group, Information for Banks, Annual Reports, General Shareholder Meeting, Financial Reports and Emitent Prospects. The *Pillar3 disclosure requirements* consists of parts: Pillar3 Semiannually Info and Pillar3 Q-terly Info. Detailed analysis of web part frequent itemsets of the Pillar3 category (*Pillar3 disclosure requirements, Pillar3 related*) in the respective quarters in the examined period was carried out in Munk, Pilkova, Benko & Blažeková (2017). The applied methodology has a similar data preparation phase for both approaches:

1. retrieving log files.
2. data cleansing – unnecessary data is removed from the log file (requests on pictures, fonts, styles, scripts, etc.). Search engines robots' access to the web portal are also removed from the log file. The result of this phase is raw data that contains only accesses to the web portal.
3. user/session identification – Reference Length method was used to identify sessions and the visitors who accessed the web were identified using the fields IP address and user agent (Cooley, Mobasher & Srivastava, 1999; Kapusta, Munk & Drlik, 2012a,b).
4. path completion – based on the visitors usage of the *Back* button of the web browser, the records of his/her path on the web portal can be reconstructed (Munk et al., 2015).
5. variables determination – the log file contains the variables in a typical Extended Log Format (ELF), so a transformation and variable definition are needed for a user behaviour analysis of the examined web portal. A dependent variable category is created, and it represents the web parts of the portal. In case the web parts have low traffic, it is appropriate to create wider categories based on their relevance to the content (Munk, Drlik et al., 2011). It is also necessary to identify independent variables – predictors that represent the time variables created from the timestamp of the access to the web category. In the case of the weeks of the year, it is the variable *week* that was created based on ISO 8601 and will have values of 0–53. The variable will be 0 in case it is a week that begins in the previous year. The next variable will be a nominal variable year representing individual years: 2009, 2010, 2011 and 2012. From the nominal variable dummy variables representing the examined years will be

created by binarization. The next nominal variable *quarterYear* served to make the quarters and specific years distinct. Similarly, dummy variables representing the specific quarter and year (2009Q1, 2009Q2, etc.) were created.

After data preparation, the experiment, divided into two approaches, is conducted. One method is focused on the time variable week and the other quarter. The first analysis is conducted using the multinomial logit model. After determining the model, it is required to identify the type of dependence for determining the degree of the polynomial and the selection of predictors, including dummy variables. The first approach was done as follows:

6. the estimation of the models' parameters α_j, β_j by maximizing the logarithm of the likelihood function. The *STATISTICA Generalized Linear Models* was used to estimate the parameters of individual values.

7. the estimation of logits η_{ij} for all predictors values $\hat{\eta}_{ij} = a_j + x_i^T b_j, j = 1, 2, ..., J - 1$.

8. the estimation of probability of accesses π_{iJ} in time i for reference web category J $\hat{\pi}_{iJ} = \frac{1}{1+\sum_{j=1}^{J-1} e^{\hat{\eta}_{ij}}}$.

9. the probability estimation of accesses π_{ij} in time i for web category $\hat{\pi}_{ij} = e^{\hat{\eta}_{ij}}\hat{\pi}_{iJ}$, $j = 1, 2, ..., J - 1$.

10. the visualization of the probabilities of web category j in time i where $j = 1, 2, ..., J$.

The model was afterwards evaluated using alternative methods to estimate the model (Munk, Drlik et al., 2011; Munk, Vrábelová & Kapusta, 2011). The evaluation consisted of the visualization of observed and expected differences of counts, extreme identification, comparison of the distribution of observed relative counts of accesses and estimated probabilities of the examined web part j in time i, and observed and expected logit visualization of each web part, except the reference web part. If the model is suitable at all levels then it is a suitable model for the analysed data.

The second approach dealt with discovering the behaviour patterns of web users during quarters in the examined period. The results were processed by association rule analysis using *STATISTICA Sequence and Association Analysis*, which is an implementation of the algorithm using a priori algorithm together with a tree-structured procedure that requires only one pass through the data (Hill & Lewicki, 2013). The aim was to extract frequent itemsets with the min support of 0.01 (Pilkova, Munk, Švec & Medo, 2015). After extracting web part frequent itemsets of web parts in the identified sessions the interest is in comparison to the proportion of incidence in the quarters of examined years. It can be summed up into the following:

11. extracting the frequent itemsets.

12. incidence matrix in the examined periods.

13. assessment of seasonality in terms of quantity (occurrence rate) in the examined years.

The results of the two different approaches will be compared based on the specified time variable. It can be assumed that the results should be similar and that the weekly analysis should offer a more detailed look at the behaviour of the web users in comparison to the quarterly analysis.

9.4 Results

Frequent itemsets (a) were extracted and probabilities of the accesses (b) were examined of web portal categories (*category*) based on time where time was represented by variables: (a) quarter and (b) week. The data saved in the log file originated from a significant domestic commercial bank operating in Slovakia. The examined log file was pre-processed, and variables were created that represented the analysed factors. First, it was important to determine whether it was significant to distinguish the individual years (variable year). In the case of the nominal variable *year*, a moderate degree of dependency with the variable *category* (*Chi-square = 389 844.7; df = 15; p = 0.000; Contingency coefficient C = 0.4; Cramer V = 0.3*) was identified. The contingency coefficient can obtain values from 0 (represents no dependence between variables) to 1 (represents the perfect dependence between variables). The contingency coefficient is statistically significant. Based on these results, dummy variables were created representing the examined years (*2009, 2010* and *2011*). These variables gain only two values: 0 or 1 meaning whether the access was done in the specific year. The dummy variable for the year 2012 is not needed as the accesses from this year will have all other variables values set to 0.

Based on the Likelihood-ratio (LR) test (Table 9.1), estimates of the theoretical counts of accesses were compared with the empirical counts of accesses. The results of the LR test helped to identify the appropriate polynomial model of the third degree for the time variable week. The value of the Pearson Chi-square approximates 1 and it means that the chosen model is suitable. Also, the maximum of the logarithm of the likelihood function helps to choose the appropriate model where the smallest value is the best.

The *STATISTICA Generalized Linear Models* was used to estimate parameters for individual data. The significance of the parameters was examined using the Wald test. The probability of access to the web portal categories has been modelled depending on time-week of access and years. Time was represented by the predictor *week* and its transformation based on the degree of the polynomial ($week^2$ and $week^3$) and the dummy variables of the examined years (*2009, 2010* and *2011*).

Based on the results (Table 9.2) of all effects test for the model, the parameters are statistically significant. In the created model, all of the years represent statistically significant features that are represented by the dummy variables. The weeks of the year represented by the variables week and its transformation based on the degree of polynomial showed also statistically significant features.

The estimated parameters for both categories were significantly dependent on the week of access and its transformations too (Table 9.3). The values of logits were significantly influenced by the examined years. The logit model provides a probability estimate at the output. The absolute size of the parameters reflects predictors with the highest influence on the examined variable. A high absolute value of the parameter refers to a large dependency. A negative value refers to indirectly proportional dependence.

Table 9.1 Evaluation of the model

	df	Stat	Stat/df
Deviance	10356140	6473096.45	0.625049
Pearson Chi-square	10356140	10445031.93	1.008584
Log-likelihood		−3236548	

Table 9.2 All effects test for the model

	df	Wald Statistic	p
Intercept	5	98888.3	<0.001
week	5	19440.9	<0.001
week²	5	25555.8	<0.001
week³	5	22826.6	<0.001
2009	5	218115.7	<0.001
2010	5	109030.4	<0.001
2011	5	80968.1	<0.001

Table 9.3 Estimate the parameters of the model

	Category	Estimate	Standard Deviation	Wald Statistic	p
week	Pillar3 related	−0.07695	0.001659	2151.0	<0.001
week²	Pillar3 related	0.00324	0.000078	1707.9	<0.001
week³	Pillar3 related	−0.00003	0.000001	968.8	<0.001
2009	Pillar3 related	−1.33753	0.008442	25100.1	<0.001
2010	Pillar3 related	−0.78993	0.008914	7852.6	<0.001
2011	Pillar3 related	0.36939	0.009105	1645.9	<0.001
week	Pillar3 disclosure requirements	0.00299	0.002050	2.1	0.1443
week²	Pillar3 disclosure requirements	−0.00106	0.000096	121.8	<0.001
week³	Pillar3 disclosure requirements	0.00002	0.000001	382.3	<0.001
2009	Pillar3 disclosure requirements	−1.78236	0.009811	33002.1	<0.001
2010	Pillar3 disclosure requirements	−1.10608	0.010141	11896.1	<0.001
2011	Pillar3 disclosure requirements	−0.60084	0.010140	3510.9	<0.001

Using the estimated parameters, it was possible to evaluate the logits for each category j in time i. The third-degree polynomial model is:

$$\hat{\eta}_{ij} = \alpha_j + \beta_{1j}week_i + \beta_{2j}week_i^2 + \beta_{3j}week_i^3 + \gamma_j year_i, \; i = 0, 1, 2, ..., 53, j = 1, 2, ..., J - 1.$$

The evaluation of the suitability of the model was conducted. The importance of thorough data preparation can be shown in the following example. The log file contained a big sample of unnecessary data that was not discovered during the data preparation phase. The evaluation of theoretical and empirical counts of accesses helped to identify this issue. During a specific week in 2012, a systematic error was identified as having occurred. It was an automated script that could be related to maintenance, backup, etc. This was identified by examining the extreme values of differences between the theoretical and empirical counts of accesses. As can be seen in Figure 9.1, during the 21st week of the year 2012, there was a high extreme value (extreme value border is depicted using the dashed line). This led to a more detailed analysis of the analysed log file and finding the issue.

After cleaning the unnecessary data from the log file, the evaluation was repeated, and the difference is shown in Figure 9.2. All of the estimated parameters already mentioned were done using the corrected log file, but it was meaningful to mention that sometimes it is possible to discover issues with the data preparation phase at the end of model evaluation.

A way to show the suitability of the model is also to evaluate theoretical and empirical logits. The idea is whether the estimated theoretical logits fit (model) the empirical logits calculated from the empirical relative counts of accesses $h_{ij} = ln\left(\frac{p_{ij}}{p_{iJ}}\right), j = 1, 2, ..., J - 1$, where p_{ij} is the empirical relative count of access to the web category j in time i and p_{iJ} is the empirical relative

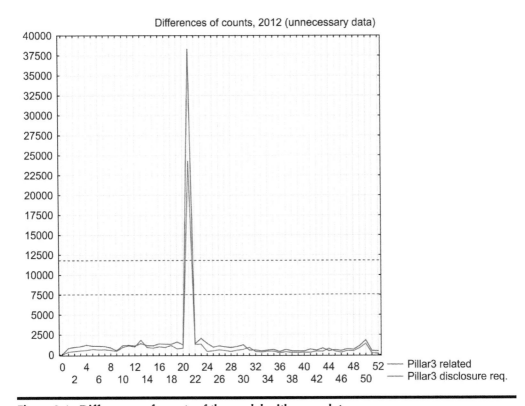

Figure 9.1 Differences of counts of the model with error data.

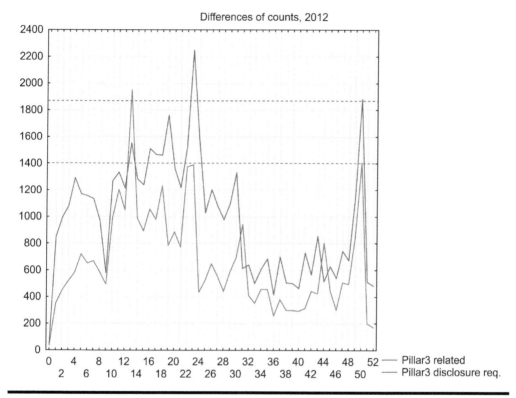

Figure 9.2 Differences of counts of the model with corrected data.

count of access to the referential web category *J* in time *i*. The visualization of observed and expected logits of each of the examined categories (except the referential web category) can show how the theoretical logits model the empirical logits. Based on the visualization for the critical year 2012 (Figures 9.3 and 9.4), it was seen that after the new data cleansing the theoretical logits fit the empirical logits better.

The plot (Figure 9.5) shows the visualization of probabilities of access to the market discipline-related web categories (Pillar3) during the year 2009. This year is taken as the year of financial crisis. It can be seen that the highest access during this year was to the web category *Pillar3 related* at the beginning of the year (the 0th week has the value 0.193, for the record this week is a week that contains days from the previous year and also from the actual year – at the turn of years). The lowest estimated values were identified later in the year (the 38th week has the value 0.160). The most interest for the category *Pillar3 disclosure requirements* was again at the turn of years but this time it was at the end of the year 2009 (the 52nd week has the value 0.100). The lowest access was in case of this category the same week as for the other category (the 38th week has the value 0.050). By studying both categories, it can be observed that both are interesting for stakeholders at the beginning of the year and then the interest lowers, whereas at the end of the year it starts to rise again. This can be analysed in more detail also using the other method by extracting the frequent itemsets of the web categories. The asterisks contained in the plot (Figure 9.5) represent the homogenous groups for occurrence of frequent itemsets of the web categories for the year

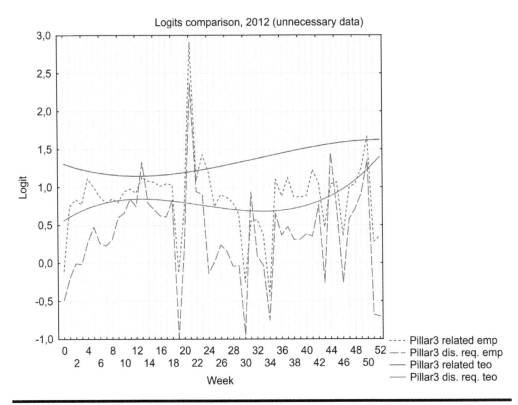

Figure 9.3 Logit visualization of the model for the year 2012 with error data.

2009. The zero hypothesis is rejected at the 5% significance level ($df = 3$, $Q = 8.258$, $p < 0.05$) for the quarters of the year 2009. Most frequent itemsets were identified in the first quarter (63.64%) and the lowest in the third quarter (38.64%). In the year 2009, two homogenous groups (2009 Q3, 2009 Q4, 2009 Q2) and (2009 Q4, 2009 Q2, 2009 Q1) were identified (Figure 9.5) based on the average occurrence of extracted frequent itemsets of the web parts. These results verify the week analysis for this year, where the most interest of the web users in Pillar3 categories was at the beginning of the year and the lowest in the third quarter (the 38th week is at the end of the third quarter where between 2009 Q1 and 2009 Q3 a statistically significant difference at the 5% significance level was identified).

The plot (Figure 9.6) shows the visualization of probabilities of access to the market discipline-related web categories (Pillar3) during the year 2010. This year is taken as the year after the financial crisis. The highest access during this year was to the web category *Pillar3 related* at the beginning of the year (the third week has the value 0.211). The lowest estimated values were identified at the end of the year in the last quarter (the 43rd week has the value 0.161). The most interest for the category *Pillar3 disclosure requirements* was at the beginning of the year at the end of the first quarter (the 11th week has the value 0.116). The lowest access was later in the year in the case of this category (the 40th week has the value 0.058). By studying both categories, it can be observed that both are interesting for the stakeholders at the beginning of the year and then

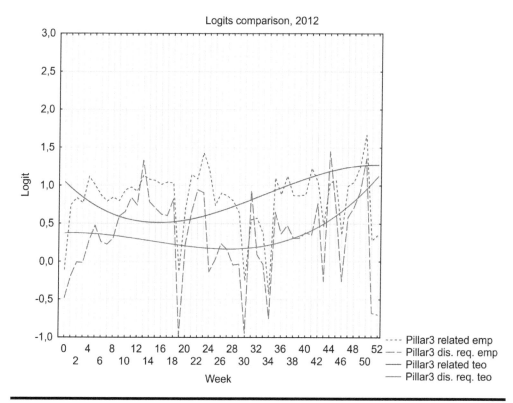

Figure 9.4 Logit visualization of the model for the year 2012 with corrected data.

the interest lowers, whereas at the end of the year it starts to rise again. Now the weekly results will be compared with the frequent itemsets. The asterisks contained in the plot (Figure 9.6) represent the homogenous groups for occurrence of frequent itemsets of the web categories for the year 2010. The zero hypothesis is rejected at the 1% significance level ($df = 3$, $Q = 12.581$, $p < 0.01$) for the quarters of the year 2010. Most frequent itemsets were identified in the first quarter (40.91%) and the lowest in the third and fourth quarters (20.45%–22.73%). In the year 2010, three homogenous groups (2010 Q4, 2010 Q3), (2010 Q3, 2010 Q2) and (2010 Q2, 2010 Q1) were identified (Figure 9.6) based on the average occurrence of extracted frequent itemsets of the web parts. The most interest of the web users in Pillar3 categories was at the beginning of the year and the lowest in the last quarters, where between 2010 Q1 and 2010 Q3/2010 Q4 and between 2010 Q2 and 2010 Q4 a statistically significant difference at the 5% significance level was identified.

The plot (Figure 9.7) shows the visualization of probabilities of access to the market discipline-related web categories (Pillar3) during the year 2011. This year can be taken as the second year after the financial crisis. The highest access during this year was to the web category *Pillar3 related* again at the beginning of the year (the fifth week has the value 0.211). The lowest estimated values were identified at the same week as in the previous year with an even lower value (the 43rd week has the value 0.151). The most interest for the category *Pillar3 disclosure requirements* was also

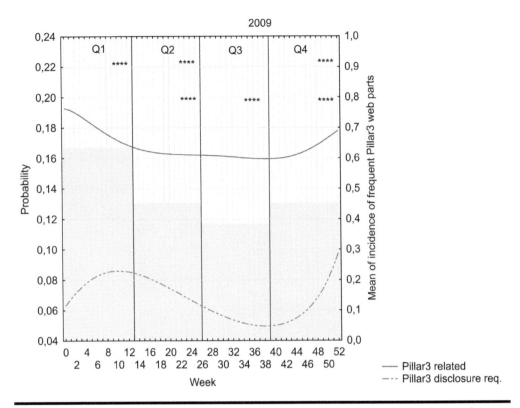

Figure 9.5 Probability visualization of market discipline-related categories during the year 2009.

the same as the previous year but with a little higher value (the 11th week has the value 0.132). The lowest access was also the same week as the previous year with an almost similar value in the case of this category (the 40th week has the value 0.059). By studying both categories, it can be observed that the behaviour is like the previous year with only a little deviation. Now the weekly results will be compared with the frequent itemsets. The asterisks contained in the plot (Figure 9.7) represent the homogenous groups for occurrence of frequent itemsets of the web categories for the year 2011. The zero hypothesis is rejected at the 1% significance level ($df = 3$, $Q = 11.539$, $df = 3$, $p < 0.01$) for the quarters of the year 2011. The second quarter contained the most frequent itemsets (38.64%) and the lowest in the first and third quarters (18.18% –20.45%). In the year 2011, two homogenous groups (2011 Q1, 2011 Q3, 2011 Q4) and (2011 Q4, 2011 Q2) were identified (Figure 9.7) based on the average occurrence of extracted frequent itemsets of the web parts. There is a little difference to the previous years. Based on the quarters the highest interest is now in the second quarter, but the week analysis shows us that it is on the period interface.

The plot (Figure 9.8) shows the visualization of probabilities of access to the market discipline-related web categories (Pillar3) during the year 2012. This year can be taken as one of the years after the financial crisis. The highest access during this year was to the web category *Pillar3 related* and has shifted more towards the end of the first quarter of the year (the 11th week has the value 0.135).

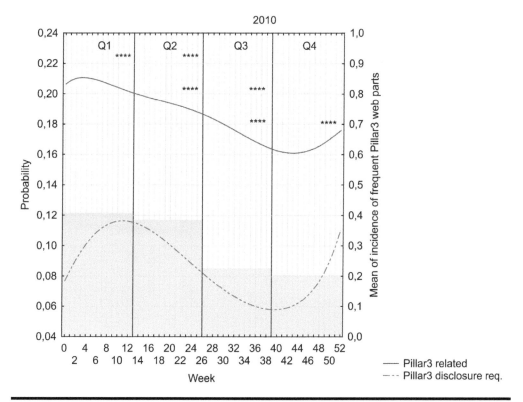

Figure 9.6 Probability visualization of market discipline-related categories during the year 2010.

The lowest estimated values were identified in the same period as in the previous two years (the 44th week has the value 0.067). The most interest for the category *Pillar3 disclosure requirements* was almost the same as the previous year (the 12th week has the value 0.107). The lowest access was in the case of this category stabilized at the same period (the 41st week has the value 0.034). By studying both categories, it can be observed that the behaviour has stabilized so that interest rises at the beginning of the year with the highest interest in the Pillar3 information at the end of the first quarter. Consequently, the interest decreases with the lowest at the beginning of the fourth quarter and then starts to rise again. It can be observed that this year has the lower interest for both categories in comparison to the previous years. In the case of frequent itemsets, statistically significant differences for the year 2012 were not found ($df = 3$, $Q = 4.154$, $p = 0.2453$). Statistically significant differences for all of the next years were also not found (*2013: df = 3, Q = 3.255, p = 0.3539; 2014: df = 3, Q = 4.565, p = 0.2066; 2015: df= 3, Q = 3.001, p = 0.3916*) and the weekly analysis for these years was also not done. It can be said that the trend for the years after the crisis is similar to the years 2010, 2011 and 2012.

The first quarters of the years 2009–2010 during the event of global financial crisis have a significant impact on the quantity of identified frequent itemsets of the parts. This can be seen also in the weekly analysis where the first quarters contained the highest interest from the examined Pillar3 web categories. On this basis, it can be concluded that the required quarterly frequency

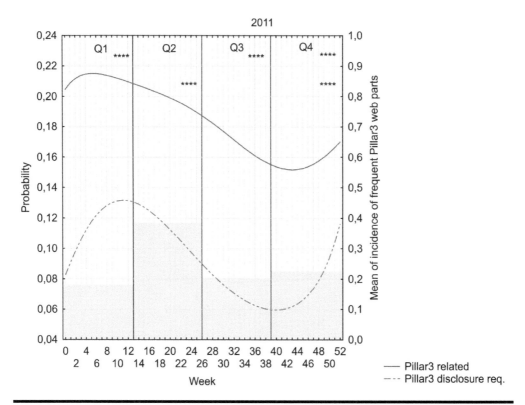

Figure 9.7 Probability visualization of market discipline-related categories during the year 2011.

publication of the results is not necessary for market discipline. It would be enough to publish this information annually, ideally in the early weeks of the year. To obtain these results, two different approaches with various time variables were used. Both approaches evaluate the behaviour of the users in time (mainly seasonality): (1) modelling the probabilities of access to the portal in time, and (2) quantitative evaluation of frequent itemsets incidence in time. The results match and based on that can be regarded as robust. The combination of these methods improved the results of the data and helped to better understand the behaviour of the stakeholders with the Pillar3 information on the web categories.

9.5 Discussion and conclusion

Pillar 3 of Basel II and Basel III regulation, called "market discipline" or according to some authors it should be named "information disclosure", is a very important component of banking supervision and regulation. Its importance has even increased after the crisis of 2007–2009. Basel supervisors have designed Pillar 3 to be an effective market discipline tool. However, its current complexity, standardization and the whole architecture also put impediments on the market discipline effectiveness. One such impediment is that regulator does not study stakeholders' interest and usage of disclosed information for some categories of commercial banks that are specific as

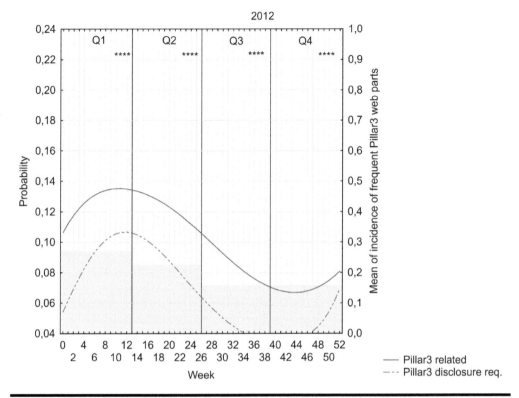

Figure 9.8 Probability visualization of market discipline-related categories during the year 2012.

far as their ownership structure, business model and funding are concerned. Usually, the impact of this situation is on one side very low interest of stakeholders in information which is not in line with their interests and on the other side, the high costs of banks related to the preparation of enormous amounts of disclosed and unused information. One such market that might suffer due to current Pillar 3 architecture is the depositors' market, specifically in CEE countries where single foreign banks/group ownership are very frequent. Therefore, in this study the interests of depositors in the disclosed two groups of information were assessed: requirement of the Pillar 3 disclosure and Pillar 3 related information during the period 2009–2012 (year of crisis and subsequent years). The analysis was based on visits of the stakeholders to the web portal of commercial banks and analysing their interest in relation to time spent on the web page (time variables) and in relation to the events of the financial crisis in 2009. The analysis of time spent on categories of the web portal was based on weekly accesses and frequent itemsets in terms of quantity (based on quarters). The findings are as follows:

1. The results of the analysis during and after the crisis suggest that stakeholders have expressed higher interest in *Pillar 3 related* information (such as annual reports, financial reports, annual reports, rating, group, general shareholder meeting, emitent prospects) rather than *Pillar 3 disclosure requirements*.

2. The highest interest of stakeholders in disclosed information was in the year of the crisis and subsequently steadily decreased.

3. The results of the analysis on the year of the financial crisis (weekly and quarterly analysis) have shown that in 2009 the highest interest was in the first quarter, at the beginning of the year (exceptionally 52nd week for *Pillar 3 disclosure requirements* in 2009), and was lowest in the third quarter for both categories.

4. In the analysis of the years 2010–2012, the years after the financial crisis, similar results have been identified, with the highest interest being at the end of the first quarter, on a period interface (exceptionally third week for *Pillar 3 related* in 2010 and fifth week for *Pillar 3 related* in 2011), and the lowest interest being identified in the fourth quarter. It is important to note that interest decreased generally during 2010–2012 in comparison to 2009.

5. The results are in line with Munk et al. (2017), whose results show that studied CEE commercial banks stakeholders are particularly interested in Pillar 3 disclosures in the first quarter and that interest in disclosures decreased after the turbulence of 2009.

6. The results also suggest that due to the significant impact of the first quarter with the highest interest of stakeholders, which was also validated by weekly analysis, quarterly disclosures seem less important for market discipline effects in comparison to annual disclosures. Annual disclosures imply higher interest than Pillar 3 disclosures and ideally should be disclosed at the beginning of the year.

The above presented results suggest that changes in information disclosures' design in commercial banks operating according to the analysed model are inevitable to enhance the efficiency of market discipline mechanisms and to add value to key stakeholders (depositors).

This chapter's conclusion fits with the study (Miklaszewska & Pawłowska, 2014, p. 264) that deeply analysed CEE banks' perspectives. In spite of fact that in the EU is currently applied complex regulatory and supervisory model, their conclusion is that it may not have produced the required more efficient and stable banking system, particularly in CEE countries that have very competitive banking environments.

Moreover, it can be agreed with Kuranchie-Pong, Bokpin & Andoh (2016) that stakeholders in the banking industry are supposed to use market discipline to make risk management more effective but to assess the bank's risk profile they need sufficient relevant information disclosures.

Finally, according to the European Banking Authority (EBA), to disclose to markets a sufficient risk profile of financial institutions is most important to ensure their correct functioning, creating trust between market participants and the efficiency of market discipline. The principles for adequate disclosures are clarity, meaningfulness, consistency over time and comparability across institutions, also in times of stress. There still exist open issues about the nature and potential impediments to disclosures in order to fulfil these principles and the authors hope that these findings and conclusions may also contribute to resolve these issues.

Due to some limitations of this research, and according to the findings, an analysis of the interest of stakeholders in the content of Pillar 3 disclosures has been identified as a future research topic.

Acknowledgements

This work was supported by the Scientific Grant Agency of the Ministry of Education of the Slovak Republic (ME SR) and Slovak Academy of Sciences (SAS) under the contract no. VEGA-1/0776/18 and by the scientific research project of the Czech Sciences Foundation Grant No. 19-15498S.

Disclosure statement

The authors declare that they have no conflict of interest.

References

Accornero, M., & Moscatelli, M. (2018). Listening to the Buzz: Social media sentiment and retail depositors' trust. *SSRN Electronic Journal*. doi:10.2139/ssrn.3160570

Arsov, S., & Bucevska, V. (2017). Determinants of transparency and disclosure – evidence from post-transition economies. *Economic Research-Ekonomska Istraživanja*, *30*(1), 745–760. doi:10.1080/1331677X.2017.1314818

Bartlett, R. (2012). Making banks transparent. *Vanderbilt Law Review*, *65*, 293–386. Retrieved from http://scholarship.law.berkeley.edu/facpubs/1824

Bartulovic, M., & Pervan, I. (2012). Comparative analysis of voluntary internet financial reporting for selected CEE countries. *Recent Researches in Applied Economics and Management*, *1*(1), 296–301.

Benli, V. F. (2015). Basel's forgotten pillar: The myth of market discipline on the forefront of Basel III. *Financial Internet Quarterly*, *11*(3), 70–91.

Berger, A. N., & Bouwman, C. H. S. (2013). How does capital affect bank performance during financial crises? *Journal of Financial Economics*, *109*(1), 146–176. doi:10.1016/j.jfineco.2013.02.008

Berger, A. N., & Davies, S. M. (1998). The information content of bank examinations. *Journal of Financial Services Research*, *14*(2), 117–144. doi:10.1023/A:1008011312729

Bischof, J., Daske, H., Elfers, F., & Hail, L. (2016). A tale of two regulators: Risk disclosures, liquidity, and enforcement in the banking sector. *SSRN Electronic Journal*. doi:10.2139/ssrn.2580569

Bouaiss, K., Refait-Alexandre, C., & Alexandre, H. (2017). *Will bank transparency really help financial markets and regulators?* Retrieved from https://hal.archives-ouvertes.fr/hal-01637917

Bouvard, M., Chaigneau, P., & Motta, A. de. (2015). Transparency in the financial system: Rollover risk and crises. *The Journal of Finance*, *70*(4), 1805–1837. doi:10.1111/jofi.12270

Calomiris, C. W. (2009). Bank regulatory reform in the wake of the financial crisis.

Cooley, R., Mobasher, B., & Srivastava, J. (1999). Data preparation for mining world wide web browsing patterns. *Knowledge and Information Systems*, *1*(1), 5–32.

Cubillas, E., Fonseca, A. R., & González, F. (2012). Banking crises and market discipline: International evidence. *Journal of Banking & Finance*, *36*(8), 2285–2298. doi:10.1016/J.JBANKFIN.2012.04.011

de Araujo, P., & Leyshon, K. I. (2016). The impact of international information disclosure requirements on market discipline. *Applied Economics*, *49*(10), 954–971. doi:10.1080/00036846.2016.1208361

Del Gaudio, B. L., Megaravalli, A. V., Sampagnaro, G., & Verdoliva, V. (2020). Mandatory disclosure tone and bank risk-taking: Evidence from Europe. *Economics Letters, 186*, 108531. doi:10.1016/j.econlet.2019.108531

Distinguin, I. (2008). Market discipline and banking supervision: The role of subordinated debt. *SSRN Electronic Journal.* doi:10.2139/ssrn.1098252

Distinguin, I., Kouassi, T., & Tarazi, A. (2012). Interbank deposits and market discipline: Evidence from Central and Eastern Europe. *SSRN Electronic Journal, 41*(2), 544–560. doi:10.2139/ssrn.2119956

Distinguin, I., Rous, P., & Tarazi, A. (2006). Market discipline and the use of stock market data to predict bank financial distress. *Journal of Financial Services Research, 30*(2), 151–176. doi:10.1007/s10693-0016-6

Drlik, M., & Munk, M. (2019). Understanding time-based trends in stakeholders' choice of learning activity type using predictive models. *IEEE Access, 7*, 3106–3121. doi:10.1109/ACCESS.2018.2887057

Ellahie, A. (2012). Capital market consequences of EU bank stress tests. *SSRN Electronic Journal.* doi:10.2139/ssrn.2157715

Evanoff, D. D., & Wall, L. D. (2000). Subordinated debt as bank capital: A proposal for regulatory reform. *Economic Perspectives*, (Q II), 40–53. Retrieved from https://ideas.repec.org/a/fip/fedhep/y2000iqiip40-53nv.25no.2.html

Faria-e-Castro, M., Martinez, J., & Philippon, T. (2017). *Runs versus lemons: Information disclosure and fiscal capacity.* Cambridge, MA. doi:10.3386/w21201

Fijalkowska, J., Zyznarska-Dworczak, B., & Garsztka, P. (2017). The relation between the CSR and the accounting information system data in Central and Eastern European (CEE) countries – The evidence of the polish financial institutions. *Journal of Accounting and Management Information Systems, 16*(4), 490–521.

Flannery, M. J., & Bliss, R. R. (2019). *Market discipline in regulation: Pre-and post-crisis.* Forthcoming, Oxford Handbook of Banking 3e.

Fonseca, A. R., & González, F. (2010). How bank capital buffers vary across countries: The influence of cost of deposits, market power and bank regulation. *Journal of Banking & Finance, 34*(4), 892–902. doi:10.1016/J.JBANKFIN.2009.09.020

Freixas, X., & Laux, C. (2011). Disclosure, transparency and market discipline. *CFS Working Paper, 11*, 1–39. Retrieved from https://www.ifk-cfs.de/fileadmin/downloads/publications/wp/2011/11_11.pdf

Frolov, M. (2007). Why do we need mandated rules of public disclosure for banks? *Journal of Banking Regulation, 8*(2), 177–191. doi:10.1057/palgrave.jbr.2350045

Gandrud, C., & Hallerberg, M. (2014). Supervisory transparency in the European banking union. *Bruegel Policy Contribution*, (2014/01). Retrieved from https://www.econstor.eu/handle/10419/106314

Giner, B., Allini, A., & Zampella, A. (2020). The value relevance of risk disclosure: An analysis of the banking sector. *Accounting in Europe.* doi:10.1080/17449480.2020.1730921

Goldstein, I., & Leitner, Y. (2015). *Stress tests and information disclosure. No 15-10, Working Papers.* Federal Reserve Bank of Philadelphia. Retrieved from https://econpapers.repec.org/paper/fipfedpwp/15-10.htm

Goldstein, I., & Sapra, H. (2014). Should banks' stress test results be disclosed? An analysis of the costs and benefits. *Foundations and Trends® in Finance, 8*(1), 1–54. doi:10.1561/0500000038

Guillemin, F., & Semenova, M. (2018). Transparency and market discipline: Evidence from the Russian Interbank Market. *Higher School of Economics Research Paper No. WP BRP 67/FE/2018*, 32. doi:10.2139/ssrn.3225061

Habek, P. (2017). CSR reporting practices in Visegrad group countries and the quality of disclosure. *Sustainability, 9*(12), 1–18.

Hadad, M. D., Agusman, A., Monroe, G. S., Gasbarro, D., & Zumwalt, J. K. (2011). Market discipline, financial crisis and regulatory changes: Evidence from Indonesian banks. *Journal of Banking & Finance, 35*(6), 1552–1562. doi:10.1016/j.jbankfin.2010.11.003

Hasan, I., Jackowicz, K., Kowalewski, O., & Kozłowski, Ł. (2013). Market discipline during crisis: Evidence from bank depositors in transition countries. *Journal of Banking & Finance, 37*(12), 5436–5451. doi:10.1016/j.jbankfin.2013.06.007

Hill, T., & Lewicki, P. (2013). *Electronic Statistics Textbook.* StatSoft Inc. Retrieved from http://www.statsoft.com/textbook/

Iren, P., Reichert, A. K., & Gramlich, D. (2014). Information disclosure, bank performance and bank stability. *International Journal Banking, Accounting and Finance, 5*(4), 39. Retrieved from https://papers.ssrn.com/sol3/papers.cfm?abstract_id=2874144

Jagtiani, J., Kaufman, G., & Lemieux, C. (1999). Do markets discipline banks and bank holding companies? Evidence from debt pricing. *Emerging Issues,* (Jun). Retrieved from http://econpapers.repec.org/article/fipfedhei/y_3a1999_3ai_3ajun_3an_3asr-99-3r.htm

Jagtiani, J., & Lemieux, C. (2001). Market discipline prior to bank failure. *Journal of Economics and Business, 53*(2), 313–324. Retrieved from http://econ.tu.ac.th/archan/Chalotorn/on%mkt%failure/jagtiani.pdf

Jordan, J. S., Peek, J., & Rosengren, E. S. (2000). The market reaction to the disclosure of supervisory actions: Implications for bank transparency. *Journal of Financial Intermediation, 9*(3), 298–319. doi:10.1006/jfin.2000.0292

Kapusta, J., Munk, M., & Drlik, M. (2012a). Cut-off time calculation for user session identification by reference length. In *2012 6th International Conference on Application of Information and Communication Technologies, AICT 2012 - Proceedings.* doi:10.1109/ICAICT.2012.6398500

Kapusta, J., Munk, M., & Drlik, M. (2012b). User session identification using reference length. In Capay, M., Mesarosova, M., & Palmarova, V. (Eds.), *DIVAI 2012: 9th International Scientific Conference on Distance Learning in Applied Informatics: Conference Proceedings, Sturovo, Slovakia* (pp. 175–184).

Karas, A., Pyle, W., & Schoors, K. (2013). Deposit insurance, banking crises, and market discipline: Evidence from a natural experiment on deposit flows and rates. *Journal of Money, Credit and Banking, 45*(1), 179–200. doi:10.1111/j.1538-4616.2012.00566.x

Kozłowski, Ł. (2016). Cooperative banks, the internet and market discipline. *Journal of Co-Operative Organization and Management, 4*(2), 76–84. doi:10.13140/RG.2.1.3768.6809

Kuranchie-Pong, L., Bokpin, G. A., & Andoh, C. (2016). Empirical evidence on disclosure and risk-taking of banks in Ghana. *Journal of Financial Regulation and Compliance, 24*(2), 197–212. doi:10.1108/JFRC-05-2015-0025

Lapteacru, I. (2019). Do bank activities and funding strategies of foreign and state-owned banks have a differential effect on risk-taking in Central and Eastern Europe? *Economics of Transition and Institutional Change, 27*(2), 541–576. doi:10.1111/ecot.12185

Li, Y., Li, C., & Gao, Y. (2020). Voluntary disclosures and peer-to-peer lending decisions: Evidence from the repeated game. *Frontiers of Business Research in China, 14*(1), 1–26. doi:10.1186/s11782-020-00075-5

Matuszak, L., & Rozanska, E. (2017). An examination of the relationship between CSR disclosure and financial performance: The case of polish banks. *Journal of Accounting and Management Information Systems, 16*(4), 522–533. Retrieved from https://econpapers.repec.org/RePEc:ami:journl:v:16:y:2017:i:4:p:522-533

Miklaszewska, E., & Pawłowska, M. (2014). Do safe banks create safe systems? Central and Eastern European banks' perspective. *Revue de l'OFCE, 132*(1), 243–267. doi:10.3917/reof.132.0243

Moreno, D., & Takalo, T. (2016). Optimal bank transparency. *Journal of Money, Credit and Banking, 48*(1), 203–231. doi:10.1111/jmcb.12295

Munk, M., Benko, L., Gangur, M., & Turčáni, M. (2015). Influence of ratio of auxiliary pages on the pre-processing phase of Web Usage Mining. *E+M Ekonomie a Management, 18*(3), 144–159. doi:10.15240/tul/001/2015-3-013

Munk, M., Drlik, M., & Vrabelova, M. (2011). Probability modelling of accesses to the course activities in the web-based educational system. In *Computational Science and Its Applications - Iccsa 2011, Pt V* (Vol. 6786, pp. 485–499).

Munk, M., Kapusta, J., & Švec, P. (2010). Data preprocessing evaluation for web log mining: Reconstruction of activities of a web visitor. In *Procedia Computer Science* (Vol. 1, pp. 2273–2280). doi:10.1016/j.procs.2010.04.255

Munk, M., Kapusta, J., Švec, P., & Turčáni, M. (2010). Data advance preparation factors affecting results of sequence rule analysis in web log mining. *E+M Ekonomie a Management, 13*(4), 143–160.

Munk, M., Pilkova, A., Benko, L., & Blažeková, P. (2017). Pillar 3: Market discipline of the key stakeholders in CEE commercial bank and turbulent times. *Journal of Business Economics and Management, 18*(5), 954–973. doi:10.3846/16111699.2017.1360388

Munk, M., Pilková, A., Drlik, M., Kapusta, J., & Švec, P. (2012). Verification of the fulfilment of the purposes of Basel II, Pillar 3 through application of the web log mining methods. *Acta Universitatis Agriculturae et Silviculturae Mendelianae Brunensis, 60*(2), 217–222.

Munk, M., Vrábelová, M., & Kapusta, J. (2011). Probability modeling of accesses to the web parts of portal. *Procedia Computer Science, 3*, 677–683. doi:10.1016/j.procs.2010.12.113

Naz, M., & Ayub, H. (2017). Impact of risk-related disclosure on the risk-taking behavior of commercial banks in Pakistan. *Journal of Independent Studies and Research-Management, Social Sciences and Economics, 15*. doi:10.31384/jisrmsse/2017.15.2.9

Nier, E. W. (2005). Bank stability and transparency. *Journal of Financial Stability, 1*(3), 342–354. doi:10.1016/J.JFS.2005.02.007

Nier, E. W., & Baumann, U. (2006). Market discipline, disclosure and moral hazard in banking. *Journal of Financial Intermediation, 15*(3), 332–361. doi:10.1016/j.jfi.2006.03.001

Niessen-Ruenzi, A., Parwada, J. T., & Ruenzi, S. (2015). Information effects of the Basel Bank capital and Risk Pillar 3 disclosures on equity analyst research an exploratory examination. *SSRN Electronic Journal.* doi:10.2139/ssrn.2670418

Parwada, J. T., Lau, K., & Ruenzi, S. (2015). The impact of Pillar 3 disclosures on asymmetric information and liquidity in bank stocks: Multi-country evidence. *CIFR Paper No. 82/2015*, 27. doi:10.2139/ssrn.2670403

Parwada, J. T., Ruenzi, S., & Sahgal, S. (2013). Market discipline and Basel Pillar 3 reporting. *SSRN Electronic Journal.* doi:10.2139/ssrn.2443189

Peristiani, S., Morgan, D. P., & Savino, V. (2010). The information value of the stress test and bank opacity. *Journal of Money, Credit and Banking, 46*(7), 1479–1500.

Pilkova, A., Munk, M., Švec, P., & Medo, M. (2015). Assessment of the Pillar 3 financial and risk information disclosures usefulness to the commercial banks users. *Lecture Notes in Artificial Intelligence, 9227*, 429–440.

Poshakwale, S., Aghanya, D., & Agarwal, V. (2020). The impact of regulations on compliance costs, risk-taking, and reporting quality of the EU banks. *International Review of Financial Analysis, 68*, 101431. doi:10.1016/j.irfa.2019.101431

Sarker, N., & Sharif, J. (2020). Simultaneity among market risk taking, bank disclosures and corporate governance: Empirical evidence from the banking sector of Bangladesh. *Academy of Accounting and Financial Studies Journal, 24*(1), 1–21.

Scannella, E. (2018). Market risk disclosure in banks' balance sheet and Pillar 3 report: The case of Italian banks. In Myriam García-Olalla & Judith Clifton (Eds.),*Contemporary Issues in Banking, chapter 3* (pp. 53–90). Palgrave Macmillan, Cham.

Scannella, E., & Polizzi, S. (2019). Do large European Banks differ in their derivative disclosure practices? A cross-country empirical study. *Journal of Corporate Accounting & Finance, 30*(1), 14–35. doi:10.1002/jcaf.22373

Sironi, A. (2003). Testing for market discipline in the European banking industry: Evidence from subordinated debt issues. *Journal of Money, Credit and Banking, 35*(3), 443–472. Retrieved from http://econpapers.repec.org/article/mcbjmoncb/v_3a35_3ay_3a2003_3ai_3a3_3ap_3a443-72.htm

Song, V., Cavusoglu, H., Lee, G. M., & Ma, L. (2020). IT risk factor disclosure and stock price crashes. doi:10.24251/HICSS.2020.738

Sowerbutts, R., Zer, I., & Zimmerman, P. (2013). Bank disclosure and financial stability. *Bank of England Quarterly Bulletin, Bank of England, 53* (4), 326–335.

Stephanou, C. (2010). Rethinking market discipline in banking: Lessons learned from the Financial Crisis. *Policy Research Working Paper, The World Bank, 5227*, 1–37.

Vauhkonen, J. (2012). The impact of Pillar 3 disclosure requirements on bank safety. *Journal of Financial Services Research, 41*(1–2), 37–49. doi:10.1007/s10693-011-0107-x

Yang, W., & Koshiyama, A. S. (2019). Assessing qualitative similarities between financial reporting frameworks using visualization and rules: COREP vs. Pillar 3. *Intelligent Systems in Accounting, Finance and Management, 26*(1), 16–31. doi:10.1002/isaf.1441

Zer, I. (2015). Information disclosures, default risk, and bank value. *Finance and Economics Discussion Series, 2015*(104), 1–43. doi:10.17016/FEDS.2015.104

Chapter 10

Machine learning in the fields of accounting, economics and finance
The emergence of new strategies

Maha Radwan, Salma Drissi and Silvana Secinaro

10.1 Introduction

In recent years, machine learning (ML) has become a fascinating field which is experiencing a renewed interest. Coming from many disciplines such as statistics, optimization, algorithms or signal processing, it is a field of study in constant mutation which has now imposed itself in our society. Already, ML has been used for decades in automatic character recognition or anti-spam filters; the uses of ML are so numerous in real life that it conquers different fields starting with designing an algorithm to estimate the value of an asset (the price of a house, or the expected gains from a shop, etc.) based on previous observations, or even analyze the composition of an email (Azencott, 2019), in particular, the content of the latter, as well as the number of occurrences of the words constituting it, etc.

Finance is also no exception since many financial activities use solutions developed by ML. Indeed, among the multiple uses of ML techniques in the finance field, we find, for example, the prediction of the percentage chance of repayment of a loan according to the track record of the assets or even predict the fluctuations of stock market, thanks to fluctuations in past or future years (Heaton et al., 2017).

In this context, ML is present everywhere: banks use it to assess the creditworthiness of a borrower or to predict and analyze all available company data (not only financial reports but also press releases, news and even sound recordings or videos transcribed) in order to identify the most interesting investments. Mentioning another field of application is in the financial sector of ML, namely, risk control and compliance (Ding et al., 2019).

In addition to use for investment decisions, risk control and compliance, marketing represents another field of application for ML. Moreover, the use of Deep Mining, for example, opens up immense potential to increase additional and transformation prospects that ensure the best possible customer service and reverse the loss of loyalty (Singh et al., 2019).

Finally, ML can be used to reduce costs and increase the productivity of financial institutions. One example in particular is the use of artificial intelligence to automate highly technical translations of financial documents, thereby saving production time and resources.

This chapter is intended as an introduction to the concepts and algorithms and uses of ML, so a more focused vision will be given to different applications of ML techniques in the fields of economics, accounting and finance. The chapter would provide insights to researchers, business experts and readers who seek to understand in a simplified way the foundations of the main algorithms used in ML as well as its applications in the fields of finance, economics and accounting through the presentation of the review of existing literature in this area.

Our chapter will be structured as follows: the first and second sections will be dedicated to presenting an overview of ML in order to establish more clearly the concept, its genesis and its main models. The third section will be reserved for the development of the main applications of ML, particularly, in the fields of algorithmic trading and portfolio management, risk management and credit scoring, insurance pricing and finally the detection of accounting and financial fraud.

10.2 General overview on machine learning

ML is currently at the heart of data science and artificial intelligence. Indeed, whether it is a digital transformation of companies, Big Data or a national strategy, ML has become essential. Its applications are many and varied, ranging from search engines and character recognition to genomics research, social network analysis, targeted advertising, computer vision, machine translation and algorithmic trading. However, what is it exactly? What do we mean by ML? How do you learn, and what does that mean for a machine? The question of learning fascinates computer and mathematics specialists from different specialties, whether neurologists, pedagogues, philosophers or artists. Indeed, a definition that applies to a computer program like a robot, a pet or a human being is that proposed by Benureau (2015) arguing that: "Learning is a modification of behavior based on an experiment".

In the case of a computer program, which is the one that interests us in this chapter, we speak of ML, at the moment, when this program has the capacity to learn without this modification being explicitly programmed, a definition advanced by Arthur Samuel (1959).

In this context, the difference between a classical program and a learning program lies in the fact that the first type uses a procedure and data which it receives as input to produce responses as output, whereas the second uses the data and the responses at the same time to produce procedures for obtaining outputs from the inputs.

To fully understand this definition, suppose a business wants to know the total amount spent by a customer from their invoices. It is therefore sufficient to apply a conventional algorithm, namely a simple addition since a learning algorithm is not necessary. However, assume the company this time seeks to use these invoices to determine which products the customer is most likely to purchase in a month. While this is likely related, the company clearly does not have all of the information it needs to do this. However, if it has the purchase history of a large number of individuals, it becomes possible to use a ML algorithm so that it derives a predictive model allowing it to provide an answer to this question.

In terms of its context of appearance, ML was born in the 1980s, and can be considered as a branch of artificial intelligence (AI, whose beginnings date back to the war). ML is intimately linked to data analysis and decision algorithms which have its origins in statistics.

Until the 18th century, statistics, assimilated "State Science", were only descriptive (Desrosières, 2016). It is only a century later that the probabilities will be linked to statistics, with, among other things, the notion of extrapolation between the observation of a sample and the characteristics of a population. We had to wait until the beginning of the 20th century for statistics to organize themselves as a separate science and to be subdivided into two disciplines: descriptive statistics and inferential statistics.

Thus, the notion of ML first refers to the understanding of human thought, which was studied by Descartes and then by G. Leibniz in his work "De Arte combinatoria" in 1666. The philosopher then tries to define the simplest reasoning thought (like an alphabet) which, when combined, will formulate very complex thoughts (Horton et a., 2009). These works were later formalized by G. Boole in 1854 in his work *An Investigation of the Laws of Thought on Which Are Founded the Mathematical Theories of Logic and Probability*.

It was not until 1956 that ML took a remarkable turn with the Dartmouth conference organized by M. Minsky and J. McCarthy, the two great emblematic figures of Artificial Intelligence. However, it will be necessary to wait for the 1980s and the development of computing capacities for ML will take on its full extent.

Nevertheless, the most striking application of ML remains that Deep Blue, the IBM supercomputer, beats the world chess champion Garry Kasparov in 1997 (Campbell et al., 2002). In 2014, Russian artificial intelligence dubbed "Eugene Goostman" was able to become the first "robot" to pass the famous Turing test [27]. Although the scientific community remains divided as to this experience, it nevertheless remains an important stage of Artificial Intelligence, and more particularly of ML (Vardi, 2014).

10.3 Data analysis process and main algorithms used

By taking advantage of new computer technologies, ML has experienced remarkable growth. Based on the development of algorithms that are capable of learning and simulating knowledge and intelligence from experiences, without the need for human intervention during their learning, nor explicitly programmed to manage this or that experience or as a specific data, ML still generates a lot of debate among researchers wanting to know if machines were capable of learning data. They learn from previous calculations in order to produce reliable and reproducible decisions and results, which requires monitoring a process whose compliance is as important as the quality of the algorithms used (Vardi, 2014). In this context, there are five phases:

1. **Defining the problem**: Data analysis is the process of examining and interpreting data in order to develop answers to questions or problems.

2. **Data collection**: Once the problem is determined and translated in terms of data analysis, it is necessary to collect data in sufficient quantity, but also take into consideration the quality of the data to be collected.

3. **Preparation of the data**: In this phase, it is necessary to clean up the acquired data.

4. **Modeling and evaluation**: Once the data is collected and the cleaning is established, it is possible to apply different algorithms for the same problem.

5. **Deployment**: One of the challenges of data analysis is to be able to provide dynamic and economically usable results. For this, it is necessary to deploy not only a solution in partnership with the departments responsible for information technology (IT) but also an interface (data visualization).

With regard to the main algorithms deployed, there are four main families of models: supervised, unsupervised, semi-supervised learning and reinforcement learning.

10.3.1 Supervised models

Supervised learning is a ML task consisting of learning a prediction function from annotated examples (Lallich et al., 2007). In other words, learning is said to be supervised if the data entering the process is already categorized and the algorithms must use it only to predict a result in order to be able to do it later when the data is not more categorized (Geron, 2017).

Among the most frequently used supervised models, there are:

(a) Support Vector Machine (SVM)

SVM represents a set of ML algorithm techniques that solve problems of discrimination and regression. This category of algorithm is often used to divide data into classes using as simple a border as possible (see Figure 10.1) so that the distance between the different groups of data and the border between them becomes maximum (Jain et al., 2020).

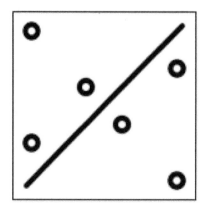

Figure 10.1 A two class support vector machine.

In this two-dimensional space, the "border" is the black line, the "support vectors" are the circled points (closest to the border) and the "margin" is the distance between the border and the line.

(b) Decision trees (AD) algorithms

Decision trees (AD) are one of the ML techniques used both in data mining and in business intelligence. The use of a hierarchical representation of the data structure in the form of decision sequences (tests) allows us to predict a result or a class. Thus, each individual (or observation), whose assignment to a well-defined class is sought, will be described by a set of variables which will then be tested at the level of the nodes of the tree (Yang and Chen, 2020). Suddenly, the tests are carried out at the level of the internal nodes and the decisions are taken in the leaf nodes. Take the case of a board of directors having to decide on the definition of a strategy to develop the turnover of their company (see Figure 10.2). Several options are possible: focus on the national market by developing new product ranges or by intensifying prospecting to gain new customers. Another alternative is possible: to develop internationally, either through a direct presence or by establishing a local partnership.

(c) Neural network(ANN)

A neural network is a software and/or hardware system that mimics the functioning of biological neurons. In other words, it is an intensely connected artificial neural network of elementary processors and which operates in parallel (Audevart and Alonzo, 2019). Each elementary processor (artificial neuron) calculates a single output based on the information it receives in both parallel and successive layers (see Figure 10.3). The first layer receives raw information as input, like the optic nerve, which processes human visual data.

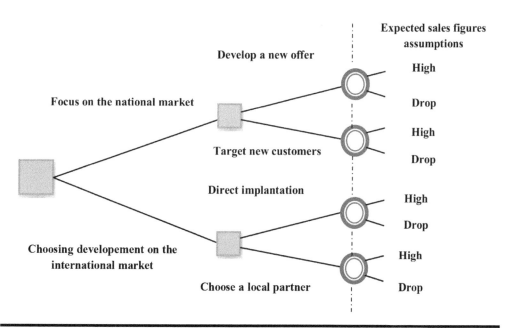

Figure 10.2 Illustration of the application of decision tree algorithms to determine possible scenarios for developing a business strategy.

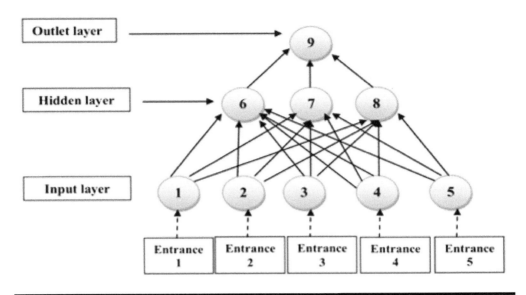

Figure 10.3 Architecture of a layered neural network.

The circles represent the neurons arranged in layers. The network represented here comprises three layers – the input layer receiving information on five neurons, and the output layer comprising a single neuron and giving the result of the internal calculation. Between these two layers is a layer called the "hidden layer" which is not visible from the outside, and is used to perform intermediate calculations.

10.3.2 Unsupervised models

Unlike supervised learning, this consists of teaching an artificial intelligence algorithm information that is neither labeled (it won't be specified that such an image is a cat or something else) nor classified to allow this algorithm to react to this information without human intervention, i.e. without supervisor (Bunker and Thabtah, 2019).

In addition, the algorithm processes the data without any prior training; it trains itself with the data it receives (Sathya and Abraham, 2013). However, just because we are talking about unsupervised learning does not mean that we should neglect the notion of categories for classification algorithms. A generally unsupervised learning algorithm is a "clustering" algorithm which will create categories from observations using categories associated with the data that is submitted to it, but it must make them emerge itself as is the case (suppose we are trying to recognize that a cat is a cat, or that an article in the journal AI is an article in the journal AI) (Love, 2002).

Another important unsupervised task is the detection of anomalies, for example to detect unusual bank card transactions in order to prevent fraud, to detect manufacturing faults or to automatically remove outliers from a dataset that we are going to provide to another learning algorithm (Lutz and Biernat, 2015) (Figure 10.4).

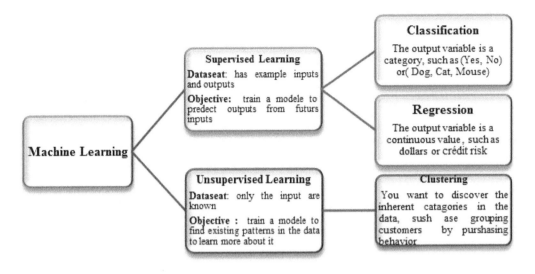

Figure 10.4 Comparative analysis between supervised learning and unsupervised learning.

10.3.3 Semi-supervised models

Regarding this third form of learning, it turns out that it has the same applications as supervised learning. However, its training relies on both tagged and untagged data (see Figure 10.5), usually a small amount from the first category and a large amount from the second category in order to produce considerable improvement in unsupervised learning accuracy (having no labeled data) (Vandewalle, 2009). Indeed, a priori labeling of all data requires the intervention of a human expert. It is a difficult operation, even tedious, when the amount of data is important without forgetting the cost associated with the labeling process.

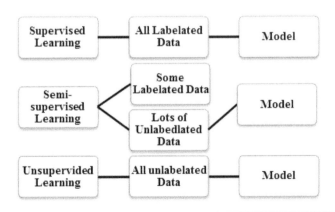

Figure 10.5 Comparative overview between the different algorithmic models of machine learning.

This form of learning is frequently used with methods such as classification, regression and prediction. Thus, it seems that semi-supervised learning is preferred when the cost of labeling is too high to justify a fully labeled learning process.

10.3.4 Reinforcement learning models

Finally, we have the last form of learning, which is reinforcement. Reinforcement learning corresponds to the case where the algorithm learns a behavior given an observation. The action of the algorithm on the environment generates a return value which then guides the learning algorithm. In other words, this mode of learning is rather applied in a class of learning problems whose objective is to learn from successive experiences, what should be done in order to apply the optimal solution (Barra et al., 2018).

Thanks to reinforcement learning, the algorithm multiplies the attempts to discover the actions bringing the greatest rewards. This form of learning involves three main components: the representative agent, the algorithm in the sense of the code, and learning or making decisions without forgetting the environment with which the agent interacts (Szepesvári, 2010).

The objective is for the agent to choose actions that maximize the rewards expected over a given period. The agent's behavior should allow choosing the actions that will maximize the sum of the rewards values in the long term (see Figure 10.6).

Unlike supervised and unsupervised learning, this form of learning is distinguished by its interactive and iterative nature. Indeed, the agent tries several solutions (exploration stage), and observes the reaction of the environment and adapts its behavior (the variables) to apply the best (Abbeel and Ng, 2004).

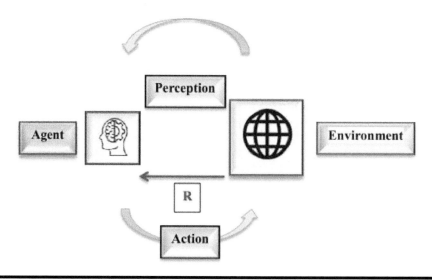

Figure 10.6 Reinforcement learning models.

10.4 Machine learning uses: cases in the fields of economics, finance and accounting

ML has seen a resurgence of interest in recent years, thanks to Big Data. Indeed, the fields of applied economics and finance inherit a long econometric tradition. Many more or less sophisticated econometric models are thus still used today (and effectively) by economics and finance practitioners to measure risks, make forecasts or manage funds (Leung et al., 2014).

In addition, since the finance industry gathers a large volume of data (Big Data) collected from its customers, it is perfectly suited to the advantages of data mining (Cecchini et al., 2010). In this context, several new financial applications based on ML algorithms are already used by banks and financial organizations in order to gain competitiveness and improve their profitability. In this section, we will expose the main uses of ML in finance.

10.4.1 Algorithmic trading

The international financial system has experienced major changes during the past three decades, accelerated in particular by the development of information and communication technologies (Aldridge, 2013). Indeed, the order execution mechanism used 50 years ago is no longer used today and it will not be the one used during the same period of time in the future. Investors have thus followed the development of transactions, thanks to technological advances that have revolutionized the financial markets (Kim, 2010). Therefore, forecasting and modeling diffusion undermines a wide range of problems encountered in forecasting stock market trends (Basak et al., 2019).

Although still little known by the general public, algorithmic trading is a form of trading that uses electronic platforms to enter stock market orders while allowing an algorithm to decide on important elements such as volume, price, opening or closing of the order (Hendershott and Riordan, 2013).

In addition, algorithmic trading contributes to better decision making regarding trading. Indeed, a mathematical model monitors new orders and trading results in real time and detects trends that can force stock prices to rise or fall. It can then act proactively to sell, hold or buy shares according to its forecasts (Bouyala, 2016; Nuti et al., 2011). Furthermore, algorithmic trading consists of two activities: stock market operations which are assisted by popular algorithms such as neural networks and support vector machines. The second is based on a completely automated form of trading.

The first form of algorithmic trading is considered to be the wisest and most recommended version for forecasting share prices and stock market indexes using external factors (Bollen et al., 2011; Kuo et al., 2001; Mittal and Goel, 2012). Indeed, by examining previous empirical studies relating to the application of Data Mining techniques in the world stock markets, it is quite obvious to note a certain preference of neural networks in terms of direction of prediction, and in particular in works of Majumder and Hussian (2007), Mizuno (1998) and Tjung et al. (2010). However, SVM has also been preferred by many researchers such as Kaur and Dharni (2019) and Kumar and Thenmozhi (2006) for whom the results of studies indicate that Data Mining techniques present significantly different performances (Schnaubelt et al., 2020).

Regarding the second form of algorithmic trading, the automated trading also known as high-frequency trading, automated trading or black box trading. The users are mainly hedge funds and investment banks trading for their own account to become major players in the financial markets in the United States and Europe (Kim, 2010). This technique takes into account computer resources and other mathematical models that can occupy an important place on the market (Biais, 2011), which is the hard version of the system.

With high-frequency trading, automation wins the decision process itself, but at a different level. The algorithm analyzes market data in real time, identifies imbalances or inefficiencies in terms of liquidity or price and then translates them into trading opportunities which will be implemented later (Aldridge, 2013). Automation and very short response times make it possible to take the advantage of minimal variations and of very short duration, which a human operator would not have been able to exploit or even detect (Henrique et al., 2019).

10.4.2 Insurance pricing

Technology has always had a huge impact on the insurance world and how it works. Indeed, the digital revolution has turned the professional world upside down, regardless of the sector of activity. The world of insurance is no exception and is being transformed by the changes brought about by digital technology and the increasing importance of Big Data. Insurance companies now have to use the right tools to exploit the vast amounts of data available. Among the processing solutions is the use of ML techniques which is fully part of the strategy implemented by companies. The proper use of this customer information appears today to be essential to guarantee its competitiveness and offer a service adapted to customer needs and expectations (Asimit et al., 2020).

Indeed, the main insurance activity is based on forecasts of future events by estimating the value and impact of these events, which requires the use of predictive modeling practices, particularly in predicting losses related to compensation. With the advent of Big Data and new data sources, such as sensors/telematics, external data sources, digital (interactions), or even social networks and the web (sentiment), organizations have never had so many opportunities to apply ML techniques to new aspects of insurance operations (Ly, 2019) to understand risk, claims and customer experience (Baudry and Robert, 2019). In addition, the fierce competition between insurers and the low costs of switching customers appeared for some time as the main motives that push insurers to use ML to determine a competitive price while covering the costs incurred (Smith et al., 2000).

Unlike traditional statistical methods, ML takes the advantage of the power of data analytics and makes it possible to relate seemingly unrelated datasets, whether structured, semi-structured or unstructured (Corlosquet-Habart and Janssen, 2017). However, empirical studies seem to disagree on the choice of the most efficient method to use. For Gu et al. (2020), regression trees remain one of the most widely used methods to improve the empirical understanding of pricing, unlike that advanced by Heaton et al. (2017) emphasizing in-depth learning for pricing.

Moreover, we can refer to the practice of "zoning"[28], to the practices of the insured (as an example, number of kilometers actually traveled or type of driving in the case of car insurance). Again, the example advanced by Boyer (2015) concerning the study of the correlations between the movements of a current account and accidents – for example the amounts paid by bank card.

Among the multiple applications of ML is personalized forecasting of future insurance costs (Verbelen et al., 2018). In this context, ML algorithms seem to be an essential asset because they allow the calculation of risk premium estimates by using a real-time analysis of the massive volume of data collected from insured customers. Data collection is facilitated by "telematics" – devices installed in the cars of policyholders thus making driving behavior measurable (for example, speeding, sudden breakdown). In combination, this allows car insurance pricing models to become more flexible and precise taking into account individual behavior (Joudaki et al., 2015; Kirchner, 2018).

10.4.3 Credit risk assessment

Although all businesses need to engage in risk management, the needs may be greater in financial institutions. Indeed, financial decision-makers today have the power and calculation methods for more precise diagnostics, forecasts and control in volatile and increasingly complex multidimensional environments capable of profoundly transforming the financial ecosystem (Hajek and Olej, 2014).

This observation indicates to us that the application of ML tools in this sector indeed concerns very diverse applications and covers a wide variety of functions, which can be divided into three strategic areas: controlling operational risk, improving management of customer relations and promoting cross-selling.

At the same time, the so-called ML methods are developing with phenomenal speed. In this direction, we can cite several empirical works which have highlighted the uses of different techniques of ML to control operational risk, as the analysis conducted by Kim et al. (2020) where he confirms that the use of a deep network can prevent operational risks by thus demonstrating the superiority of deep learning over ML and rule-based repositories. Algorithms based on decision trees (such as Stacking (Artis, 2002)). As for Aziz and Dowling (2019), the application of decision trees for the management of operational risk poses many challenges, in particular that concerning the over-adjustment of existing data which subsequently impacts its predictive power with new data and in new situations. Rather, it recommends support vector machines (SVMs) despite their complexities for mapping risk.

Other work has focused on the contribution of ML techniques and new data sources (new data) for credit risk modeling. Indeed, credit scoring was historically one of the first areas of application for ML techniques (Ghoddusi et al., 2019).

In the study by Cao et al. (2018), the choice of a reasonable model becomes the most important problem due to the rapid development of algorithm technology. That said, this work exposes the use of a new approach based on a set of deep genetic cascades of different support vector machine (SVM) classifiers. A kind of hybrid model that combines the advantages of several models including Deep Learning. Another study carried out by Plawiak et al. (2019) comes to join the results of the previous study on the performance of the method (DGCEC) in keeping the risk of credit default at an acceptable level. The two studies recommend combining various learning algorithms to improve the results obtained.

The sovereign risk ratings provided by the rating agencies also represent one of the most answered fields of application of ML techniques. Indeed, in the aftermath of the 2008 financial crisis, rating agencies were very strongly criticized for their poor assessment of the risk relating to real estate financial securities, which are also called "structured subprime products". The vast majority of AAA ratings were awarded to these stocks, yet the value of these assets plummeted as property prices plummeted, triggering the financial crisis (Coffinet and Kien, 2020). Such a situation has led to sharp criticism of the credit rating process from investors and bond issues, especially after having introduced a subjective component into the model used for credit ratings (De Moor et al., 2018).

However, the use of ML to manage bank credit risk should remain limited and certainly very tightly controlled. Indeed, bank supervisors generally require that the risk models be clear and simple in order to be understandable, verifiable and appropriate to be validated (Yu et al., 2008).

Whatever the case, these techniques generate significant productivity gains as soon as they render a certain number of preprocessing on the data obsolete; the essential advantage of ML is that it allows the use of new data (New Data) likely to better reflect credit risk (Khandani et al., 2010).

Moreover, the innovative aspect is appreciated here compared to the customer data usually used in score models such as payment history and income. However, the central question is whether this data diversity allows infinite access to credit from individuals or companies previously considered too risky in traditional databases (Kruppa, 2013). In addition, these new data can be considered Big Data if the number of predictors observed for each individual is very large (Yue et al., 2007).

10.4.4 Financial fraud detection

With a perspective of financial accounting fraud, particularly in the current economic context, the detection and identification of financial accounting fraud has been the subject of research, discussion and even controversy among a large number of investors, university researchers, media, the financial community and regulators. Among these researches, we can cite the analysis presented by Kumar et al. (2019) which uses techniques such as logistic regression, random forest and ML support vector to create a new alert model for the protection of elderly customers in a financial institution. Other ML techniques have been recommended like the work advanced by Yang et al. (2019) which studies the quality effect of Big N audit using double automatic learning with gradient reinforcement to carry out audit missions.

That said, and due to the emergence of a number of large-scale financial frauds discovered and reported in large companies such as Enron, Lucent, WorldCom and Satyam over the past decade, the requirement to detect, define and report increased financial accounting fraud (Yue et al., 2007).

In search of a more scientific definition of the concept of fraud, we find the definition advanced by the *Oxford English Dictionary* (McLean and McMillan, 2009) which defines fraud as "error" or criminal deception intended to result in personal financial gain. The difference between fraud and error is not obvious to everyone. In the context of the literature review, fraud is defined as any act leading to the abuse of the system of a for-profit organization without necessarily leading to direct legal consequences (Phua et al., 2010). Although a universally accepted definition of financial fraud is lacking in the literature, researchers have defined it as a deliberate act contrary to law, rule or policy with the intention of obtaining a financial benefit unauthorized and intentional inaccuracies or omissions of amount in the financial statements (Kou et al., 2004; Phua et al., 2010; Wang et al., 2006).

Often difficult to find a complete definition, financial fraud nevertheless presents in several forms ranging from the gross forgery of an identity card to the use of very sophisticated social engineering techniques. And to top it all off, the fraud mechanism is said to be "adversarial", that is, fraudsters are constantly trying to bypass existing detection procedures and systems in order to exploit any potential defect.

A majority of anti-fraud systems currently found are based on rules set by a human actor for the simple reason that the results obtained are relatively simple to understand and deemed transparent by the profession (Ahmed et al., 2016). If we look at financial fraud as an example, we find that effective fraud detection has always been an important but also complex task for accounting professionals (Ngai et al., 2011).

Moreover, the use of traditional internal audit techniques to detect accounting fraud seems to be obsolete (Fanning et al., 1995). First, auditors generally do not have the requisite knowledge regarding accounting fraud. Second, the lack of experience and expertise on the part of auditors in the detection and prevention of fraud negatively impacts their mission and can generate a very significant operational risk. Finally, while admitting the limits of an audit mission, the financial and accounting managers affirmed that the traditional and standard audit procedures are certainly easy to set up and effective; however, they become very difficult to maintain and perpetuate as the number of rules to be applied increases. This situation prompted several researchers to develop and empirically test predictive fraud detection audit models with practical applications for audit operations (Hajek and Henriques, 2017). Therefore, by analyzing the actual accounting data, the proposed model can identify abnormal transactions which allow it to focus directly on exceptions for a more thorough investigation in real time, which naturally leads to a significant reduction in manual intervention and processing time in audit assignments (Singh et al., 2019).

In addition, due to the asymmetry of information between corporate insiders and external investors, the uncertainty of the financial market as to the existence of fraud can hamper the normal functioning of the financial markets and the economic growth of a country (Li and Hoi, 2014).

The term "Data Mining" refers to the analysis and identification of interesting data and models from different perspectives and the transformation of this data into useful and statistically reliable information by establishing relationships between previously unknown and exploitable data (Grossrieder, 2013).

The convergence between Data Mining and the detection of accounting and financial fraud is illustrated in the fact that data mining as an advanced analytical tool can help auditors make decisions and detect fraud (Sharma and Panigrahi, 2013).

Indeed, Data Mining techniques have the potential to resolve the contradiction between the effect and the effectiveness of fraud detection (Wang, 2010). Exploration or data mining allows users to analyze data from different angles, to categorize it and to synthesize the relationships identified in order to extract and discover the hidden models in a very large collection of data. In traditional control models, an auditor can never be sure of the legitimacy and the intention of a fraudulent transaction. To treat this situation, the most optimal and cost-effective option is to find sufficient evidence of fraud from the available data using specialized, complex and sophisticated mathematical and computer algorithms to segment the data and assess future probabilities (Wang, 2010).

10.5 Conclusions

If artificial intelligence (AI) broadly designates a science aimed at imitating human capabilities, ML is its subset which consists of forming a machine to learn by itself. Besides, thanks to new computer technologies, ML has experienced remarkable growth in recent years. This renewed interest can be explained by the recognition of trends and the theory that computers can learn without being programmed to perform specific tasks. While many ML algorithms have been around for a long time, the computing capabilities and new data available today allow us to improve the accuracy of predictive analyses.

This renewed interest in ML is explained by the combination of several factors which also contributed to its incredible popularity – in particular Data Mining as well as the multiplication and diversification of available data.

In this chapter, the objective was to review the growing role as well as the functioning of the main algorithms representing the engines of ML. In general, two main types of ML algorithms are used today, supervised learning and unsupervised learning, as well as these different fields of application, particularly in the field of finance, which obviously does not escape to this revolutionary science.

This becomes a competitive advantage in various fields such as pricing, default risk, fraud detection and portfolio management. As such, it is essential for those involved in finance to understand the principles and applications of ML in order to have a clear and complete vision of these models deployed within their organization and subsequently benefit from the enormous opportunities allowing the times to stand out from the competition and reinvent their business.

References

Abbeel, P., & Ng, A. Y. (2004). Apprenticeship learning via inverse reinforcement learning. In *Paper Presented at the Proceedings of the Twenty-First International Conference on Machine Learning*, Banff, Canada.

Ahmed, M., Mahmood, A. N., & Islam, M. R. (2016). A survey of anomaly detection techniques in financial domain. *Future Generation Computer Systems, 55*, 278–288.

Ahmed, S. R. (2004). Applications of data mining in retail business. In *International Conference on Information Technology: Coding and Computing 2004*. Proceedings. ITCC 2004, 455–459.

Aldridge, I. (2013). *High-frequency trading: A practical guide to algorithmic strategies and trading systems*, Vol. 604, John Wiley & Sons.

ArtÂThs, M., Ayuso, M., & Guillén, M. (2002). Detection of automobile insurance fraud with discrete choice models and misclassified claims. *Journal of Risk and Insurance, 69*(3), 325–340.

Asimit, V., Kyriakou, I., & Nielsen, J. P. (2020). Special issue "Machine Learning in Insurance". *Risks, 8*(2), 54.

Audevart, A., & Alonzo, M. (2019). *Apprendre demain: Quand intelligence artificielle et neurosciences révolutionnent l'apprentissage*. Dunod.

Azencott, C.-A. (2019). *Introduction au machine learning*. Dunod.

Aziz, S., & Dowling, M. (2019). Machine learning and AI for risk management. In *Disrupting Finance*, Lynn, T., Mooney, J.G., Rosati, P., & Cummins, M. (Eds.), 33–50.

Barra, V., Miclet, L., & Cornuéjols, A. (2018). *Apprentissage artificiel: Concepts et algorithmes*. Ed. 3: Eyrolles.

Basak, S., Kar, S., Saha, S., Khaidem, L., & Dey, S. R. (2019). Predicting the direction of stock market prices using tree-based classifiers. *The North American Journal of Economics and Finance*, *47*, 552–567.

Baudry, M., & Robert, C. Y. (2019). A machine learning approach for individual claims reserving in insurance. *Applied Stochastic Models in Business and Industry*, *35*(5), 1127–1155.

Benureau, F. (2015). *Self exploration of sensorimotor spaces in robots*. Université de Bordeaux. Available at https://tel.archives-ouvertes.fr/tel-01251324/document.

Biais, B. (2011). *High frequency trading*. European Institute of Financial Regulation. Available at https://repository.nu.edu.sa/bitstream/123456789/2206/1/High frequency trading Bruno Biais (Toulouse School of Economics).pdf.

Bollen, J., Mao, H., & Zeng, X. (2011). Twitter mood predicts the stock market. *Journal of Computational Science*, *2*(1), 1–8.

Bolton, R. J., & Hand, D. J. (2002). Statistical fraud detection: A review. *Statistical Science*, *17*(3), 235–249.

Bouyala, R. (2016). *La révolution FinTech*. RB édition.

Boyer, J.-M. (2015). La tarification et le big data: quelles opportunités? *Revue d'Economie Financière*, *4*, 81–92.

Bunker, R. P., & Thabtah, F. (2019). A machine learning framework for sport result prediction. *Applied Computing and Informatics*, *15*(1), 27–33.

Campbell, M., Hoane Jr, A. J., & Hsu, F.-h. (2002). Deep blue. *Artificial Intelligence*, *134*(1–2), 57–83.

Cao, A., He, H., Chen, Z., & Zhang, W. (2018). Performance evaluation of machine learning approaches for credit scoring. *International Journal of Economics, Finance and Management Sciences*, *6*(6), 255–260.

Cecchini, M., Aytug, H., Koehler, G. J., & Pathak, P. (2010). Making words work: Using financial text as a predictor of financial events. *Decision Support Systems*, *50*(1), 164–175.

Coffinet, J., & Kien, J.-N. (2020). Detection of rare events: A Machine Learning toolkit with an application to banking crises. *The Journal of Finance and Data Science*, *5*(4), 183–207.

Corlosquet-Habart, M., & Janssen, J. (2017). *Le big data pour les compagnies d'assurance*. Vol. 1, ISTE Group.

De Moor, L., Luitel, P., Sercu, P., & Vanpée, R. (2018). Subjectivity in sovereign credit ratings. *Journal of Banking & Finance*, *88*, 366–392.

Desrosières, A. (2016). *La politique des grands nombres: histoire de la raison statistique*. La découverte.

Ding, K., Lev, B., Peng, X., Sun, T., & Vasarhelyi, M. A. (2019). *Machine learning improves accounting estimates*. Available at SSRN 3253220.

Fanning, K., Cogger, K. O., & Srivastava, R. (1995). Detection of management fraud: A neural network approach. *Intelligent Systems in Accounting, Finance and Management*, *4*(2), 113–126.

Galland, M. (2012). *La régulation du trading haute fréquence*. Bull. Joly Bourse mars.

Géron, A. (2017). *Machine Learning avec Scikit-Learn*. Dunod.

Ghoddusi, H., Creamer, G. G., & Rafizadeh, N. (2019). Machine learning in energy economics and finance: A review. *Energy Economics*, *81*, 709–727.

Grossrieder, L., Albertetti, F., Stoffel, K., & Ribaux, O. (2013). Des données aux connaissances, un chemin difficile: réflexion sur la place du data mining en analyse criminelle. *Revue Internationale de Criminologie et de Police Technique et Scientifique*, *66*(1), 99–116.

Gu, S., Kelly, B., & Xiu, D. (2020). Empirical asset pricing via Machine Learning. *The Review of Financial Studies*, *33*(5), 2223–2273.

Hajek, P., & Henriques, R. (2017). Mining corporate annual reports for intelligent detection of financial statement fraud–A comparative study of machine learning methods. *Knowledge-Based Systems*, *128*, 139–152.

Hajek, P., & Olej, V. (2014). Predicting firms' credit ratings using ensembles of artificial immune systems and machine learning âĂŞ An over-sampling approach. In *IFIP International Conference on Artificial Intelligence Applications and Innovations*, 29–38. Berlin: Springer.

Heaton, J., Polson, N., & Witte, J. H. (2017). Deep learning for finance: deep portfolios. *Applied Stochastic Models in Business and Industry*, *33*(1), 3–12.

Hendershott, T., & Riordan, R. (2013). Algorithmic trading and the market for liquidity. *Journal of Financial and Quantitative Analysis*, *48*(4), 1001–1024.

Henrique, B. M., Sobreiro, V. A., & Kimura, H. (2019). Literature review: Machine learning techniques applied to financial market prediction. *Expert Systems with Applications*, *124*, 226–251.

Horton, R., Morrissey, R., Olsen, M., Roe, G., & Voyer, R. (2009). Mining eighteenth century ontologies: Machine learning and knowledge classification in the Encyclopédie. *Digital Humanities Quarterly*, *3*(2), 1–15.

Huang, G., Song, S., Gupta, J. N., & Wu, C. (2014). Semi-supervised and unsupervised extreme learning machines. *IEEE Transactions on Cybernetics*, *44*(12), 2405–2417.

Jain, M., Narayan, S., Balaji, P., Bhowmick, A., & Muthu, R. K. (2020). *Speech emotion recognition using support vector machine*. arXiv preprint arXiv:2002.07590.

Joudaki, H., Rashidian, A., Minaei-Bidgoli, B., Mahmoodi, M., Geraili, B., Nasiri, M., & Arab, M. (2015). Using data mining to detect health care fraud and abuse: a review of literature. *Global Journal of Health Science*, *7*(1), 194–202.

Kaur, J., & Dharni, K. (2019). Predicting daily returns of global stocks indices: Neural networks vs support vector machines. *Journal of Economics, Management and Trade*, *24*(6), 1–13.

Khandani, A. E., Kim, A. J., & Lo, A. W. (2010). Consumer credit-risk models via machine-learning algorithms. *Journal of Banking & Finance*, *34*(11), 2767–2787.

Kim, A., Yang, Y., Lessmann, S., Ma, T., Sung, M.-C., & Johnson, J. E. (2020). Can deep learning predict risky retail investors? A case study in financial risk behavior forecasting. *European Journal of Operational Research*, *283*(1), 217–234.

Kim, K. (2010). *Electronic and algorithmic trading technology: The complete guide*. Academic Press.

Kirchner, T. (2018). *Predicting your casualtiesâĂŞHow machine learning is revolutionizing insurance pricing at AXA*, Available at https://digital.hbs.edu/platform-rctom/submission/predicting-your-casualties-how-machine-learning-is-revolutionizing-insurance-pricing-at-axa/.

Kou, Y., Lu, C. T., Sirwongwattana, S., & Huang, Y. P. (2004). Survey of fraud detection techniques. In *IEEE International Conference on Networking, Sensing and Control*, Vol. 2, 749–754. IEEE.

Kruppa, J., Schwarz, A., Arminger, G., & Ziegler, A. (2013). Consumer credit risk: Individual probability estimates using machine learning. *Expert Systems with Applications*, *40*(13), 5125–5131.

Kumar, G., Muckley, C. B., Pham, L., & Ryan, D. (2019). Can alert models for fraud protect the elderly clients of a financial institution? *The European Journal of Finance*, *25*(17), 1683–1707.

Kumar, M., & Thenmozhi, M. (2006). Forecasting stock index movement: A comparison of support vector machines and random forest. In *Indian Institute of Capital Markets 9th Capital Markets Conference Paper*, Mumbai, India, 1–16.

Kuo, R. J., Chen, C., & Hwang, Y. (2001). An intelligent stock trading decision support system through integration of genetic algorithm based fuzzy neural network and artificial neural network. *Fuzzy Sets and Systems*, *118*(1), 21–45.

Lallich, S., Lenca, P., & Vaillant, B. (2007). *Construction d'une entropie décentrée pour l'apprentissage supervisé*. Available at https://hal.archives-ouvertes.fr/hal-02121562/.

Leung, C. K.-S., MacKinnon, R. K., & Wang, Y. (2014). A machine learning approach for stock price prediction. In *18th International Database Engineering & Applications Symposium*, Porto Portugal, 274–277.

Li, B., & Hoi, S. C. (2014). Online portfolio selection: A survey. *ACM Computing Surveys (CSUR), 46*(3), 1–36.

Li, B., Yu, J., Zhang, J., & Ke, B. (2016). Detecting accounting frauds in publicly traded US firms: A machine learning approach. In *Asian Conference on Machine Learning*.

López de Prado, M., & Lewis, M. J. (2019). Detection of false investment strategies using unsupervised learning methods. *Quantitative Finance, 19*(9), 1555–1565.

Love, B. C. (2002). Comparing supervised and unsupervised category learning. *Psychonomic Bulletin & Review, 9*(4), 829–835.

Lutz, M., & Biernat, E. (2015). *Data science: fondamentaux et études de cas: Machine Learning avec Python et R*. Editions Eyrolles.

Ly, A. (2019). *Algorithmes de Machine Learning en assurance: solvabilité, textmining, anonymisation et transparence*. Université Paris-Est.

Majumder, M., & Hussian, M. A. (2007). Forecasting of Indian stock market index using artificial neural network. *Information Science*, 98–105.

McLean, I., & McMillan, A. (2009). *The concise Oxford dictionary of politics*. OUP Oxford.

Mittal, A., & Goel, A. (2012). *Stock prediction using twitter sentiment analysis*. Standford University, CS229, available at http://cs229.stanford.edu/proj2011/GoelMittal-StockMarketPredictionUsing TwitterSentimentAnalysis.pdf.

Mizuno, H., Kosaka, M., Yajima, H., & Komoda, N. (1998). Application of neural network to technical analysis of stock market prediction. *Studies in Informatic and Control, 7*(3), 111–120.

Moualek, D. Y. (2017). *Deep Learning pour la classification des images*. 07-03-2017. Available at http://dspace.univ-tlemcen.dz/handle/112/12583.

Ngai, E. W., Hu, Y., Wong, Y. H., Chen, Y., & Sun, X. (2011). The application of data mining techniques in financial fraud detection: A classification framework and an academic review of literature. *Decision Support Systems, 50*(3), 559–569.

Nuti, G., Mirghaemi, M., Treleaven, P., & Yingsaeree, C. (2011). Algorithmic trading. *Computer, 44*(11), 61–69.

Oxford, O. E. (2009). *Oxford English Dictionary*. Oxford University Press.

Phua, C., Lee, V., Smith, K., & Gayler, R. (2010). *A comprehensive survey of data mining-based fraud detection research*. arXiv preprint arXiv:1009.6119.

PÅĆawiak, P., Abdar, M., & Acharya, U. R. (2019). Application of new deep genetic cascade ensemble of SVM classifiers to predict the Australian credit scoring. *Applied Soft Computing, 84*, 105740.

Sánchez, D., Vila, M., Cerda, L., & Serrano, J.-M. (2009). Association rules applied to credit card fraud detection. *Expert Systems with Applications, 36*(2), 3630–3640.

Sang, C., & Di Pierro, M. (2019). Improving trading technical analysis with tensorflow long short-term memory (LSTM) neural network. *The Journal of Finance and Data Science, 5*(1), 1–11.

Sathya, R., & Abraham, A. (2013). Comparison of supervised and unsupervised learning algorithms for pattern classification. *International Journal of Advanced Research in Artificial Intelligence, 2*(2), 34–38.

Schnaubelt, M., Fischer, T., & Krauss, C. (2020). Separating the signal from the noiseâĂŞfinancial machine learning for Twitter. *Journal of Economic Dynamics and Control*, 103895.

Sharma, A., & Panigrahi, P. K. (2013). *A review of financial accounting fraud detection based on data mining techniques.* arXiv preprint arXiv:1309.3944.

Singh, N., Lai, K. h., Vejvar, M., & Cheng, T. E. (2019). Data-driven auditing: A predictive modeling approach to fraud detection and classification. *Journal of Corporate Accounting & Finance, 30*(3), 64–82.

Smith, K. A., Willis, R. J., & Brooks, M. (2000). An analysis of customer retention and insurance claim patterns using data mining: A case study. *Journal of the Operational Research Society, 51*(5), 532–541.

Szepesvári, C. (2010). Algorithms for reinforcement learning. *Synthesis Lectures on Artificial Intelligence and Machine Learning, 4*(1), 1–103.

Thomas, T. P. V., Vijayaraghavan, A. P., & Emmanuel, S. (2020). *Machine learning approaches in cyber security analytics.* Springer.

Tjung, L. C., Kwon, O., Tseng, K., & Bradley-Geist, J. (2010). Forecasting financial stocks using data mining. *Global Economy and Finance Journal, 3*(2), 13–26.

Vandewalle, V. (2009). Estimation et sélection en classification semi-supervisée. Available at https://tel.archives-ouvertes.fr/tel-00447141/.

Vardi, M. Y. (2014). Would Turing have passed the Turing test? *Communications of the ACM, 57*(9), 5–5.

Verbelen, R., Antonio, K., & Claeskens, G. (2018). Unravelling the predictive power of telematics data in car insurance pricing. *Journal of the Royal Statistical Society: Series C (Applied Statistics), 67*(5), 1275–1304.

Wang, J.-H., Liao, Y.-L., Tsai, T.-M., & Hung, G. (2006). Technology-based financial frauds in Taiwan: issues and approaches. In *2006 IEEE International Conference on Systems, Man and Cybernetics*, 1120–1124. IEEE.

Wang, S. (2010). A comprehensive survey of data mining-based accounting-fraud detection research. In *2010 International Conference on Intelligent Computation Technology and Automation*, Changsha, China, 50–53.

Yafooz, W. M., Bakar, Z. B. A., Fahad, S. A., & Mithon, A. M. (2020). Business intelligence through big data analytics, data mining and machine learning data management, analytics and innovation. Sharma N., Chakrabarti A., & Balas V. (Eds.), *Data Management, Analytics and Innovation. Advances in Intelligent Systems and Computing*, vol. *1016*, Springer, Singapore, 217–230.

Yang, J.-C., Chuang, H.-C., & Kuan, C.-M. (2019). Double machine learning with gradient boosting and its application to the big n audit quality effect. *USC-INET Research Paper(19-05)*.

Yang, S.-B., & Chen, T.-L. (2020). Uncertain decisiontree for bank marketing classification. *Journal of Computational and Applied Mathematics, 371*, 112710.

Yu, L., Wang, S., & Lai, K. K. (2008). Credit risk assessment with a multistage neural network ensemble learning approach. *Expert Systems with Applications, 34*(2), 1434–1444.

Yue, D., Wu, X., Wang, Y., Li, Y., & Chu, C.-H. (2007). A review of data mining-based financial fraud detection research. In *2007 International Conference on Wireless Communications, Networking and Mobile Computing*, 5519–5522. IEEE.

Zhang, D., & Zhou, L. (2004). Discovering golden nuggets: Data mining in financial application. *IEEE Transactions on Systems, Man, and Cybernetics, Part C (Applications and Reviews), 34*(4), 513–522.

Chapter 11

Handling class imbalance data in business domain

Md. Shajalal, Mohammad Zoynul Abedin and
Mohammed Mohi Uddin

11.1 Introduction

Due to the recent advancement in computer science and communication technology, the availability of the raw data has been immensely increased over the decade. As a result, a huge opportunity has been created to mine some new data patterns and knowledge from the data (He and Garcia, 2009; Van Hulse, Khoshgoftaar, and Napolitano, 2007). But at the same time, this huge data created major problems like data imbalance (Aurelio et al., 2019). Especially in the classification task, imbalance data is a curse where well-reputed algorithms might fail to classify with efficient accuracy. The major reason is that the number of labeled data points for one specific class is extremely higher than the number of labeled data points for the other class/classes (Han, Wang, and Mao, 2005; Lemaître, Nogueira, and Aridas, 2017). Conventionally, the class having more data points is called the majority class and the other class (classes) is (are) known as a minority. Hence, the algorithm may learn the majority class examples' patterns with higher accuracy, maybe more than 99%. On the contrary, for minority class, the performance is worst, even less than 10%.

However, the data imbalance problem is a common scenario in some renowned research domains in business such as credit card fraud direction (Wei et al., 2013) and product backorder prediction (de Santis, de Aguiar, and Goliatt, 2017; Hajek and Abedin, 2020). There are some other fields where the data imbalance problem is common, including information retrieval (Chang et al., 2003; Chen et al., 2011; Zheng, Wu, and Srihari, 2004), detecting unreliable telecommunication customers (Burez and Van den Poel, 2009), learning word pronunciations, network intrusion (Cieslak, Chawla, and Striegel, 2006; Rodda and Erothi, 2016) and oil-spill detection (De Maio et al., 2016). Researchers tried different approaches to solving data imbalance problems that are broadly categorized as data-level approaches and algorithm-level approaches.

From many business applications, however, the credit card fraud detection has been taken as a study example in this chapter. For banks and card issuers, credit card fraud is an alarming event. Due to credit card anomalies, financial institutions count a huge amount of monetary losses every year. Thereby, credit card fraud discovery is an integral part of banks that screens fake transactions in advance of their authorization by card issuers. Although credit card anomalies happen infrequently, they result in huge impacts as most fake transactions have large values. As of privacy issues, there is a lack of empirical research on evidencing real-world transaction data. Hence, it is significant to classify and predict whether a transaction is fraudulent. Moreover, a sufficient prediction of fraud transactions permits stakeholders to take timely actions that can potentially prevent extra fraud or monetary losses.

In this chapter, we will mainly discuss the data-level approaches for detecting credit card fraud. The oversampling and undersampling approach tries to duplicate the minority class examples and remove some majority class examples, respectively. In some cases, the combination of both sampling techniques might be an effective solution. Other data-level methods generate new samples for minority class applying some data patterns and hypothesis. The SMOTE (Chawla et al., 2002) and borderline-SMOTE (Han, Wang, and Mao, 2005; Nguyen, Cooper, and Kamei, 2009) are the popular examples of such approaches. The evaluation metrics that suited to judge the performance of classification methods on such datasets include AUC (Yang et al., 2017), ROC curve and precision-recall curve (He and Garcia, 2009).

The rest of the chapter is organized as follows: we first define the data imbalance problem in Section 11.2. Then, we discuss the possible solution for the imbalanced dataset in Section 11.3. Section 11.4 presents the evaluation metrics to measure the performance of any method having an imbalance problem. A case study on credit card fraud detection dataset is also presented in Section 11.5. Finally, we conclude the chapter with some future research directions in Section 11.6.

11.2 Data imbalance problem

Usually, the dataset with unequal distribution of different class examples is an imbalanced one. But in the classification task, when any dataset exhibits the property that the number of majority class examples is significantly larger than the number of minority class examples, it will be treated as imbalanced one (He and Garcia, 2009). Moreover, in some cases, the difference between the number of data points over classes might be extremely unequal. The severely imbalanced dataset can be defined by the ratio between the number of inter-class data points, and the ratio could be 100:1, 1000:1 or 10000:1 (Krawczyk, 2016). That means a 100:1 extremely imbalanced dataset has 100 majority class examples per one minority class example and is analogous for other ratios.

For example, in the product backorder prediction task (Hajek and Abedin, 2020), only one product went backorder per 137 orders. In ratio, the rarity of the backordered product can be defined as 137:1, which indicates this is a highly imbalanced dataset. We can illustrate the distribution of the example over two different class by using Figure 11.1. Similarly, for the credit card

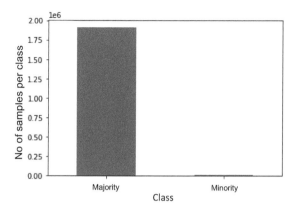

Figure 11.1 Class distribution in product backorder prediction dataset.

fraud detection dataset, only 0.17% data points are labeled as fraud and the rest of the examples (99.87%) are successful valid transactions. Hence, the algorithms need some level of superiority to learn the pattern of credit card fraud. This is next to impossible for any classical method due to the lack of data points for the minority class. Hence, the minority class examples should be increased in some way so that the algorithm can learn the minority class and eventually predict correctly. It can be done in two ways: one is to duplicate the examples and another is to generate some examples synthetically considering the data patterns.

11.3 Balancing techniques

11.3.1 Random sampling-based method

As the classical algorithms perform with standard accuracy in the balanced dataset, randomly duplicating the minority class examples or removing random majority class data points might be one solution. Previous studies also suggested that classical algorithms could provide high accuracy on a balanced dataset after applying random sampling. To overcome the imbalanced problem, one of the most easiest and widely used first step solutions is random oversampling or/and random undersampling (Douzas and Bacao, 2017). By maintaining an inter-class ratio of data points, some minority class examples can be oversampled. For the same reason, if the number of minority class examples is reasonable, some majority class examples can be removed randomly to achieve a balanced ratio (Cao et al., 2013). The common practice is to exploit the combination of random oversampling and undersampling before applying the classification algorithm.

11.3.2 SMOTE oversampling

Generally, the misclassification cost is comparatively higher when an abnormal object is predicted as normal than the opposite error cost. The loss of a classifier might increase because of copying minority class examples randomly to achieve the balance in the distribution of examples in the dataset. To create minority class examples artificially, a widely used technique called SMOTE-(**S**ynthetic **M**inority **O**ver-sampling **TE**chnique) was proposed by Chawla et al. (2002). Unlike random oversampling, SMOTE can create synthetic examples of a particular minority class artificially (Last, Douzas, and Bacao, 2017).

To choose minority class examples, SMOTE leverages the synthetic examples along the ling segments (Sharma et al., 2018). At first, considering the nearest neighbors it selected k minority examples by joining the line with all. Here, k nearest minority examples are chosen based on the desired number of over-sampled examples. The difference between the feature vectors of the considered sample and its nearest neighbor is exploited to create synthetic minority class examples for selection. A random number in [0,1] is multiplied with the difference and added to the feature vector of the considered sample. Therefore, the random point along the line is selected between two features and it will be the more effective decision region.

However, depending on the percentage of the oversampling examples, SMOTE decides how many synthetic samples are needed. For example, we need to generate new example for each instance if the oversampling percentage is 100%; hence, the size of the minority class will be twice. Let the percentage be n, given that $n > 100$; the SMOTE oversampling technique's working steps are as follows:

1. SMOTE first identifies k nearest neighbors such that $k = ceil\left[\frac{n}{100}\right]$ from minority class X by exploiting traditional Euclidean distance (Guo et al., 2003):

$$d(\boldsymbol{P}, \boldsymbol{Q}) = \sqrt{\sum_{i=1}^{n} \left(p_i - q_i\right)^2}$$

   where P and Q indicate the vector representation of features of a particular minority sample and one neighbor, respectively.

2. Then, we need to calculate the difference between the feature vectors of the negative class example and neighbor. In total, we have k feature difference vectors.

3. Each feature value of the vector is multiplied by a random number on a scale [0,1].

4. Finally, the summation vector among the difference vectors is used as a minority class example.

11.3.3 Borderline-SMOTE

Most classification algorithms try to learn the borderline examples of each class. Because the rate of misclassification might depend on how the algorithms learn borderline examples. It is also common for any method that classifies the borderline data points as the wrong class. Therefore a special version of SMOTE has been introduced considering the above scenario that is widely known as borderline-SMOTE (Han, Wang, and Mao, 2005). Note that SMOTE first selects k nearest neighbors in the minority class and generates the class examples for the minority class. But borderline-SMOTE only creates and oversampled the borderline data points of the minority class (Nguyen, Cooper, and Kamei, 2009). In summary, first, borderline-SMOTE finds out the borderline examples, then generates the synthetic data points and adds them to the training set as minority class examples. Given a labeled training dataset, let $\{p_1, p_2, \ldots, p_a\}$ and

$\{n_1, n_2, \ldots, n_b\}$ be the minority and majority class examples having the size a and b, respectively. Then the steps of borderline-SMOTE are described as follows:

1. Calculate the m nearest neighbors for each minority class example, p_i, in the dataset. Let m' be the number of majority examples such that $0 \le m' \le m$

2. When $m' = m$, such that all the nearest neighbors are from majority examples, that p_i is considered as noise. If the number nearest of neighbors of p_i from the majority class is larger than the neighbors from minority class such that $\frac{m}{2} \le m' < m$, then p_i could be easily misclassified. Therefore, that p_i is put into the DANGER set. These are the borderline examples of minority class.

3. The members in the DANGER set are from minority examples and they are borderline data points. Mathematically,

$$DANGER = \{p'_1, p'_2, p'_3, \ldots, p'_H\}$$

where $DANGER \subset P$ and $0 \le H < a$.

4. For a positive integer s lies in $[1, K]$, $s \times H$ number for positive data points are generated. Then for each example in DANGER, this method randomly selects s nearest neighbors from its k nearest neighbors. This step is similar to the SMOTE that has been explained in the previous section.

11.3.4 Class weight boosting

The prominent classification algorithms usually are applied to the dataset that has an equal weight for each class. But, for the imbalanced dataset, one sensible approach is to use different class weights for specific classes. As we noted earlier, minority samples are very rare in the real world. Hence, providing greater weight to the minority class can boost the classification performance. The minority class samples are very challenging to accurately classify which makes the classification performance very poor. However, the majority class samples are easier to predict. This scenario might increase the loss of a particular classification algorithm. Hence, weight boosting might be effective to apply and handle the imbalance in the dataset (Sun, Kamel, and Wang, 2006).

11.4 Evaluation metrics

The performance of any classifier is estimated usually by *Accuracy*, *Precision* and *Recall*. However, the performance estimation of a classifier handling data imbalance is somewhat different than the conventional one. Hence, some other metrics such as the area under the curve (AUC), receiver operating characteristics (ROC) curve, precision-recall curve, etc. are employed to test the performance of a method applied on imbalanced data. Exploiting a matrix with different statistics refereed as a confusion matrix (Figure 11.2) (Chawla et al., 2002), the above-mentioned metrics are estimated.

In summary, the confusion metrics consist of four statistics: True Negative, False Negative, False Positive and False Negative. These can be summarized as follows:

	Predicted Negative	Predicted Positive
Actual Negative	**TN** True Negative	**FP** False Positive
Actual Positive	**FN** False Negative	**TP** True Positive

Figure 11.2 Confusion matrix (see Moula, Guotai, and Abedin, 2017, p. 165).

- **True Negative (TN):** How many negative examples are predicted appropriately as negative examples?
- **False Positive (FP):** How many negative examples are predicted inappropriately as positive examples?
- **False Negative (FN):** How many positive examples are predicted inappropriately as negative examples?
- **True Positive (TP):** How many positive examples are predicted inappropriately as positive examples?

Accuracy is the most widely used metrics (Moula, Guotai, and Abedin, 2017) to judge the performance of any classifier which can be defined as follows:

$$Acc = \frac{TP + TN}{TP + FN + FP + FN}$$

Besides the *Accuracy Acc* metric, *loss* $= 1 - Acc$ is a considerable metric to estimate the system's performance. Due to the imbalance in the class distribution, the losses are also unequal throughout the classes. Therefore, the *Accuracy* is not sufficient to measure the performance of the classifier (Chawla et al., 2002). Moreover, accuracy is a general metric that does not indicate how many correctly classify samples of a particular class. For imbalance dataset, ROC is employed widely as a better metric to evaluate the performance of the classification algorithm (Chawla et al., 2002).

$$F = \frac{FP}{FP + TN}$$

The precision p is another evaluation metric that is based on the accuracy of the classifier when it classifies only the positive examples. Precision is calculated as follows:

$$P = \frac{TP}{TP + FP}$$

The ability of any particular classifier to predict positive samples is measured by the recall R:

$$R = \frac{TP}{TP + FN}$$

Receiver operating characteristics (ROC) curves: ROC curve is widely used to measure the performance of any classifier applied on imbalanced dataset (Yang et al., 2017). This curve can be constructed by using two measures: *true positive* rate and *false positive* rate. These can be calculated by the following equations (see Moula, Guotai, and Abedin, 2017, p. 165):

$$TP\_rate = \frac{TP}{TP + FN}; \ FP\_rate = \frac{FP}{FP + TN}$$

ROC curve can be drawn by plotting the *TP_rate* and *FP_rate*. Note that any point in the curve represents the performance of the classifier in certain distribution. The curve also represents the trade-off between true positive and false positive. They also correspond to the benefit and cost of the classifier, respectively.

As an example, an ROC curve is illustrated in Figure 11.3. The ROC points in the diagonal BD represent the random guess of the class labels, which means random classifier. The blue and green curves in Figure 11.3 indicate the typical ROC curves. If the curve is closer to point A, the performance is better compared to the others. Here, we can see that the performance of any method having the blue ROC curve is better than the classifier having the green ROC curve. According to the curve, we can also say that the classifier might have a higher number of true positive examples by raising the false positive examples. However, any ROC curve going through the shaded part in the figure is the worst classifier than the random classifiers.

Precision-Recall curve: Precision-Recall curve is quite similar to the ROC curve. This curve can be used for a highly imbalanced dataset (He and Garcia, 2009). In the same fashion, this curve can be generated by plotting the value of precision and recall of the classifier. The characteristics are similar to the ROC curve. But for a severely imbalanced dataset where the number of negative examples is extremely larger than the positive example, the ROC cannot be the only curve to measure the performance. However, if the curve is similar for both ROC and precision-recall, then the performance can be validated.

Area Under Curve (AUC): The most important evaluation metric to test is the efficiency of a classifier under data imbalance in AUC (Area Under Curve) (Chawla et al., 2002; Yang et al., 2017). Basically, AUC is estimated considering the ROC curve or the precision recall curve. This metric is single-handedly well enough to indicate the performance of any classifier under data imbalance problem. This evaluation metric is estimated as follows:

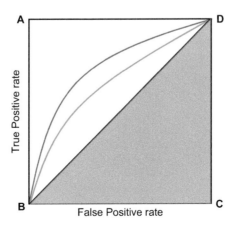

Figure 11.3 Receiver operating characteristics (ROC) curves.

$$AUC = \frac{1 + P - F}{2}$$

The area under the blue curve illustrates the AUC of the classifier with blue ROC in Figure 11.3.

11.5 Case study: credit card fraud detection

To visualize the performance of different data-level balancing techniques discussed throughout this chapter, we applied those techniques on an imbalanced business dataset. We collected *Credit Card Fraud Detection* dataset from Kaggle.

The dataset has the transaction details of European cardholders from September 2019. According to the statistics of the class distribution, this is a highly imbalanced dataset. The number of valid transactions by the cardholders is 284,807; on the contrary, the fraud transactions have happened only 492 times. In other words, the amount of minority class (fraud transaction) is only 0.17%. The distribution is illustrated in Figure 11.4. However, each transaction has 30 different feature values – though the feature values are not the original ones. The organizers applied the principal component analysis technique to transform the data values for confidentiality purposes.

We applied different data-level approaches to balance the dataset before applying the classification method. A typical deep neural network-based (Kraus, Feuerriegel, and Oztekin, 2020) classification technique has been applied to train the method. The dataset has been split and 80% was used for training and the rest of the samples have been utilized for testing. After applying the DNN-based method, we evaluated the performance of different data-level balancing techniques. The performance of different methods is reported in Figure 11.5. We can see that, among four different balancing techniques, borderline-SMOTE outperformed others.

In terms of AUC, we can see that the other balancing techniques were also performed effectively. Note that borderline-SMOTE always tries to find out the borderline samples that tend to be misclassified. Therefore, by applying this particular technique, the method can learn and select better candidates to resample the dataset. However, SMOTE oversampling generates the samples synthetically rather than randomly. The performance also visualizes the superiority of SMOTE over random oversampling and weight boosting. We also illustrated the performance in terms of the ROC curve in Figure 11.6. The curves also represent the performance of different balancing techniques.

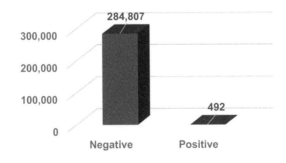

Figure 11.4 The distribution of valid transaction and fraud transaction in *Credit Card Fraud* detection dataset.

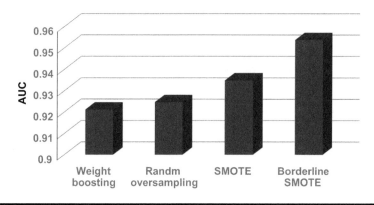

Figure 11.5 Performance of different data balancing techniques on credit card fraud detection dataset in terms of AUC.

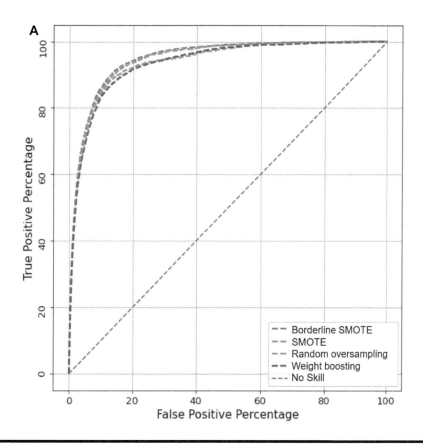

Figure 11.6 Performance of different data balancing techniques on credit card fraud detection dataset in terms of ROC curve.

11.6 Conclusion

In summary, the class imbalanced dataset has a skewed distribution of data points over the classes. In a highly imbalanced dataset, the number of majority class examples might be extremely higher than the number of minority class examples. In this chapter, we presented some data-level challenges and the solution to overcome the imbalanced problem. The techniques to solve the imbalanced problems include random oversampling and undersampling, SMOTE and borderline-SMOTE synthetic sampling and class weight boosting. To measure the performance of any classifier on such data, there are several effective evaluation metrics such as ROC curve, precision-recall curve and AUC. Future research can use a larger dataset from multi-countries perspectives in order to test the effectiveness of various techniques. Research on innovative methods in tackling classification challenges with imbalance data is warranted.

References

Aurelio, Yuri Sousa, Gustavo Matheus de Almeida, Cristiano Leite de Castro, and Antonio Padua Braga. 2019. "Learning from imbalanced data sets with weighted cross-entropy function." *Neural Processing Letters* 50 (2): 1937–1949.

Burez, Jonathan, and Dirk Van den Poel. 2009. "Handling class imbalance in customer churn prediction." *Expert Systems with Applications* 36 (3): 4626–4636.

Cao, Hong, Xiao-Li Li, David Yew-Kwong Woon, and See-Kiong Ng. 2013. "Integrated oversampling for imbalanced time series classification." *IEEE Transactions on Knowledge and Data Engineering* 25 (12): 2809–2822.

Chang, Edward Y, Beitao Li, Gang Wu, and Kingshy Goh. 2003. "Statistical learning for effective visual information retrieval." In *Proceedings 2003 International Conference on Image Processing (Cat. No. 03CH37429)*, Vol. 3, III–609. IEEE.

Chawla, Nitesh V, Kevin W Bowyer, Lawrence O Hall, and W Philip Kegelmeyer. 2002. "SMOTE: Synthetic minority over-sampling technique." *Journal of Artificial Intelligence Research* 16: 321–357.

Chen, Enhong, Yanggang Lin, Hui Xiong, Qiming Luo, and Haiping Ma. 2011. "Exploiting probabilistic topic models to improve text categorization under class imbalance." *Information Processing & Management* 47 (2): 202–214.

Cieslak, David A, Nitesh V Chawla, and Aaron Striegel. 2006. "Combating imbalance in network intrusion datasets." In *2006 IEEE International Conference on Granular Computing*, 732–737. Atlanta.

De Maio, Antonio, Danilo Orlando, Luca Pallotta, and Carmine Clemente. 2016. "A multifamily GLRT for oil spill detection." *IEEE Transactions on Geoscience and Remote Sensing* 55 (1): 63–79.

de Santis, Rodrigo Barbosa, Eduardo Pestana de Aguiar, and Leonardo Goliatt. 2017. "Predicting material backorders in inventory management using machine learning." In *2017 IEEE Latin American Conference on Computational Intelligence (LA-CCI)*, 1–6. IEEE.

Douzas, Georgios, and Fernando Bacao. 2017. "Geometric SMOTE: Effective oversampling for imbalanced learning through a geometric extension of SMOTE." *arXiv preprint arXiv:1709.07377*.

Guo, Gongde, Hui Wang, David Bell, Yaxin Bi, and Kieran Greer. 2003. "KNN model-based approach in classification." In *OTM Confederated International Conferences "On the Move to Meaningful Internet Systems"*, 986–996. Springer.

Hajek, Petr, and Mohammad Zoynul Abedin. 2020. "A profit function-maximizing inventory backorder prediction system using big data analytics." *IEEE Access* 8: 58982–58994.

Han, Hui, Wen-Yuan Wang, and Bing-Huan Mao. 2005. "Borderline-SMOTE: A new over-sampling method in imbalanced data sets learning." In *International Conference on Intelligent Computing*, 878–887. Springer.

He, Haibo, and Edwardo A Garcia. 2009. "Learning from imbalanced data." *IEEE Transactions on Knowledge and Data Engineering* 21 (9): 1263–1284.

Kraus, Mathias, Stefan Feuerriegel, and Asil Oztekin. 2020. "Deep learning in business analytics and operations research: Models, applications and managerial implications." *European Journal of Operational Research* 281 (3): 628–641.

Krawczyk, Bartosz. 2016. "Learning from imbalanced data: Open challenges and future directions." *Progress in Artificial Intelligence* 5 (4): 221–232.

Last, Felix, Georgios Douzas, and Fernando Bacao. 2017. "Oversampling for imbalanced learning based on k-means and smote." *arXiv preprint arXiv:1711.00837* .

Lemaître, Guillaume, Fernando Nogueira, and Christos K Aridas. 2017. "Imbalanced-learn: A python toolbox to tackle the curse of imbalanced datasets in machine learning." *The Journal of Machine Learning Research* 18 (1): 559–563.

Moula, Fahmida E, Chi Guotai, and Mohammad Zoynul Abedin. 2017. "Credit default prediction modeling: An application of support vector machine." *Risk Management* 19 (2): 158–187.

Nguyen, Hien M, Eric W Cooper, and Katsuari Kamei. 2009. "Borderline over-sampling for imbalanced data classification." In *Proceedings: Fifth International Workshop on Computational Intelligence & Applications*, Vol. 2009, 24–29. IEEE SMC Hiroshima Chapter.

Rodda, Sireesha, and Uma Shankar Rao Erothi. 2016. "Class imbalance problem in the network intrusion detection systems." In *2016 International Conference on Electrical, Electronics, and Optimization Techniques (ICEEOT)*, 2685–2688. IEEE.

Sharma, Shiven, Colin Bellinger, Bartosz Krawczyk, Osmar Zaiane, and Nathalie Japkowicz. 2018. "Synthetic oversampling with the majority class: A new perspective on handling extreme imbalance." In *2018 IEEE International Conference on Data Mining (ICDM)*, 447–456. IEEE.

Sun, Yanmin, Mohamed S Kamel, and Yang Wang. 2006. "Boosting for learning multiple classes with imbalanced class distribution." In *Sixth International Conference on Data Mining (ICDM'06)*, 592–602. IEEE.

Van Hulse, Jason, Taghi M Khoshgoftaar, and Amri Napolitano. 2007. "Experimental perspectives on learning from imbalanced data." In *Proceedings of the 24th International Conference on Machine Learning*, 935–942. New York, USA.

Wei, Wei, Jinjiu Li, Longbing Cao, Yuming Ou, and Jiahang Chen. 2013. "Effective detection of sophisticated online banking fraud on extremely imbalanced data." *World Wide Web* 16 (4): 449–475.

Yang, Zhiyong, Taohong Zhang, Jingcheng Lu, Dezheng Zhang, and Dorothy Kalui. 2017. "Optimizing area under the ROC curve via extreme learning machines." *Knowledge-Based Systems* 130: 74–89.

Zheng, Zhaohui, Xiaoyun Wu, and Rohini Srihari. 2004. "Feature selection for text categorization on imbalanced data." *ACM Sigkdd Explorations Newsletter* 6 (1): 80–89.

Chapter 12

Artificial intelligence (AI) in recruiting talents
Recruiters' intention and actual use of AI

Md. Aftab Uddin, Mohammad Sarwar Alam,
Md. Kaosar Hossain, Tarikul Islam, and Md. Shah Azizul Hoque

12.1 Introduction

Artificial intelligence (AI) is a fast-growing field of study in the computer science domain that emulates specific human characteristics to catch up with the rapid advances in human life (Hmoud and Laszlo, 2019; Tambe et al., 2019; Zhou and Shen, 2018). AI can be defined as the ability of computer technology to model human behavior without minimum human intervention (Black and van Esch, 2020; Hamet and Tremblay, 2017). Unlike the nature of human intelligence, AI research has focused on only a few components of intelligence such as learning, knowledge, perception, problem-solving, planning, ability to manipulate and move objects as well as advance and correct uses of language. Since its beginning back in 1921 as a robot (the earliest form of AI), mentioned in Hamet and Tremblay (2017), AI contributes to numerous fields including business, education, transportation, agriculture, entertainment, engineering, etc. (Popa, 2011; Ramesh et al., 2004). AI is used to accomplish administrative tasks faster, better, and cheaper with absolute accuracy (Bhalgat, 2019; Kolbjornsrud et al., 2016). AI is becoming more popular day by day because of its three salient features such as recruitment and on-boarding, internal mobility and employee retention, and automation of administrative tasks in a cheaper, quicker, and smoother manner (Iqbal, 2018; O'Connor, 2020).

Nowadays, human resources are treated as the strategic weapon for businesses to outperform competitors, and it is believed that knowledge, skill, abilities, and other characteristics embodied in the human capital can elicit sustainable competitive advantage (Black and van Esch, 2020; Patel et al., 2019). However, acquiring the right talent is considered as one of the toughest issues managers face in a competitive global marketplace (Park et al., 2004). The talent acquisition function within HR is assigned with the responsibility to acquire people with the highest possible potentialities (Palshikar et al., 2019). Moreover, recruiting talents using traditional mode is very challenging, particularly screening in the right resumes, sorting the desired skill sets objectively, and eliciting the matched profile for the firm (Wilfred, 2018). Particularly, recruiters need to scan and analyze the complete resumes/curriculum vitae, profiles, and other referrals to screen the right candidate, which prevents effective recruitment because of human limitations caused by unconscious biases, favoritism, preconceived perceptions, and time constraints (Hmoud and Laszlo, 2019; Johansson and Herranen, 2019).

In the current tech-based workplace, hiring managers always strive to apply new techniques to source the right talents for making sure of person-job fit (Dennis, 2018; Gupta et al., 2018a; Wilfred, 2018). If we conclude based on the survey, there are tremendous opportunities for HR professionals to adopt AI in their processes and reap the benefits of using this advanced technology (Deloitte, 2019; Iqbal, 2018). Entelo, Harver, and HireVue are some examples of AI-based recruitment applications used by thousands of organizations (Vedapradha, 2019). Bersin (2017) revealed that around 96% of recruiters believe that AI facilitates talent acquisition and retention significantly, and 13% of HR managers already see evidence of AI becoming a regular part of HR.

By using the software HR professionals are getting advantages in performing tasks such as viewing and updating employee information, access to HR business transaction data, team training, automation of repetitive, low-value tasks, and the hiring process without any human intervention (McGovern et al., 2018; Vardarlier and Zafer, 2020). Henceforth, these automated systems in recruitment are proposed to overcome the problems of manual processing and analysis for saving time and cost of right talent recruitment (Tambe et al., 2019; van Esch et al., 2019; Vedapradha, 2019). Organizations use AI (such as data mining, artificial neural network, expert systems, machine learning, and knowledge-based search engines) for numerous purposes. AI is a very time- and cost-saving option for the organizations that replaces tiresome manual processes rapidly (Hmoud and Laszlo, 2019; Wilfred, 2018). It has been employed to generate candidate pool – screening candidates initially, evaluating them, and finally selecting them as the best possible ones (Geetha and Bhanu, 2018; Nawaz, 2019). Even the failed candidates are tracked as potential future employees. The investment in AI can be validated for HR functions by HR professionals' time in administrative tasks, eliminating the loads of shared service centers by providing HR services and answers for routine works; recruiting, selecting, and retaining; and reducing bias in decision-making on HR-related issues (Bhalgat, 2019).

Although a good number of studies were found on different recruitment tools in numerous countries (Ball, 2001; Bamel et al., 2014; Boudreau and Cascio, 2017; Kmail et al., 2015; Mehrabad and Brojeny, 2007; Palshikar et al., 2019; Quaosar, 2018), there is an insignificant number of study on the use of AI technology in talent acquisition; particularly, study on the recruiters' and human resource professionals' acceptance behavior of AI-directed talent acquisition tools is absent in the Bangladesh context. Other estimates reported in Tambe et al. (2019) about Wharton School showed that 41% of CEOs are not prepared to make proper use of new data analytic tools and only 4% claim that they are "to a large extent" prepared.

In many countries such as Bangladesh different brands of AI software such as the HR cloud solution Success Factors (SF), with conversational AI capabilities through IBM Watson, SAP Leonardo ML Foundation, Recast.AI, ServiceNow, and Microsoft Azure/Skype are used to conduct day-to-day activities by HR professionals. AI adoption is slow in Bangladesh as well as in the rest of the world because of the talent gap, concern over privacy, ongoing maintenance, integration capabilities, and limited proven applications (McGovern et al., 2018). The existing literature shows that AI is increasingly used for talent recruitment; however, little is known about the documentation to its user acceptance. The research questions in this project were based on the essence of the UTAUT that blends other fragmented theories such as diffusion of innovation theory (DOI), the theory of planned behavior (TPB), the social cognitive theory (SCT), and the technology acceptance model (TAM) (Uddin et al., 2020). Henceforth, this study will look forward to answering the following research questions:

RQ1. What factors drive the recruiters/HR professionals to use or implement AI in recruiting talents in Bangladeshi business organizations?

RQ2. What significance does UTAUT provide in the implementation of AI at home and abroad?

The study contributes to advance the theory and knowledge by providing new insights and empirical evidence in numerous ways. This study is an attempt to figure out the influential factors associated with the adoption of AI-based software for talent acquisition and the magnitude of their impacts on the adoption of AI technology using UTAUT (Khanam et al., 2015). We noticed that the majority of studies on the use and implementations of AI using the UTAUT model were conducted mostly in the advanced countries. Thereby, this study is going to be the first in the context of South Asian perspectives, particularly in Bangladesh, which will, directly and indirectly, help to advance prior knowledge. Second, we add two new variables, such as technology anxiety (TA) and resistance to change (RC) with the previous UTAUT model, which might add fresh evidence to the previously held knowledge. Finally, we will investigate the moderating effect of age status of HR professionals or recruiters because it is common that old adults resist any new technology more than young adults do. Since AI adoption is unique in the case of Bangladesh perspective, old adults might be reluctant to adopt AI-based technology to recruit talents. This effect might also provide new dimensions of understanding AI adoption from age perspectives of recruiters and HR professionals.

12.2 Theory and hypothesis development

In the past decades, we observed that technology acceptance, and, finally, adoption had become the talk of the topic. Numerous theories were used such as DOI, TPB, motivation theory, TAM, institutional theory, SCT, UTAUT, and the model of perceived credibility theory (Alam et al., 2018; Alam and Uddin, 2019; Uddin et al., 2020). However, theorists advocated that those fragmented theories failed to grip the wholesome view of the model in a dynamic situation (Venkatesh et al., 2003, 2012).Venkatesh et al. (2012) and Uddin et al. (2020) signposted to using a holistic model that clustered all the fragmented concepts together to adopt and use any technology.

Consequently, the UTAUT is extensively used to discover the adoption and the actual use of technology (Uddin et al., 2020), which is represented by facilitating conditions (FC), effort expectancy (EE), social influence (SI), performance expectancy (PE), behavioral intention (BI) to use, and actual use (AU) (Venkatesh et al., 2003, 2012). Venkatesh et al. (2003) posited that the

UTAUT had undergone considerable progress as opposed to any other models that accounted for nearly 69% of BI, which is the strongest predictor of AU. However, AI is currently a novel technology in Bangladesh and most HR professionals limitedly use AI at their work. Therefore, if we only consider actual use it may lead to an imprecise conclusion about HR professionals' AI adoption behavior. The extent of the HR professionals' willingness to adopt AI-tool can be defined as a BI to use AI in recruiting talents. Specifically, we used potential factors included in the original UTAUT model along with two additional variables and one moderating variable for manifesting an accurate preview of AI adoption for recruiting talents by HR professionals in Bangladesh.

12.2.1 Technology anxiety and intentions to use

As a negative affective response of end users toward any new technology, TA received considerable focus in information system studies (Powell, 2013). TA can be defined as the degree of users' apprehension and fear as they are going to use new technology (Venkatesh, 2000). Scholars extended the UTAUT model with many auxiliary variables (Alam and Uddin, 2019; Nuq and Aubert, 2013; Oh and Yoon, 2014; Slade et al., 2013; Uddin et al., 2020) and TA has been examined as a sheer concern which influences users' intention to adopt a system. Technology is a negative emotional response where it is observed that young adults exhibited more technology skills and self-efficiency than old adults (Czaja et al., 2006). Importantly, it holds that irrespective of age groups, people experience fear and discomfort while using new technology (Meuter et al., 2003). Therefore, we can develop the following hypothesis:

H1. TA influences BI to use AI

12.2.2 Performance expectancy and intentions to use

PE in the UTAUT model is one of the most censorious determinants that explains BI. Venkatesh et al. (2003) described PE as the extent to which using a particular technology ends with a specific solution that users value. Thus, PE is a deciding factor stimulating the intention to choose or use a technology (Alam et al., 2018; Alam and Uddin, 2019). Prior studies also exemplified the findings that PE positively impacts intention to use technology (Rahi et al., 2019; Raza et al., 2019; Soliman et al., 2019). Similar to the adoption of any new technology and method, recruiters and professionals will have firm faith on the predicted performance of AI while developing their intention to use AI (Alam et al., 2018; Khanam et al., 2015; Rajan, 2015). Based on the above empiric and theoretical underpinnings, the following hypothesis is formulated:

H2. PE influences the BI to use AI

12.2.3 Effort expectancy and intentions to use

Venkatesh (2000) explained that EE is the magnitude of ease related to technology use. This construct is developed considering the perceived ease of use and the complexities associated with the use of a technology (Alam and Uddin, 2019). In other words, EE in AI adoption reflects the users' capability to use AI technology. Moreover, EE is a precursor of individuals' intention to use any technology (Aggelidis and Chatzoglou, 2009). Prior studies showed that EE and intention to use technology are positively concomitant (Dwivedi et al., 2019; Raza et al., 2019; Rozmi et al.,

2019; Uddin et al., 2020; Wrycza et al., 2017). Therefore, we expect that EE is very vital for HR professionals when using AI at the time of recruiting talents. Subsequently, we developed the following hypothesis:

H3. EE influences BI to use AI.

12.2.4 Social influence and intention to use

SI refers to the magnitude to which users accept that essential others in their society believe and expect users should use the new technology (Uddin et al., 2020; Venkatesh et al., 2012). Studies opined that social norms and images and important others are essential during deciding as to adopt the technology (Dwivedi et al., 2019; Rahi et al., 2019; Rajan, 2015). Specifically, SI in AI adoption refers to the degree that individuals' business and social groups believe that using AI in recruiting talents is associated with group norms. The social impact theory professed that people behave in compliance with their group norms because individuals think that aligning with a particular group is essential to them (Latane, 1981). Lu et al. (2005) stated that SI puts a premium on users' BI at the beginning of a new technological breakthrough.

Additionally, the surrounding environment shapes and navigates human thoughts and understanding, which is a stimulator of aiming at the decision to use new technology (Dong, 2009). Thus, SI is the strongest predictor of how an individual intends to adopt new technology, exceptionally when people are marginally involved with it. Moreover, a substantial number of studies identified the significant influence of SI on the actual use of an object, such as e-government services, cloud computing, brand identification, and ERP adoption (Uddin et al., 2019a). Therefore, looking at the above findings, there are reasons to believe that essential others would strongly influence the HR professionals' intention to use AI in recruiting talents in their social groups. Thus, we developed the following hypothesis:

H4. SI influences BI to use AI.

12.2.5 Resistance to change and intentions to use

Generally, people do resist when they encounter any new thing or process, which results in delaying or terminating any change effort (Huy, 1999). Audia and Brion (2007) reasoned in their multi-level study that all forces do resist to change initiatives. Generally, it is observed that people resist to subside their susceptibility to potential threat or submissiveness or to lose of self-control over the status quo (Gupta et al., 2018b). It is highlighted in the study of Rouhani and Mehri (2018) that people not only apprehend to new technology but also try to resist it. Guo (2013) and Hasan et al. (2018) provided that RC among the users results in declining intention to adopt a technology. It is thus pinpointed that intention to adopt AI will also observe RC among users. Consequently, the following hypothesis is endorsed:

H5. RC has a negative influence on BI to use AI.

12.2.6 Facilitating conditions and intentions to use

The adoption of technology requires proper organizational and technical supports to get expected utility from using a novel technology. FC included perceived compatibility, and infrastructural and technological support in a new system (Venkatesh, 2000; Venkatesh et al., 2003). In numerous studies, intention to adopt technology is significantly influenced by related FC in the specified technology (Rozmi et al., 2019; Soliman et al., 2019; Uddin et al., 2020; Yi et al., 2006). In general, it seems that users seek assistance if the devices are new to them. Moreover, the unavailability of technical and infrastructural supports increases ambiguity among them, which prevents the former from accepting a novel technology (Dong, 2009). Uddin et al. (2020) and Alam and Uddin (2019) provided evidence in the context of Bangladesh that FC influences the BI to adopt the technology. Accordingly, recruiters and HR professionals might be interested in using AI in the recruitment process if they are assured of the availability of FC (Upadhyay and Khandelwal, 2018; Wilfred, 2018). Hence, we recommend the following hypothesis:

H6. FC predicts BI to use AI.

12.2.7 Behavioral intention to use and actual use

BI to use refers to the extent of positive and evaluative impacts that users relate the technology with their target job (Venkatesh et al., 2003). Conversely, actual use is the demonstration of visible reply toward a given target (Uddin et al., 2020). Related studies highlighted the impact of the BI to use on AU behavior (Barrane et al., 2018; Rahman et al., 2017; Raza et al., 2019; Tarhini et al., 2016; Uddin et al., 2020). Studies pressed on the importance of inciting users' intention to use new technology for driving them actually to use the same. Hence, it can be synthesized that ignited BI to use AI among the recruiters is a must to using AI (Gupta et al., 2018a; Kmail et al., 2015; NiharikaReddy et al., 2019; Palshikar et al., 2019). Thus, adopting AI in recruiting, one's BI to use will strongly influence the AU behavior. So, the following hypothesis is proposed:

H7. BI to use predicts the AU of AI.

12.2.8 Moderating effects of age status

Despite there is a considerable difference between young and old as to technology and newness, little is known about the intervening effects of age regarding technology adoption (Kwateng et al., 2019; Morris and Vankatesh, 2000; Soliman et al., 2019; Venkatesh et al., 2003; Wrycza et al., 2017). Venkatesh et al. (2003) stressed the fact that young adults are more intrinsically motivated to accept change and adopt technology than old adults. They further cited that old adults try less to adopt any change and have less likelihood that increased efforts would result in the increased outcome (Kwateng et al., 2019; Soliman et al., 2019). Subsequently, old adults' TA prevents their BI to adopt AI. Venkatesh et al. (2003) underscored that the young displayed their profound interest in PE while building their intention to accept technology than their counterparts. Likewise, the study of Rhodes (1983) denoted that older people showed their profound knack for affiliation needs that inspire them to seek social approval of their activities. Thus, their score on SI for building BI to accept AI will get higher than young adults. Kwateng et al. (2019) investigated the moderating influence of age in a modified UTAUT context and found that older employees emphasized the availability of adequate supports and scored low on accepting change, which is also mentioned in Hall and Mansfield (1975).

As incited above, Venkatesh et al. (2003) also put more premium on credible supports and PE for convincing old adults to adopt technology over young adults. Despite the fact that the study of Laguna and Babcock (1997) revealed that there are almost no differences in TA or RC between young adults and old adults, Zajicek and Hall (2000) and Arning and Ziefle (2007) professed that older adults display more inertia to change and fear of failure to their counterparts because of their low level of technical efficacy. Basing on the prior studies' observation, we identified that the age difference between young adults and old adults moderates the influence of predictor variables on BI to use AI in recruiting talents. In consequence, the hypotheses are:

H8. The influence of TA on the intention to use AI would be more substantial for young adults than old adults.

H9. The impact of PE on the intention to use AI would be stronger for young adults than old adults.

H10. The effect of EE on the intention to use AI would be stronger for young adults than old adults.

H11. The influence of SI on the intention to use AI would be more substantial for young adults than old adults.

H12. The impact of RC on the intention to use AI would be stronger for young adults than old adults.

H13. The influence of FC on the intention to use AI would be stronger for young adults than old adults (Figure 12.1).

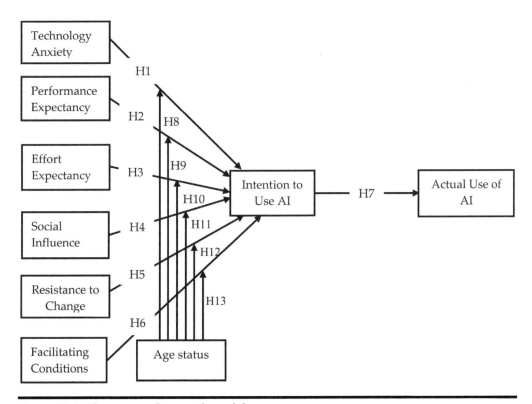

Figure 12.1 The proposed research model.

12.3 Research design

12.3.1 Survey design

This project would follow a very well-articulated technological map to frame the required activities. Multi-item survey instruments were designed to conduct the survey, which was collected from prior studies conducted in English-speaking countries. Therefore, following the understanding of Brislin (1970), the back-translation method was followed to translate it into native-Bangla (Uddin et al., 2019b). In this regard, the survey instruments were sent to academics and professional to ensure its face and content validities and few necessary changes were made to items (reworded and simplified) for the comprehension of the meaning to the native-Bangladeshi (Mahmood et al., 2019; Uddin et al., 2020). We followed the deductive reasoning approach to study predicted relationships. The deductive method following positivism philosophy sounds justified when researchers are interested in testing the theory.

12.3.2 Data collection procedure and participants' information

To perform the empirical examination of the model, we collected data from talent recruiters and human resource professionals of the human resource department who have been working at different organizations in Bangladesh. A cover letter with a self-addressed envelope was sent to the respondent to send us the data easily. The cover letter was addressed to the head of the human resource/talent acquisition/personnel/administration department of each organization to select one of their recruiters to respond to the survey. To avoid response bias, we assured them that information would be kept private and confidential and we will report on the general industrial recruitment phenomenon in place of a firm-specific data, which prevents them from pleasing any (Azim et al., 2019; Mahmood et al., 2019).

We considered each organization as a unit and, hence, sent 396 questionnaires to organizations, and we received 259 surveys with a response rate of 65%, which is considered adequate for conducting the study (Mahmood et al., 2019; Uddin et al., 2019b). Finally, 252 responses were used, leaving unmatched cases and missing data. We collected data from diverse groups recruiting professionals in terms of gender, age, tenure, educational profile, the size of the firm, and type of industry. Table 12.1 shows that talent recruiters are male-dominated (80.2%) and age ranges from a minimum of 23 years to a maximum of 60 years with a mean age of 33.40 years, which reflects that the human resource profession is at its fancy. Specifically, the most significant number of respondents belongs to 30–39 years old (151 respondents, 60%). Likewise, the tenure of the participants also ranged from 1 year to 35 years, with a mean age of 6.10 years. Sixty-one percent of the respondents have a tenure experience of one to five years. Educational backgrounds highlighted that maximum professionals have a master degree (80%), followed by a bachelor (19%) and others (1%). The study represented small (9%), medium (38%), and large (53%) organizations, and service firms (69%) responded more than manufacturing firms (31%).

12.3.3 Measurement tools

As mentioned before, we adopted items representing the construct from the previous year (**Appendix 1**). Few changes were tailored to items for suiting it to AI adoption and face validity to

Table 12.1 Demographic information (*n* = 252)

Characteristics	Classifications	Frequencies	Percentage
Gender	Male	202	80
	Female	50	20
Age Mean age = 33.40 years	20 to 29 years	62	25
	30 to 39 years	151	60
	41 and above	39	15
Tenure Mean age = 6.10 years	1 to 5 years	155	61
	6 to 10 years	65	26
	More than 10 years	43	13
Education	Undergrad	47	19
	Master	201	80
	PhD	4	1
Size of the firm	Small	22	9
	Medium	95	38
	Large	135	53
Type of industry	Service industry	174	69
	Manufacturing industry	78	31

generate accurate replies. We adopted items for constructs representing PE, EE, FC, SI, TA, and BI to use developed and refined by Venkatesh et al. (2003) and Venkatesh et al. (2012). Finally, we adopted items from Rajan (2015) and Laumer et al. (2016) to measure AU and RC, respectively.

12.3.4 Results and hypotheses testing

12.3.4.1 Analytical technique

We used the multivariate data analytic technique to analyze the data because it engenders data using the whole model in an integrated manner (Hair et al., 2014a). Henceforth, PLS-based structural equation modeling (PLS-SEM), SmartPLS3, is used for three reasons (Hair et al., 2017a; Hair, 2017b). First, it guarantees to estimate the model with any sample size. Second, the present study contains both direct effects and indirect effects, which can be measured simultaneously using PLS-SEM (Hair et al., 2014b). Another distinctiveness of PLS-SEM is its capability to evaluate both the measurement model and the structural model for ensuring the genuineness of the results (Azim et al., 2019; Uddin et al., 2019a).

12.3.4.2 Measurement model evaluation

In our measurement model evaluation, we examined the constructs' reliabilities and validities underlying the study. Thereby, reliabilities are tested in Cronbach's alpha and composite reliability. Any score above 0.70 is recommended adequate (Hair et al., 2017a, 2014a; Hair, 2017b). Scores in Cronbach's alpha and composite reliability (Tables 12.2 and 12.3) ranged from 0.826 to 0.962, which are within the cut-off value.

Table 12.2 Measurement model evaluation

Variables	1	2	3	4	5	6
Control variables						
1. Age	1					
2. Tenure	0.799	1				
3. Education	0.062	−0.006	1			
4. Size	0.019	0.044	0.254	1		
5. Gender	0.093	0.057	−0.012	0.005	1	
6. Type	−0.123	−0.079	−0.159	−0.211	−0.015	1
Latent variables						
7. AU	−0.133	−0.129	0.038	−0.019	0.050	−0.089
8. EE	−0.060	−0.075	0.043	−0.033	0.086	−0.025
9. FC	−0.085	−0.092	0.072	0.048	0.015	0.053
10. BI	−0.112	−0.053	0.018	0.108	0.028	−0.023
11. PE	−0.155*	−0.108	−0.051	−0.006	−0.142	−0.024
12. RC	0.091	0.060	0.068	0.086	0.000	−0.108
13. SI	−0.087	−0.055	−0.114	−0.051	0.059	0.075
14. TA	0.033	0.063	−0.107	−0.004	0.001	0.046
Mean	33.401	6.103	–	–	–	–
Standard deviation	6.180	5.419	–	–	–	–
Cronbach's alpha	–	–	–	–	–	–
Composite reliability	–	–	–	–	–	–
AVE	–	–	–	–	–	–

TA, technology anxiety; PE, perceived performance; EE, effort expectancy; SI, social influence; RC, resistance to change; FC, facilitating conditions.

Convergent validity refers to the clustering of its item into the same construct, whereas discriminant validity indicates the construct's distinctiveness from other constructs (Hair et al., 2017a, 2014a; Hair, 2017b). According to Hair (2017b), convergent validities will be achieved when a construct's average variance extracted (AVE) exceeds 0.50. Table 12.2 reports that AVE ranged from 0.656 to 0.882, which demonstrated that constructs' convergent validity is maintained. We measured discriminant validity using the approach of Fornell and Larcker (1981), which posits that the square root of any construct's AVE needs to be larger than its correlation with other scores. Likewise, Table 12.2 also depicts the diagonal italicized score (the square root

Table 12.3 Measurement model evaluation – cont.

Variables	7	8	9	10	11	12	13	14
Latent variables								
7. AU	*0.934*							
8. EE	0.183	*0.875*						
9. FC	0.269	0.323	*0.917*					
10. BI	0.464	0.468	0.412	*0.939*				
11. PE	0.270	0.460	0.244	0.446	*0.810*			
12. RC	−0.195	−0.264	−0.042	−0.230	−0.296	*0.929*		
13. SI	0.243	0.369	0.252	0.401	0.302	−0.187	*0.912*	
14. TA	−0.199	−0.204	−0.070	−0.411	−0.174	0.110	−0.146	*0.901*
Mean	3.579	3.650	3.550	3.595	3.831	1.787	3.514	2.197
Standard deviation	0.892	0.826	0.952	1.029	0.748	0.965	0.933	0.961
Cronbach's alpha	0.927	0.898	0.937	0.933	0.826	0.948	0.933	0.923
Composite reliability	0.953	0.929	0.955	0.957	0.884	0.962	0.952	0.945
AVE	0.872	0.766	0.841	0.882	0.656	0.864	0.832	0.812

TA, technology anxiety; PE, perceived performance; EE, effort expectancy; SI, social influence; RC, resistance to change; FC, facilitating conditions.

of the related construct's AVE) which is higher than scores beneath it. Thus, there is no concern about reliability and validity.

12.3.4.3 Structural model evaluation

The structural model is tested using collinearity testing, β, p-value, and R^2. Collinearity means that standardized regression weights among variables are not stable and subject to high standard errors. Mainly, the variance inflation factor (VIF), an indicator of collinearity, above 3.00, is problematic and leads to a damaging effect on the results (Mahmood et al., 2019). Notably, the maximum VIF resulted here is 1.477 (EE), which is within the threshold limit. Figure 12.2 presents the results on the predicted paths along with their estimates. The figure displays the strength of the relationships in β and the overall predictability of the model (R^2).

Subsequently, all the path coefficients are documented significantly along with their significance levels, except the paths exhibiting the influence of RC on BI (Hair et al., 2017a, 2014b). To investigate the strength of R^2, we used the references of Cohen (1977) and Hair et al. (2014a). Cohen (1977) mentioned that R^2 scores with 0.10, 0.25, and 0.30 are small, medium, and significant, respectively, and conversely, Hair et al. (2014a) asserted that any score above 0.20 (R^2) in a behavioral science discipline is satisfactory. Remarkably, Figure 12.2 posits that R^2 for both cases is above 0.20. Thus, the strength of the paths and the overall predictability of the model are acceptable.

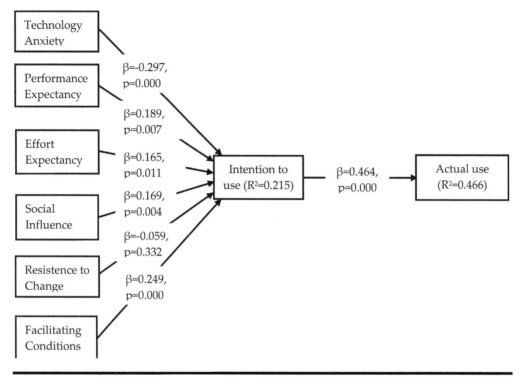

Figure 12.2 The structural model with the path estimates.

12.3.4.4 Testing of direct effects

Results exposed in Table 12.4 discovered that all the hypotheses (H1: $\beta = -0.297$; $p = 000$, H2: $\beta = 0189$; $p = 007$, H3: $\beta = 0.165$; $p = 011$, H4: $\beta = 0.169$; $p = 004$, H6: $\beta = 0.249$; $p = 000$, and H7: $\beta = 0.464$) are supported, excepting H5 ($\beta = -0.059$; $p = 332$). As a result, the present research found that all the hypotheses are significant. However, H5 accentuating the influence of RC on the BI to use the AI-enabled tool is insignificant because most of the respondents in recruiting talents are young who have no apathy to any sort of change.

12.3.4.5 Testing of moderating effects

Consistent with our hypothesized research framework, we tested the moderating influence of respondents' age of the influence of exogenous variables (predictors of intention to use AI-tool) on the endogenous variable (intention to use AI-tool). Henceforth, multi-group analysis (MGA) is used to estimate the moderating effect on the underlying path relations (Hair et al., 2017a; Sarstedt et al., 2011). Accordingly, we split the respondents into two mutually exclusive groups: young adults who are below 33 (135, 53.6%) and old adults who are 33 and above (117, 46.4%) (Lowry and Gaskin, 2014).

Table 12.4 displays moderating effects of age on the influence of TA, PE, EE, SI, RC, and FC on IU. Results in Table 12.5 revealed that the negative influence of TA on IU (H8) for old

Table 12.4 **Test statistics of direct effects**

Hypotheses	Path relations	β	STER	t-statistics	p-value	Decision
Hypothesis 1	TA → BI to use	−0.297	0.055	5.423	0.000	Supported
Hypothesis 2	PE → BI to use	0.189	0.072	2.681	0.007	Supported
Hypothesis 3	EE → BI to use	0.165	0.064	2.532	0.011	Supported
Hypothesis 4	SI → BI to use	0.169	0.058	2.890	0.004	Supported
Hypothesis 5	RC → BI to use	−0.059	0.057	0.970	0.332	Not supported
Hypothesis 6	FC → BI to use	0.249	0.061	4.064	0.000	Supported
Hypothesis 7	BI to use → AU	0.464	0.060	7.772	0.000	Supported

TA, technology anxiety; PE, perceived performance; EE, effort expectancy; SI, social influence; RC, resistance to change; FC, facilitating conditions; STER, standard error; Bold and italicized diagonal value indicates square root of the corresponding variable's average variance extracted (AVE).

adults is higher than young adults. Unfortunately, the difference between old and young adults is not significant ($\beta = -0.175; p = 0.123$). Likewise, the impacts of PE, EE, and SI on IU have also differed concerning old and young adults. Akin to H8, the influences of PE ($\beta = 0.217; p = 0.122$), EE ($\beta = -0.070; p = 0.555$), and SI ($\beta = 0.081; p = 0.462$) on IU are not significantly different between old and young adults.

Furthermore, the effect of RC on IU is found insignificant among old adults; however, the same effect is found significant among young adults. Surprisingly, the difference is found significant ($\beta = -0.296; p = 0.007$). Finally, in H13, the influence of FC on IU reported that the effect is also different between old and young adults, and the difference is found significant ($\beta = -0.269; p = 0.021$). Therefore, Table 12.4 indicates that hypotheses 8–11 are not supported, whereas hypotheses 12 and 13 are supported.

12.4 Discussion and conclusion

The present study investigated the adoption and the AU of AI in recruiting talents from a developing country's perspective, specifically in Bangladesh. Hypotheses and research questions were developed from the ideation of UTAUT. Adoption and implementation of AI for recruiting talent by the human resource professionals might result in efficient and effective recruitment promptly. In our proposed study, a conceptual model is developed with extensions to original UTAUT by TA and RC along with the moderating mechanism of age status, and examines the determinants of AI adoption and its actual use in recruiting talents by Bangladeshi recruiters.

As illustrated before, results showed that impacts of all predictors on the intention to use AI are statistically significant. The study also revealed that there is a substantial influence of BI to adopt AI on the actual use of AI in recruiting talents. Surprisingly, the impact of RC on the BI to use AI is found insignificant. Since there is no study on the adoption of AI in recruiting

Table 12.5 Moderating effects of age hypothesized relationships

Hypothesis	Path relations	Old adults			Young adults			Difference in β	p-Value	Decision
		B	STER	p-Value	β	STER	p-Value			
Hypothesis 8	TA -> IU	−0.348	0.089	0.000	−0.174	0.069	0.012	−0.175	0.123	Not supported
Hypothesis 9	PE -> IU	0.249	0.119	0.037	0.032	0.072	0.656	0.217	0.122	Not supported
Hypothesis 10	EE -> IU	0.165	0.089	0.064	0.235	0.078	0.003	−0.070	0.555	Not supported
Hypothesis 11	SI -> IU	0.205	0.081	0.011	0.124	0.077	0.108	0.081	0.462	Not supported
Hypothesis 12	RC -> IU	0.092	0.083	0.268	−0.204	0.064	0.002	0.296	0.007	Supported
Hypothesis 13	FC -> IU	0.155	0.081	0.055	0.424	0.081	0.000	−0.269	0.021	Supported

TA, technology anxiety; PE, perceived performance; EE, effort expectancy; SI, social influence; RC, resistance to change; FC, facilitating conditions; STER, standard error.

talents, in consequence, no relevance was noticed. However, the results found consistent with the findings of UTAUT, which were studied in other settings (Alam and Uddin, 2019; Kwateng et al., 2019; Rozmi et al., 2019; Uddin et al., 2020; Venkatesh et al., 2003; Wrycza et al., 2017). This study surely will contribute to putting forward the unique insights for AI adoption and the AU of it from the conceptualization of UTAUT in acquiring talents. This study will also provide an understanding of the processes and mechanisms of AI adoption and its AU by the recruiters and HR professionals in recruiting talents.

Using the premise of the UTAUT model, this study reviewed several factors influencing the adoption and the AU of AI in the context of Bangladesh. The observed results delineate that when TA, PE, EE, SI, and FC of AI increase, actual users' BI to use of AI fluctuates, which is found relevant in the context of the UTAUT model (Asamoah and Andoh-Baidoo, 2018). Likewise, the impact of RC on the BI to use AI is not found significant. Studies show that HR professionals are relatively young (33.40 years), and it is also found that they are highly educated (79.80% have master degrees), which signifies that they will have less inertia to change.

We have examined the moderating effects of age from the ideation of the original study (Venkatesh et al., 2003). The results of the moderating effects of age status associated with AI indicate that age plays an insignificant role regarding the influence of EE, TA, SI, and RC on the BI to use AI because the age difference is very low among the recruiting professionals in Bangladesh. The result is found consistent with the findings of Venkatesh et al. (2012) and Laguna and Babcock (1997). Similar to the observations of Arning and Ziefle (2007), Soliman et al. (2019), Kwateng et al. (2019), Venkatesh et al. (2003), and Zajicek and Hall (2000), the study shows that young and old adults demonstrated different results as to the influence of RC and FC on the BI to use AI (Hall and Mansfield, 1975; Kwateng et al., 2019; Soliman et al., 2019).

12.4.1 Limitation of study and future research directions

The present study is the first attempt in its type to unearth the factors impacting the adoption and the AU of AI in recruiting talents by recruiters, specifically in Bangladesh. Although the study contributes in numerous ways to advance the literature and provides novel insights by proposing AI technology replacing traditional recruitments, it inherently contains some constraints that inhibit the generalization of the findings. First, we collected data from talent recruiters and human resource professionals of the human resources department who were working at different organizations in Bangladesh, which still lack industry comprehensiveness. Second, respondents are too young with a very less tenure experience to understand the real state of AI adoption and the AU of it. Hence, future researchers are expected to go for including more respondents with experienced recruiters for developing a real scenario on AI adoption in Bangladesh. Third, the sample size and cross-sectional data prevent the findings from generalizability and causality. Thereby, we recommend using more responses in a longitudinal survey in a mixed-method design. Finally, the study on the adoption of AI in recruiting is in its infancy. It might not be adequate to generalize the findings based on research in Bangladesh. Therefore, we will recommend to future researchers to conduct more studies in other countries and cross-culture settings to have a holistic glimpse of it.

References

Aggelidis, V. P., & Chatzoglou, P. D. (2009). Using a modified technology acceptance model in hospitals. *International Journal of Medical Informatics, 78*(2), 115–126. doi:10.1016/j.ijmedinf.2008.06.006

Alam, M. S., Uddin, K. M. K., & Uddin, M. A. (2018). End users' behavioral intention to use an enterprise resource planning (ERP) system: An empirical explanation of the UTAUT Model. *The Comilla University Journal of Business Studies, 5*(1), 73–86.

Alam, M. S., & Uddin, M. A. (2019). Adoption and implementation of Enterprise Resource Planning (ERP): An empirical study. *Journal of Management and Research, 6*(1), 84–116.

Arning, K., & Ziefle, M. (2007). Understanding age differences in PDA acceptance and performance. *Computers in Human Behavior, 23*(6), 2904–2927. doi:10.1016/j.chb.2006.06.005

Asamoah, D., & Andoh-Baidoo, F. K. (2018). Antecedents and outcomes of extent of ERP systems implementation in the Sub-Saharan Africa context: A panoptic perspective. *Communications of the Association for Information Systems, 42*, 581–601. doi:10.17705/1cais.04222

Audia, P. G., & Brion, S. (2007). Reluctant to change: Self-enhancing responses to diverging performance measures. *Organizational Behavior and Human Decision Processes, 102*(2), 255–269. doi:10.1016/j.obhdp.2006.01.007

Azim, M. T., Fan, L., Uddin, M. A., Jilani, M. M. A. K., & Begum, S. (2019). Linking transformational leadership with employees' engagement in the creative process. *Management Research Review, 42*(7), 837–858. doi:10.1108/MRR-08-2018-0286

Ball, K. S. (2001). The use of human resource information systems: A survey. *Personnel Review, 30*(6), 677–693. doi:10.1108/eum0000000005979

Bamel, N., Bamel, U. K., Sahay, V., & Thite, M. (2014). Usage, benefits and barriers of human resource information system in universities. *VINE: The Journal of Information and Knowledge Management Systems, 44*(4), 519–536. doi:10.1108/VINE-04-2013-0024

Barrane, F. Z., Karuranga, G. E., & Poulin, D. (2018). Technology adoption and diffusion: A new application of the UTAUT model. *International Journal of Innovation and Technology Management, 15*(06), 1950004–1950023. doi:10.1142/s0219877019500044

Bersin, J. (2017). *Robotics, AI and Cognitive Computing Are Changing Organizations Even Faster than We Thought.* Forbes.

Bhalgat, K. H. (2019). *An Exploration of How Artificial Intelligence Is Impacting Recruitment and Selection Process.* Dublin Business School. Retrieved from https://esource.dbs.ie/handle/10788/3956

Black, J. S., & van Esch, P. (2020). AI-enabled recruiting: What is it and how should a manager use it? *Business Horizons, 63*(2), 215–226. doi:10.1016/j.bushor.2019.12.001

Boudreau, J., & Cascio, W. (2017). Human capital analytics: Why are we not there? *Journal of Organizational Effectiveness: People and Performance, 4*(2), 119–126. doi:10.1108/JOEPP-03-2017-0021

Brislin, R. W. (1970). Back-translation for cross-cultural research. *Journal of Cross-Cultural Psychology, 1*(3), 185–216. doi:10.1177/135910457000100301

Cohen, J. (1977). *Statistical Power Analysis for the Behavioral Sciences.* New York: Academic Press.

Czaja, S. J., Charness, N., Fisk, A. D., Hertzog, C., Nair, S. N., Rogers, W. A., & Sharit, J. (2006). Factors predicting the use of technology: Findings from the center for research and education on aging and technology enhancement (create). *Psychology and Aging, 21*(2), 333–352. doi:10.1037/0882-7974.21.2.333

Deloitte. (2019). *Deloitte's 2019 Global Human Capital Trends survey.* Accessed on July 6, 2020, Retrieved from https://www2.deloitte.com/content/dam/Deloitte/cz/Documents/human-capital/cz-hc-trends-reinvent-with-human-focus.pdf

Dennis, M. J. (2018). Artificial intelligence and recruitment, admission, progression, and retention. *Enrollment Management Report, 22*(9), 1–3. doi:10.1002/emt.30479

Dong, J. Q. (2009). User acceptance of information technology innovations in the Chinese cultural context. *Asian Journal of Technology Innovation, 17*(2), 129–149. doi:10.1080/19761597.2009.9668676

Dwivedi, Y. K., Rana, N. P., Jeyaraj, A., Clement, M., & Williams, M. D. (2019). Re-examining the Unified Theory of Acceptance and Use of Technology (UTAUT): Towards a revised theoretical model. *Information Systems Frontiers, 21*(3), 719–734. doi:10.1007/s10796-017-9774-y

Fornell, C., & Larcker, D. F. (1981). Evaluating structural equation models with unobservable variables and measurement error. *Journal of Marketing Research, 18*(1), 39–50. doi:10.1177/002224378101800104

Geetha, R., & Bhanu, S. R. D. (2018). Recruitment through artificial intelligence: A conceptual study. *International Journal of Mechanical Engineering and Technology, 9*(7), 63–70.

Guo, X., Sun, Y., Wang, N., Peng, Z., & Yan, Z. (2013). The dark side of elderly acceptance of preventive mobile health services in China. *Electronic Markets, 23*(1), 49–61. doi:10.1007/s12525-012-0112-4

Gupta, P., Fernandes, S. F., & Jain, M. (2018). Automation in recruitment: A new frontier. *Journal of Information Technology Teaching Cases, 8*(2), 118–125. doi:10.1057/s41266-018-0042-x

Gupta, S., Misra Subhas, C., Kock, N., & Roubaud, D. (2018). Organizational, technological and extrinsic factors in the implementation of cloud ERP in SMEs. *Journal of Organizational Change Management, 31*(1), 83–102. doi:10.1108/JOCM-06-2017-0230

Hair, J., Hollingsworth, C. L., Randolph, A. B., & Chong, A. Y. L. (2017). An updated and expanded assessment of PLS-SEM in information systems research. *Industrial Management & Data Systems, 117*(3), 442–458. doi:10.1108/IMDS-04-2016-0130

Hair Jr, J. F., Black, W. C., Babin, B. J., & Anderson, R. E. (2014). *Multivariate Data Analysis: A Global Perspective.* 7 ed. London: Pearson.

Hair Jr., J. F., Hult, G. T. M., Ringle, C. M., & Sarstedt, M. (2017). *A Primer on Partial Least Squares Structural Equation Modeling (PLS-SEM).* Los Angeles: Sage Publication.

Hair Jr, J. F., Sarstedt, M., Hopkins, L., & Kuppelwieser, V. G. (2014). Partial least squares structural equation modeling (PLS-SEM). *European Business Review, 26*(2), 106–121. doi:10.1108/ebr-10-2013-0128

Hall, D. T., & Mansfield, R. (1975). Relationships of age and seniority with career variables of engineers and scientists. *Journal of Applied Psychology, 60*(2), 201–210. doi:10.1037/h0076549

Hamet, P., & Tremblay, J. (2017). Artificial intelligence in medicine. *Metabolism, 69*, S36–S40. doi:10.1016/j.metabol.2017.01.011

Hasan, M. S., Ebrahim, Z., Mahmood, W. H. W., & Rahmanm, M. N. A. (2018). Factors influencing enterprise resource planning system: A review. *Journal of Advanced Manufacturing Technology, 12*(1), 247–258.

Hmoud, B., & Laszlo, V. (2019). Will artificial intelligence take over humanresources recruitment and selection. *Network Intelligence Studies, 7*(13), 21–30.

Huy, Q. N. (1999). Emotional capability, emotional intelligence, and radical change. *Academy of Management Review, 24*(2), 325–345. doi:10.5465/amr.1999.1893939

Iqbal, F. M. (2018). Can artificial intelligence change the way in which companies recruit, train, develop and manage human resources in workplace? *Asian Journal of Social Sciences and Management Studies, 5*(3), 102–104.

Johansson, J., & Herranen, S. (2019). *The application of Artificial Intelligence (AI) in human resource management: Current state of AI and its impact on the traditional recruitment process.* Bachelor Degree Thesis, Jönköping University, Sweden.

Khanam, L., Uddin, M. A., & Mahfuz, M. A. (2015). Students' behavioral intention and acceptance of e-recruitment system: A Bangladesh perspective. In *12th International Conference on Innovation and Management, ICIM 2015*, 1297–1303. Wuhan, China.

Kmail, A. B., Maree, M., Belkhatir, M., & Alhashmi, S. M. (2015). An automatic online recruitment system based on exploiting multiple semantic resources and concept-relatedness measures. In *2015 IEEE 27th International Conference on Tools with Artificial Intelligence (ICTAI)*, 620–627. IEEE.

KolbjÂÿrnsrud, V., Amico, R., & Thomas, R. J. (2016). How artificial intelligence will redefine management. *Harvard Business Review*, *2*, 1–6.

Kwateng, K. O., Atiemo, K. A. O., & Appiah, C. (2019). Acceptance and use of mobile banking: An application of UTAUT2. *Journal of Enterprise Information Management*, *32*(1), 118–151. doi:10.1108/JEIM-03-2018-0055

Laguna, K., & Babcock, R. L. (1997). Computer anxiety in young and older adults: Implications for human-computer interactions in older populations. *Computers in Human Behavior*, *13*(3), 317–326. doi:10.1016/S0747-5632(97)00012-5

Latané, B. (1981). The psychology of social impact. *American Psychologist*, *36*(4), 343–356. doi:10.1037/0003-066X.36.4.343

Laumer, S., Maier, C., Eckhardt, A., & Weitzel, T. (2016). User personality and resistance to mandatory information systems in organizations: A theoretical model and empirical test of dispositional resistance to change. *Journal of Information Technology*, *31*(1), 67–82. doi:10.1057/jit.2015.17

Lowry, P. B., & Gaskin, J. (2014). Partial least squares (PLS) structural equation modeling (SEM) for building and testing behavioral causal theory: When to choose it and how to use it. *IEEE Transactions on Professional Communication*, *57*(2), 123–146. doi:10.1109/TPC.2014.2312452

Lu, J., Yao, J. E., & Yu, C.-S. (2005). Personal innovativeness, social influences and adoption of wireless Internet services via mobile technology. *The Journal of Strategic Information Systems*, *14*(3), 245–268. doi:10.1016/j.jsis.2005.07.003

Mahmood, M., Uddin, M. A., & Luo, F. (2019). Influence of transformational leadership on employees' creative process engagement: A multi-level analysis. *Management Decision*, *57*(3), 741–764. doi:10.1108/MD-07-2017-0707

McGovern, S. L. P., Vinod, Gill, S., Aldrich, T., Myers, C., Desai, C., Gera, M., & Balasubramanian, V. (2018). *The new age: Artificial intelligence for human resource opportunities and functions*. Retrieved from https://www.ey.com/Publication/vwLUAssets/EY-the-new-age-artificial-intelligence-for-human-resource-opportunities-and-functions/

Mehrabad, M. S., & Brojeny, M. F. (2007). The development of an expert system for effective selection and appointment of the jobs applicants in human resource management. *Computers & Industrial Engineering*, *53*(2), 306–312. doi:10.1016/j.cie.2007.06.023

Meuter, M. L., Ostrom, A. L., Bitner, M. J., & Roundtree, R. (2003). The influence of technology anxiety on consumer use and experiences with self-service technologies. *Journal of Business Research*, *56*(11), 899–906. doi:10.1016/S0148-2963(01)00276-4

Morris, M. G., & Venkatesh, V. (2000). Age differences in technology adoption decisions: Implications for a changing work force. *Personnel Psychology*, *53*(2), 375–403.

Nawaz, N. (2019). How far have we come with the study of artificial intelligence for recruitment process. *Internatinal Journal of Scientific and Technology Research*, *8*(7), 488–493.

Niharika Reddy, M., Mamatha, T., & Balaram, A. (2019). Analysis of e-recruitment systems and detecting e-recruitment fraud. In *International Conference on Communications and Cyber Physical Engineering 2018*, 411–417. Singapore: Springer.

Nuq, P. A., & Aubert, B. (2013). Towards a better understanding of the intention to use eHealth services by medical professionals: The case of developing countries. *International Journal of Healthcare Management, 6*(4), 217–236. doi:10.1179/2047971913Y.0000000033

O'Connor, S. W. (2020). *Artificial Intelligence in Human Resource Management.* Accessed on July 6, 2020, Retrieved from https://www.northeastern.edu/graduate/blog/artificial-intelligence-in-human-resource-management/

Oh, J.-C., & Yoon, S.-J. (2014). Predicting the use of online information services based on a modified UTAUT model. *Behaviour & Information Technology, 33*(7), 716–729. doi:10.1080/0144929X.2013.872187

Palshikar, G. K., Srivastava, R., Pawar, S., Hingmire, S., Jain, A., Chourasia, S., & Shah, M. (2019). Analytics-led talent acquisition for improving efficiency and effectiveness. In A. K. Laha (Ed.), *Advances in Analytics and Applications*, 141–160. Singapore: Springer.

Park, H. J., Gardner, T. M., & Wright, P. M. (2004). HR practices or HR capabilities: which matters? Insights from the Asia Pacific region. *Asia Pacific Journal of Human Resources, 42*(3), 260–273. doi:10.1177/1038411104045394

Patel, C., Budhwar, P., Witzemann, A., & Katou, A. (2019). HR outsourcing: The impact on HR's strategic role and remaining in-house HR function. *Journal of Business Research, 103*, 397–406. doi:10.1016/j.jbusres.2017.11.007

Popa, C. (2011). Adoption of Artificial Intelligence in Agriculture. *Bulletin of the University of Agricultural Sciences and Veterinary Medicine Cluj-Napoca Agriculture, 68*(1), 284–293. doi:10.15835/buasvmcn-agr:6454

Powell, A. L. (2013). Computer anxiety: Comparison of research from the 1990s and 2000s. *Computers in Human Behavior, 29*(6), 2337–2381. doi:10.1016/j.chb.2013.05.012

Quaosar, G. M. A. A. (2018). Adoption of human resource information systems in developing countries: An empirical study. *International Business Research, 11*(4), 133–141. doi:10.5539/ibr.v11n4p133

Rahi, S., Mansour, M. M. O., Alghizzawi, M., & Alnaser, F. M. (2019). Integration of UTAUT model in internet banking adoption context. *Journal of Research in Interactive Marketing, 13*(3), 411–435. doi:10.1108/JRIM-02-2018-0032

Rahman, M. M., Lesch, M. F., Horrey, W. J., & Strawderman, L. (2017). Assessing the utility of TAM, TPB, and UTAUT for advanced driver assistance systems. *Accident Analysis & Prevention, 108*, 361–373. doi:10.1016/j.aap.2017.09.011

Rajan, C. A., & Baral, R. (2015). Adoption of ERP system: An empirical study of factors influencing the usage of ERP and its impact on end user. *IIMB Management Review, 27*(2), 105–117. doi:10.1016/j.iimb.2015.04.008

Ramesh, A. N., Kambhampati, C., Monson, J. R. T., & Drew, P. J. (2004). Artificial intelligence in medicine. *Annals of the Royal College of Surgeons of England, 86*(5), 334–338. doi:10.1308/147870804290

Raza, S. A., Shah, N., & Ali, M. (2019). Acceptance of mobile banking in Islamic banks: evidence from modified UTAUT model. *Journal of Islamic Marketing, 10*(1), 357–376. doi:10.1108/JIMA-04-2017-0038

Rhodes, S. R. (1983). Age-related differences in work attitudes and behavior: A review and conceptual analysis. *Psychological Bulletin, 93*(2), 328–367. doi:10.1037/0033-2909.93.2.328

Rouhani, S., & Mehri, M. (2018). Empowering benefits of ERP systems implementation: empirical study of industrial firms. *Journal of Systems and Information Technology, 20*(1), 54–72. doi:10.1108/JSIT-05-2017-0038

Rozmi, A. N. A., Bakar, M. I. A., Abdul Hadi, A. R., & Imran Nordin, A. (2019). Investigating the Intentions to Adopt ICT in Malaysian SMEs Using the UTAUT Model. In *International Visual Informatics Conference*, 477–487. Cham: Springer.

Sarstedt, M., Henseler, J., & Ringle, C. M. (2011). Multigroup analysis in partial least squares (PLS) path modeling: Alternative methods and empirical results. *Measurement and Research Methods in International Marketing*, 22, 195–218.

Slade, E. L., Williams, M. D., & Dwivedi, Y. (2013). An extension of the UTAUT 2 in a healthcare context. Paper presented at the UK Academy for Information Systems Conference, UK.

Soliman, M. S. M., Karia, N., Moeinzadeh, S., Islam, M. S., & Mahmud, I. (2019). Modelling intention to use ERP systems among higher education institutions in Egypt: UTAUT perspective. *International Journal of Supply Chain Management*, 8(2), 429–440.

Tambe, P., Cappelli, P., & Yakubovich, V. (2019). Artificial intelligence in human resources management: Challenges and a path forward. *California Management Review*, 61(4), 15–42. doi:10.1177/0008125619867910

Tarhini, A., El-Masri, M., Ali, M., & Serrano, A. (2016). Extending the UTAUT model to understand the customers' acceptance and use of internet banking in Lebanon: A structural equation modeling approach. *Information Technology and People*, 29(4), 23–38.

Uddin, M. A., Alam, M. S., Mamun, A. A., Khan, T.-U.-Z., & Akter, A. (2020). A study of the adoption and implementation of enterprise resource planning (ERP): Identification of moderators and mediator. *Journal of Open Innovation: Technology, Market, and Complexity*, 6(1), 2–19.

Uddin, M. A., Mahmood, M., & Fan, L. (2019). Why individual employee engagement matters for team performance? Mediating effects of employee commitment and Organizational citizenship behaviour. *Team Performance Management: An International Journal*, 25(1/2), 47–68. doi:10.1108/TPM-12-2017-0078

Uddin, M. A., Priyankara, H. P. R., & Mahmood, M. (2019). Does a creative identity encourage innovative behaviour? Evidence from knowledge-intensive IT service firms. *European Journal of Innovation Management*. doi:10.1108/EJIM-06-2019-0168

Upadhyay, A. K., & Khandelwal, K. (2018). Applying artificial intelligence: implications for recruitment. *Strategic HR Review*, 17(5), 255–258. doi:10.1108/SHR-07-2018-0051

van Esch, P., Black, J. S., & Ferolie, J. (2019). Marketing AI recruitment: The next phase in job application and selection. *Computers in Human Behavior*, 90, 215–222. doi:10.1016/j.chb.2018.09.009

Vardarlier, P., & Zafer, C. (2020). Use of artificial intelligence as business strategy in recruitment process and social perspective. In U. Hacioglu (Ed.), *Digital Business Strategies in Blockchain Ecosystems: Transformational Design and Future of Global Business*, 355–373. Cham: Springer.

Vedapradha, R., Hariharan, R., & Shivakami, R. (2019). Artificial intelligence: A technological prototype in recruitment. *Journal of Service Science and Management*, 12(3), 382–390.

Venkatesh, V. (2000). Determinants of perceived ease of use: Integrating control, intrinsic motivation, and emotion into the technology acceptance model. *Information Systems Research*, 11(4), 342–365.

Venkatesh, V., Morris, M. G., Davis, G. B., & Davis, F. D. (2003). User acceptance of information technology: Toward a unified view. *MIS Quarterly*, 27(3), 425–478.

Venkatesh, V., Thong, J. Y., & Xu, X. (2012). Consumer acceptance and use of information technology: extending the unified theory of acceptance and use of technology. *MIS Quarterly*, 36(1), 157–178.

Wilfred, D. (2018). AI in recruitment. *NHRD Network Journal*, 11(2), 15–18. doi:10.1177/0974173920180204

Wrycza, S., Marcinkowski, B., & Gajda, D. (2017). The enriched UTAUT model for the acceptance of software engineering tools in academic education. *Information Systems Management, 34*(1), 38–49. doi:10.1080/10580530.2017.1254446

Yi, M. Y., Jackson, J. D., Park, J. S., & Probst, J. C. (2006). Understanding information technology acceptance by individual professionals: Toward an integrative view. *Information & Management, 43*(3), 350–363. doi:10.1016/j.im.2005.08.006

Zajicek, M., & Hall, S. (2000). *Solutions for Elderly Visually Impaired People Using the Internet.* London: Springer.

Zhou, J., & Shen, M. (2018). When human intelligence meets artificial intelligence. *PsyCh Journal, 7*(3), 156–157. doi:10.1002/pchj.216

Index

Note: **Bold** page numbers refer to tables figures.